THE
MENTAL HEALTH
MINISTRY
OF THE
LOCAL CHURCH

"Within our community God has appointed . . .
those who have gifts of healing, or ability
to help others or power to guide them."
—I Cor. 12:28 (NEB)

THE
MENTAL HEALTH
MINISTRY
OF THE
LOCAL CHURCH

HOWARD J. CLINEBELL, JR.

Abingdon Press • Nashville • New York

THE MENTAL HEALTH MINISTRY
OF THE LOCAL CHURCH

Originally published as
Mental Health Through Christian Community

Copyright © 1965, 1972 by Abingdon Press

Apex Edition published 1972

ISBN 0-687-24829-9

Library of Congress Catalog Card Number: 73-185551

Scripture quotations unless otherwise noted are
from the Revised Standard Version of the Bible,
copyrighted 1946 and 1952 by the Division of
Christian Education, National Council of Churches,
and are used by permission.

Scripture quotations noted NEB are from *The New
English Bible.* © the delegates of the Oxford
University Press and the Syndics of the Cambridge
University Press 1961, 1970. Reprinted by permission.

Scripture quotations noted Phillips are from *The
New Testament in Modern English,* copyright 1958
by J. B. Phillips.

MANUFACTURED BY THE PARTHENON PRESS, AT
NASHVILLE, TENNESSEE, UNITED STATES OF AMERICA

To
Charlotte
John, Donald, and Susan

ACKNOWLEDGEMENTS

Among the many persons to whom I owe appreciation for contributing to my thinking in the area of the church and mental health, my largest debt is to my former parishioners at Brick Chapel, De Kalb, Oak Park, Lake Ronkonkoma, Stony Brook, Woodhaven, Great Neck, and Pasadena. For what I learned with and from them, I am grateful. The same is true of those who were patients at the Methodist Hospital of Southern California during my period as chaplain there. Four years at the Pasadena Area Pastoral Counseling Center were particularly fruitful ones for me, involving as they did counseling relationships with several hundred men, women, and youth who brought their problems to that center. I am indebted to these persons for what they taught me from their perspectives of suffering and growth. My association with David W. Morgan, psychiatric consultant at that center, opened new doors into the depths of the human spirit. Without the support of the Pasadena Methodist Foundation and the guidance of the First Methodist Church's Mental Health Committee, the center would not have been possible.

Opportunities have been manifold to test and rework many of the ideas in this book through interaction with seminary students and parish ministers. In particular, I recall stimulating discussions in three summer school courses on "The Local Church and Mental Health," at the Pacific School of Religion, Iliff School of Theology, and the School of Theology at Claremont, respectively. I stand in debt to my faculty colleagues—K. Morgan Edwards, David D. Eitzen, Paul B. Irwin, Frank W. Kimper, and Harvey J. Seifert—and to Harvey H. Potthoff of the Iliff faculty, for their insightful comments concerning various chapters of the manuscript. The same applies to John B. Cobb, Jr., of the Claremont faculty, who also suggested the title which appears on this volume.

My thanks also to Robert Hilton, Robert Hagelbarger, and Paul Pretzel for their assistance at many points, to Miss A. Esther Smith who typed and retyped the manuscript, and to the trustees of the School of Theology for time off from my teaching duties to complete this project. A special word of gratitude to my family for their patience during my period of obsession with this book.

Howard J. Clinebell, Jr.
Claremont, California

INTRODUCTION

There is a growing commitment throughout our country to the development of comprehensive community-based programs for the treatment and prevention of mental illness. Such programs have acquired the name of "community psychiatry" or "community mental health." The church's capacity to involve itself in every aspect of community life has served as a model for the development of certain aspects of the community mental health centers. At the same time, these centers bring a new set of challenges and possibilities to the church. The discovery of new healing powers and methods for dealing with human ills has provided resources which the church must recognize and use in its ministry to human beings.

A distinctive feature of Christianity from its beginning has been its deep concern with the fate of the individual. Since the problem of health is a problem of the state of the individual, it is understandable how Christianity has been permeated with concern with health. Formerly, religious healing became one of its central bases of validation.

The church at times has equated salvation with "being saved," while neglecting the dimension of *being healed* or *making whole* which the root *salvus* denotes. This has resulted in theology and medicine losing some of the intimate connection they originally had and always should have. The message conveyed by the healing stories in the New Testament is that the kingdom of God would come as the healing power on earth.

The church in its beginning and in its greatest periods has seen no basic conflict between the role of the healer and the role of the bishop. It has held the conviction that the totality of human need cannot be met where people try to compartmentalize man into body, soul, or psyche, but that man's needs are best met when he is seen as a whole person and when all of the resources of man and God are appropriated to meet that need. It has continually stressed that God works through the knowledge of science and the sources of healing that he has placed in nature.

Healing power is latent in man because it is latent in the nature of things. We live in a universe where positive values are actualized through an interplay of natural, human, and divine creativity. Every therapist counts on the drive for recovery, deep within his patient, that goes beyond the conscious devising of himself and his patients. The therapist's task is to participate in the releasing of healing processes rather than to invent them.

Dr. Clinebell has written a challenging guidebook for making the church's ministry more effective in the field of mental health. Several years ago, an eminent theologian mentioned that one of the difficulties in the effective correlation of "religious and scientific psychotherapy" was the lack of the institutional means of cooperation. Clinical pastoral training and community psychiatry are two recent developments that represent major steps toward furnishing the institutional means.

The central message in *The Mental Health Ministry of the Local Church* is that the church as a healing-redemptive fellowship is inescapably concerned with mental health in both the preventive and therapeutic dimensions. Dr. Clinebell carefully shows that the contemporary mental health thrust in the churches, while having the advantage of new insights from the sciences of man and new helping techniques from the psychotherapeutic disciplines, is essentially the same concern for the healing and growth of persons as was found in the ministry of Jesus and throughout the church's history.

It is to Dr. Clinebell's credit that he is not advocating the "use" of the clergy and the resources of the church in the service of the nation's mental health. Rather, he establishes the place of the local church as a mental health resource without distorting the ultimate goals of the church or the prevailing forms of her functioning. He contends that each activity in the church should make itself count by contributing significantly to the growth of persons in their ability to live creatively and to love fully themselves, others, and God. His examination of each of the areas of a local church's life is done in the perspective of how each area may make the maximum contribution to the spiritual health and growth of persons.

Of all the phases of church life that Dr. Clinebell discusses, his comments on the group life of the church are of particular interest. Applicants to medical school often identify this group life as the major integrating factor in their lives during the stormy period of adolescent development. This is only one example; many can be given.

In studying the biblical healing stories, one notes that healing seems to have taken place almost invariably in some corporate context. The group atmosphere in the New Testament healing episodes was a most significant factor in the preparation and support of the healing process. In the life of the early church, where healing became more and more associated with the corporate worship and the sacramental life of the believing community, the element of group atmosphere became a factor of prime importance.

Today, a neglected area of church life is the use of the congregation as an instrument of therapy. The church as a therapeutic and redemptive community can have profound influence upon the health of the individual and the group. The patient with an emotional problem is often lonely and isolated, desperately needing to feel a sense of community with others. The congregation has within its very structure the ability to heal his isolation, to rescue the alcoholic, to answer the cry for help of the suicide candidate, to give direction and structure to the adolescent. The church also has a great opportunity with the "marginal" person who is living on the edge of life and who is in danger of dropping out of his family and of society. Also, the church can function as one of the finest stabilizing forces for senior citizens, providing a sense of purpose and significance to their lives and incorporating them meaningfully and creatively into the religious group life of the church and the community. And above all, the individual in psychotherapy at some point in his search for healing runs head on into the religious question. He often turns to the church, especially if encouraged to do so, to explore fundamental questions related to the nature and destiny of man and his ever-present existential anxiety and guilt.

But the group life of the church is only one among many of the prevailing forms of church functioning which Dr. Clinebell evaluates. He examines in the perspective of community mental health the major functions of the church, such as worship, preaching, the prophetic ministry, the church school, family-life programs, administration, evangelism, and other areas. He offers valuable and constructive approaches for renewal.

Dr. Clinebell has lucidly translated his concerns and knowledge regarding mental health into a blueprint for action in the local church. He brings to his subject extensive clinical experience and theoretical sophistication. He covets for every aspect of the church's ministry a central position in the community's search for wholeness. The author has the rare gift of stating theological presuppositions in such a way that the religious dimension in all of life is illuminated and accepted. He has worked for years with refreshing originality and great effectiveness in bringing the new developments of the behavioral sciences to the church and, at the same time, has been a good interpreter of the theological to the professionals in the behavioral sciences.

Hopefully, both laymen and professionals in the religious and behavioral science fields will use this book, and use it collaboratively, in seeking to attain "mental health through Christian community."

James A. Knight, M.D.
Professor of Psychiatry
Associate Dean
Tulane University School of Medicine
New Orleans, Louisiana

CONTENTS

THE
MENTAL HEALTH
MINISTRY
OF THE
LOCAL CHURCH

CHAPTER 1

The Mental Health Mission of the Local Church

*Stir up the gift of God, which is in thee. . . . For God
hath not given us the spirit of fear; but of power,
and of love, and of a sound mind.—II Tim. 1:6-7
(KJV)*

The message of this book has three themes: (a) *Mental health is
a central and inescapable concern of any local church that is a healing-redemptive fellowship.* (b) *A local church today has an un-
precedented opportunity to multiply its contributions to both the
preventive and the therapeutic dimensions of mental health.* (c) *A
church can seize this opportunity most effectively by allowing mental
health to become a leavening concern, permeating all areas of its
life.* When this occurs, the spirit of Christian community flourishes
in the many facets of a church's program, causing it to become a
center of healing and growth.

Churches have always been major contributors to personality
health. As Karl Menninger has observed, "religion has been the
world's psychiatrist throughout the centuries." [1] Without the stabilizing, undergirding, nurturing, value-supporting ministries of the
churches, millions of persons in every age would have been diminished in their abilities to handle life situations constructively.
Further, they would have been much more vulnerable to mental,
emotional, and spiritual illnesses.

The mental health contributions of the past have been significant
but they do not compare with the remarkable potentialities of the
foreseeable future! A heartening upsurge of concern for mental

---

[1] *Man Against Himself* (New York: Harcourt, Brace and World, Inc., 1938), p. 449.

13

health is occurring in society at large and in many churches. There are clear indications that the time is ripe for the churches to make a major breakthrough in the area of mental health. This is the hope and challenge of our present situation. The purpose of this book is to wrestle with *how* a local church can share in this breakthrough by fulfilling its mental health mission.

The local church is in a strategic position on the front lines of mental health, in both its preventive and therapeutic aspects. Year in, year out, most churches are contributing significantly to the growth of persons and the healing of their inner wounds. We know from a recent study that nearly as many troubled people seek counseling from clergymen as from all other helping professions combined.[2] The churches have face-to-face relationships with over 120,000,000 adults and youth—more than any other institution in our society. Think of the opportunity for enhancing positive mental health which this gives the churches!

The various aspects of a local church's program help many people in a wide variety of ways. But the *potential* contributions of the many-faceted program of a local church are like a vein of rich ore which we have only begun to discover and mine. This book aims at applying some insights from pastoral psychology to the major dimensions of a church's program—worship, preaching, the prophetic ministry, the church school, the group life, the family-life program, administration and evangelism—as a way of mining this ore. My intention is to develop a practical guidebook for maximizing a local church's mental health ministry.

To the superficial observer, the typical church has the appearance of a three-ring circus. Some churches are just that! But an effective, person-centered church, when known from the inside, is recognized as being much more like a large, busy family than a circus. During any given week, a remarkable variety of meaningful activities occurs within its program, involving persons of all ages. These many activities offer frequent opportunities for personal growth.

The widespread concern, shared by dedicated laymen and ministers alike, is that their church's buzzing schedule not be, like Ezekiel's vision, merely wheels within wheels. Each activity should

[2] Gerald Gurin, *et al.*, *Americans View Their Mental Health* (New York: Basic Books, Inc., 1960), p. 307.

make itself count by contributing significantly to the growth of persons in their ability to live creatively and to love themselves, others, and God more fully. It is to this concern that the chapters ahead seek to speak a clear word. To do so, they will examine each of the areas of a local church's life from the perspective of a single, guiding question: *How can this area of the life of a church make the maximum contribution to the spiritual health and growth of persons?* This question will be used as a searchlight in exploring the untapped resources for wholeness which exist so abundantly in that living, interpersonal organism which is the local church.

The hope of any church is inherent in those laymen and ministers who love it and know that its timeless gospel is still "good news." Such persons are keenly aware of the meaning and challenge which the Christian religion has brought to their lives and to millions of their fellows. They know that the churches, with all their weaknesses, are often remarkably effective channels for helping persons develop their fullest personhood. They believe that the message and the fellowship of the church are crucially important resources for helping all of us to be more alive in this "age of nerves."

These churchmen are also aware that the stresses of life distort many people into "inferior caricatures of what they might have been," [3] as one of the pioneers of modern psychiatry has put it. They feel the immense tragedy of this fact. They long for the fullest flowering of God-given potentialities in themselves and in others. They want no part of the Miltown approach to religion. Naturally they want *peace* of mind, but they also want both *strength* of mind [4] and vivid awareness of the needs of others. They suspect that the churches have only begun to apply the fresh insights of the sciences of man to their life and work. They are eager to help enhance the person-centeredness of the churches in which they provide leadership. It is of such people that the former director of the National Institute of Mental Health, Robert H. Felix, speaks when he declares: "Religious leaders are in the forefront of professional people who recognize the need to apply scientific findings about human person-

[3] Harry Stack Sullivan, *Conceptions of Modern Psychiatry* (New York: W. W. Norton & Co., 1953), p. 27.

[4] Joint Commission on Mental Illness and Health, *Action for Mental Health* (New York: Basic Books, Inc., 1961), p. xxvii.

ality to their work with people." [5] It is to these ministers and lay leaders that this book is addressed.

To find the hidden veins of precious mental health ore in your church will not be an easy task, but this is precisely the challenge. My hope is that this book will help you respond to this challenge in ways that will allow your church to grow in the greatness of its service to persons.

WHAT IS POSITIVE MENTAL HEALTH?

Mental health is desired and cherished by most people, for themselves and their loved ones. Ordinarily we do not call it "mental health," but when we long for happiness, inner serenity, and effectiveness in living, we are actually searching for mental health. The simple description of mental health—*happiness experienced at a deep level*—is useful in communicating its positive quality. This description is, of course, an oversimplification, since mental health includes the capacity to experience a wide variety of deep feelings including sorrow, disappointment, anger, and empathy, as well as what is usually meant by happiness.[6]

Social psychologist Marie Jahoda made an exhaustive study of positive mental health concepts.[7] She found that the term is extremely elusive and ambiguous in current psychological thought, but she was able to identify six major approaches by various schools of thought. Combining and paraphrasing these as criteria, we could say that a person is mentally healthy to the degree that: (a) His attitudes toward himself are characterized by self-acceptance, self-esteem, and accuracy of self-perception. (b) He actualizes his potentialities through personal growth. (c) His inner drives are focused and his personality integrated (the opposite of being fragmented by inner conflicts.) (d) He has a dependable sense of inner identity and values so that he is not overly dependent on the influence of others. (e) He is able to see reality—the world and other people—with accuracy because his subjective needs do not distort

[5] "The Hard Core of Counseling," *Pastoral Psychology*, April, 1950, p. 37.

[6] Happiness, by itself, is not an adequate criterion for measuring mental health because some people defend themselves against unconscious feeling of despair by a facade of "happiness." They are the so-called "smiling depressives." Further, many other people are happy to the degree that life brings them close to what they desire. Thus, external circumstances rather than mental health could be the decisive factor in determining such a person's happiness.

[7] *Current Concepts of Positive Mental Health* (New York: Basic Books, Inc., 1958).

his perceptions. (f) He is able to take what life gives him; master his environment; and enjoy love, work, and play.[8]

As these criteria indicate, mental health is a *positive* condition and not merely the absence of mental illness. The absence of incapacitating psychological problems is a *necessary* but not a *sufficient* sign of mental health. The term "mental health" should give us the feeling of warmth and sunlight, not merely the absence of cold and shadow. Erich Fromm's description in *The Sane Society* carries this positive emphasis:

The mentally healthy person is the productive and unalienated person; the person who relates himself to the world lovingly, and who uses his reason to grasp reality objectively; who experiences himself as a unique individual entity, and at the same time feels one with his fellow-man; who is not subject to irrational authority, and who accepts willingly the rational authority of conscience and reason; who is in the process of being born as long as he is alive, and considers the gift of life the most precious chance he has.[9]

Elsewhere in the same volume, Fromm points out that mental health is characterized "by the ability to love and to create." [10]

Mental health is more of a road than a goal. It is movement in a certain direction, not the achievement of a psychological halo. Lawrence K. Frank emphasizes the growth aspect: "Healthy personalities are to be viewed as individuals who continue to grow, develop, and mature, accepting the requirements and opportunities of each successive stage of life . . . and finding the fulfillment they offer." [11]

Many descriptions of mental health make it sound like a very big order.[12] Unless one remembers that even the most fortunate person achieves these qualities only to a limited degree, mental health becomes a burdensome rather than a releasing idea. That paragon of

---

[8] For other paraphrases of these six approaches see Jahoda, p. xi and Richard V. McCann, *The Churches and Mental Health* (New York: Basic Books, Inc., 1962), p. 5.

[9] Erich Fromm, *The Sane Society* (New York: Holt, Rinehart & Winston, 1955), p. 275.

[10] *Ibid.*, p. 69.

[11] "The Promotion of Mental Health," *Annals of American Academy of Political and Social Science*, 286 (1953), 169.

[12] *Mental Health Education: A Critique* (Philadelphia: Pennsylvania Mental Health, Inc., 1960), is a candid and realistic evaluation of the use of the concept of mental health in educational efforts.

perfect mental health sometimes encountered in Sunday supplement articles does not exist in flesh and blood. The research studies of so-called normal people—that is, people who have families, hold jobs and are involved in no major conflicts with the laws of society—disclose "rich pathological material" in the average man's personality. Most people have temporary psychological upsets from time to time.

From the perspective of a religious orientation, most definitions of mental health are deficient in that they omit an emphasis on the vertical dimension of life—the dimension of values, meanings, and the spiritual reality which we call God. Spiritual health—the adequacy of one's philosophy of life and the maturity of one's relationship with God—is an indispensable aspect of mental health. Inadequacies in this area are often causative factors in producing mental disturbance. In the light of this, "mental health," as the term is employed in this book, includes a satisfying and growing relationship with God, as the person understands him. The term mental health, then, has four major aspects—the ability to relate constructively with oneself (inner unity), with other people, and with God, and the ability to cope with the demands of life.

To offset the perfectionism which tends to make a burden of the idea of mental health, it is helpful to point out what mental health is not (as stated by a group of experts in the mental health disciplines, meeting at Cornell University in 1958). Mental health is *not:*

1. *Adjustment under all circumstances.* There are many circumstances to which man should not adjust, otherwise there would be no progress. 2. *Freedom from anxiety and tensions.* Anxiety and tension are often prerequisites and accompaniments of creativity and self-preservation. . . . 3. *Freedom from dissatisfaction.* . . . 4. *Conformity.* One criterion of maturity is the ability to stand apart from the crowd when conditions indicate. . . . 5. *Constant happiness.* In this imperfect world, a sensitive, mature person often experiences unhappiness. 6. *A lessening of accomplishment and creativity.* Mental health is characterized by the ability of the individual to use his powers ever more fully. 7. *The absence of personal idiosyncrasies.* Many such idiosyncrasies which do not interfere with function enrich the life of the individual and those who come in contact with him. 8. *The undermining of authority.* Mental health is

characterized by the increased ability of the individual to use and respect realistic authority while deprecating the use of authority as an oppressive force. . . . 9. *Opposition to religious values.* Mental health facilitates and complements the aims of religion inasmuch as it fosters the highest spiritual and social values.[13]

WHY A CENTRAL CONCERN OF THE CHURCH?

A church's concern for mental health is at the very center of its mission, at the heart of its God-given task. It is not a frill nor a fad, but a logical, inescapable expression of a church's central mission on earth. Here are four reasons why mental health is an essential part of the church's mission:

(1) *Mental health is directly linked to the fundamental purpose of the church.* In their classic study, reported in *The Purpose of the Church and Its Ministry,* H. Richard Niebuhr and his collaborators concluded that "no substitute can be found for the definition of the goal of the Church as the *increase among men of the love of God and neighbor.*" [14] One basic function that is impaired in the mentally ill person is his ability to give and receive love. A teacher of psychiatry has observed that the two great commandments of Jesus provide a test of mental health. To the extent that a person is able to love God and neighbor, he is mentally healthy. When one sees the basic purpose of the church and the nature of mental health in juxtaposition, their interrelationship becomes clear. To say to a person who is crippled in his ability to love, "What you need is to love God and your neighbor," is like saying to a man clinging to a log in mid-ocean, "What you need is dry land." Nothing could be truer or less helpful. In working for positive mental health or for the improved treatment of personality problems the church is implementing its basic purpose by enhancing the *ability* of persons to love God and neighbor.

In other words, mental health deals with the well-being of that which in Christian ethics is regarded as the most precious part of God's creation—*personality.* George Albert Coe's familiar definition of religion as "the discovery of persons" points in the same direction.

[13] *Ibid.,* pp. 13-14.
[14] *The Purpose of the Church and Its Ministry* (New York: Harper & Brothers, 1956) , p. 31.

Mental health is enhanced when persons are discovered—discovered on the level where they hope and hurt, on the level of their hunger and despair. A parent who discovers his child—that is, discovers how to satisfy the child's deep personality hungers—will enhance the child's mental health.

(2) *Spiritual health and mental health are inseparably related.* As indicated above, spiritual health is an indispensable aspect of mental health. The two can be separated only on a theoretical basis. In live human beings, spiritual and mental health are inextricably interwoven. Whatever hurts or heals one's relationship with oneself and others will tend to hurt or heal one's relationship with God, and vice versa. Robert H. Felix has pointed out that the more human personality is studied from the medical viewpoint the more we become aware of the important role of religious faith in maintaining mental and emotional health. On the other hand, psychiatrist Richard G. Johnson has stated that "a healthy mind is necessary for a person to get the most out of his religion." [15] (It is significant that the words "health," "hale," "whole," and "holy" come from the same Anglo-Saxon root.[16]) Morris L. West writes: "The sick mind is a defective instrument in the great symphony which is God's dialogue with man." [17]

The relationship between mental health and religious awareness is often complex. Many brilliant religious insights have been produced by persons whose mental health was anything but robust. A chronic depressive such as Kierkegaard, the father of existentialism, is a superb illustration of this. Is it that emotional disturbances force people like the "gloomy Dane" to look below the surface of the so-called "normal" world? It may be, as Rollo May has suggested, that some people experience mental difficulties *because* they are more sensitive than others to the injustices, cruelties, and irrationalities of life. In any case, the church should reject any easy identification of optimum spiritual development with culture-bound definitions of

[15] Former psychiatric director of the Mental Health Clinic at the Westwood, California, Methodist Church in a lecture at the Veterans Administration Seminar, 1958.
[16] Paul B. Maves (ed.), *The Church and Mental Health* (New York: Charles Scribner's Sons, 1953), p. 1.
[17] *The Shoes of the Fisherman* (New York: Dell Publishing Co., 1963), p. 79.

mental health.[18] Having said this, it is important to reemphasize the many continuities and correlations which *are* found between a person's experiences with people and his relationship with God.

(3) *Mental health has been a central concern of the Christian community throughout the centuries.* Mental health is a modern label for an ancient concern. In the Christian church it is as ancient as the life of a young carpenter who is said to have declared, "I came that they may have life, and have it abundantly" (John 10: 10) . It is as ancient as the Christian concern for *wholeness in persons.* A sense of the deep roots in our tradition of passion for personality wholeness can help the mental health concern catch fire in a local congregation. Halford Luccock once declared, "There are a lot of people chattering about the 'new psychology' who never heard of the old psychology." [19] A study such as *Pastoral Care in Historical Perspective* gives convincing evidence that the church at its best has always had a vital interest in what we now call mental health.[20]

The contemporary mental health thrust in the churches has the advantage of new insights from the sciences of man and new helping techniques from the psychotherapeutic disciplines. But essentially, it is the same concern for the healing and growth of persons as was found in the ministry of Jesus, in the apostolic church, in the work of John Chrysostom (the church father who thought of himself as a "physician of souls") , in the ministry of Martin Luther with his "Letters of Spiritual Counsel," and of great pastors such as Richard Baxter of the Puritan period and Horace Bushnell of the nineteenth century.

(4) *Mental health is a central concern of the church because of the tragic toll of human agony caused by its absence.* Anything that hurts a single child of God is of immediate concern to a Christian.

[18] A line from William James's Gifford lectures is relevant at this point: "At any rate you must all be ready now to judge the religious life by its results exclusively, and I shall assume that the bugaboo of morbid origin will scandalize your piety no more." From *The Varieties of Religious Experience* (Modern library ed.; New York: Random House, 1936) , p. 2.

[19] Halford Luccock, *Marching Off the Map, and Other Sermons* (New York: Harper & Row, 1952) , p. 162.

[20] W. A. Clebsch and C. J. Jaekle (Englewood Cliffs, N. J.: Prentice-Hall, 1964) ; see also John T. McNeill, *A History of the Cure of Souls* (New York: Harper & Brothers, 1951) and Charles F. Kemp, *Physicians of the Soul* (New York: The Macmillan Company, 1947) .

The weight of raw human suffering caused by the absence of mental health defies comprehension.

Let us say that an hypothetical minister serves a congregation which includes five hundred adults representing a cross-section of the American population.[21] Based on various research studies, it could be estimated that approximately twenty-five of his members have been hospitalized for major mental illness in the past, twenty-four are alcoholics, another fifty are severely handicapped by neurotic conflicts, and another one hundred by moderate neurotic symptoms.[22]

One hundred fifteen members of his congregation would answer "yes" to the question, "Have you ever felt you were going to have a nervous breakdown?" Seventy would have sought professional help with a personal or marital problem in the past.[23] Over six of his parishioners will be hospitalized for mental illness in any given year. An average of one member of his congregation will attempt suicide every other year. Eight members of his congregation will be involved in serious crimes in a given year. If the married persons in his congregation were asked to rate the relative happiness of their nuptial relationship, fewer than half would rate them as "very happy." [24]

When projected on a national scale the statistics are as follows:[25]

Hospitalized during a year for psychiatric treatment	1,450,000
Hospitalized at any one time for mental illness	800,000
Children and youth treated for mental disturbances	269,200
Total children and youth needing psychiatric help	1,000,000
Alcoholics	5,000,000
Drug addicts	50,000
Suicides per year	18,000
Serious crimes per year	1,800,000
Juveniles arrested per year	1,500,000
Children living in homes broken by divorce or death	6,000,000

[21] This would, of course, be an atypical Protestant congregation since the middle class tends to be overrepresented in such groups.

[22] W. L. Holt, Jr., "The Mental Disease Problem as Seen by the Practicing Physician," *Health Week* (November, 1955), pp. 17-18.

[23] *Americans View Their Mental Health*, p. 304.

[24] *Ibid.*, p. 92.

[25] Unless otherwise noted, these figures are from "Facts About Mental Illness," National Association of Mental Health, 1962.

Divorces per year 400,000
Persons incapacitated by major neurotic conflicts 17,000,000
Spent on tranquilizers per year $150,000,000

Even if one chooses to make sizable deductions from these figures to allow for possible overestimates, the picture is still one of overpowering darkness and despair. The cold statistics represent an immense load of pain. To those who are seriously enough disturbed to become statistics must be added the anonymous millions whose God-given creativity is crippled by self-doubt, guilt, and anxiety. In every church and every community a considerable percentage of "normal" people exist as emotional cripples, living half-lives at only a small fraction of their potentialities. The possibilities for good which a positive program of mental health can have for such persons defies the imagination.

Nearly everyone has read statistics like these time and again in the popular press. They are what the volume *Action for Mental Health* describes as "shocking figures that no longer shock." A seminary professor of ethics has described Christian love as "the ability to read statistics with compassion." [26] Somehow we must get behind the statistics on mental illness to the suffering human beings they represent—persons with the same basic feelings that you and I have.

For the sake of its spiritual integrity, the church must take an interest in the problems of mental illness. A local church can so easily become a polite, middle-class club—comfortable and irrelevant to human agony. Firsthand contact with the grimly discouraging work of helping the hurt and the troubled can keep a church close to the infected wounds of our society. Based on McCann's research concerning what the churches are doing in the field of mental illness and mental health, the authors of *Action for Mental Health* wrote this indictment of our lethargy and unconcern: "The prevalence of religion in modern American society, as measured by church membership . . . does not seem to have had any measurable positive or negative effect on mental health. . . . Moreover, *the churches, as nearly as this study was able to determine, are not devoting much more attention to mental health than is society at large.*" [27] The familiar

[26] Waldo Beach, Duke Divinity School.
[27] *Action for Mental Health*, pp. 139-40.

words of Dean Inge are relevant here: "In religion, nothing fails like success."

Consider this modern paraphrase of a familiar story:

A certain man went down the rocky twisted road on his inner journey. The thieves of unhappy experiences, disappointments, and anxieties robbed him of his mental and spiritual well-being, leaving him broken and bleeding beside the road of life. A minister came along, and later, a leading layman. Both saw the man broken in spirit beside the road. But they were very busy with other important matters. So they walked by on the other side. After a while, a social worker (or a member of AA, Gambler's Anonymous, or Recovery) came by that way. He saw the man broken in spirit and had compassion on him, binding up his mental and spiritual wounds. Then he took him to a halfway house where he could regain his health. Who, then, was neighbor to him who fell among the thieves of mental health?

This modern parable is obviously unjust to the ministers and laymen I described earlier in this chapter. Many of them are actively engaged in mental health activities. But if McCann's findings are accurate the parable speaks the truth about many local churches.

THE THINGS THAT MAKE FOR MENTAL HEALTH

Positive mental health, like a plant, grows best in a certain environment. The interpersonal environment within which mental health flourishes is one in which basic personality needs are satisfied (see chap. 6). When human relationships in a family, a church, or a community are of such a quality as to satisfy the heart-hungers of persons, they grow toward the fulfillment of their potentialities. When relationships block the satisfaction of these needs, persons stop growing and become vulnerable to personality illnesses. When the personality needs of parents and children are relatively well-satisfied in a home, the marriage is sturdy and parent-child relationships flower. Temporary personality malnutrition produces garden-variety unhappiness and conflict. Severe and continuing deprivation produces personality warping and illnesses.

A local church is part of the *extended family*—a part of that web of meaningful relationships which encircle and undergird the inner circle of the family. As in the case of the family, the health and effectiveness of a church are directly related to its success in satisfying the needs of people. A "good church," like a "good marriage," is one within which persons find a quality of relatedness which satisfies their heart-hungers. The inspiration, fellowship, and sense of belonging which come from involvement in the life of a church where people are "members one of another" (Rom. 12:5) is an important source of psychological nourishment. This satisfaction of inner needs helps nurture mental health and prepares one to meet the needs of others.

CHAPTER 2
The Christian Message and Mental Health

*The manner in which a man utilizes his religion—
whether it be to enrich and ennoble his life or to excuse his selfishness and cruelty, or to rationalize his
delusions and hallucinations, or to clothe himself in
a comforting illusion of omnipotence—is a com-
mentary on the state of his mental health.*[1]
—*Karl A. Menninger*

THE RELIGION THAT HURTS VERSUS THE RELIGION THAT HEALS

Sad to say, the church has not always been on the side of the angels
in the treatment of the mentally ill; nor has the Christian religion
uniformly been used in ways that enhance positive mental health. In
reflecting on the *History of Medical Psychology*,[2] Aldous Huxley
commented in a satirical vein:

The tormentors of the insane have been drawn, in the main, from
two professions—the medical and the clerical. To which shall we award
the palm? Have clergymen been responsible for more gratuitous suffering than doctors? Or have doctors made up for a certain lack of intensity
in their brand of torture (after all, they never went so far as to burn
anyone alive for being mad) by its longer duration and greater number
of victims? It is a nice point. To prevent hard feelings, let us divide the
prize equally between the two contenders.[3]

[1] *The Human Mind* (3rd ed.; New York: Alfred A. Knopf, 1946), p. 467.
[2] Gregory Zilboorg, *History of Medical Psychology* (New York: W. W. Norton &
Company, 1941).
[3] "Madness, Badness, and Sadness," *Esquire* (June, 1956), p. 50.

26

Huxley points out that, during most of the centuries of the Christian age, the mentally ill have been subjected to almost ceaseless torture. During the sixteenth century, for instance, religious leaders burned at the stake a vast number of "witches" (estimated at from one hundred thousand to several million). They did it for what they believed to be the soundest of theological reasons (which must have been small comfort to the "witches"). More recent examples could be cited.

Unfortunately, tragic mistakes in the area of mental health by religious leaders are not all in the past. In preparing a report for an international congress on mental health, a group of clinically trained chaplains summarized the insights derived from their work in mental hospitals and prisons:

American Protestantism has frequently made critical and tragic errors in its presentation of the Christian religion—errors which have contributed to emotional and spiritual conflict and immaturity in our people. Most of those errors find a focus in a stern, legalistic, absolute, and Pharisaical moralism which is the characteristically American form of Protestantism.[4]

The Christian message is frequently distorted in ways that cause it to hurt rather than to heal, to block rather than to stimulate personality growth. Any minister who has worked in a mental hospital has had to face this painful truth—that distorted religion has contributed to the immaturity, guilt, isolation, fear, and rage of some of the crippled souls to whom he ministers.

Through the centuries, religious leaders have been handling psychological dynamite with little awareness of the tremendous power for good or ill in their hands. In recent decades, thanks to the behavioral sciences and the psychotherapeutic disciplines, tools for testing the impact of various forms of religion on people's lives have begun to become available. It behooves those of us who have responsibilities for teaching the Christian message—ministers, church school teachers, and parents in particular—to become aware of the probable psychological effects of certain interpretations of that message.

[4] "American Protestantism and Mental Health," *Journal of Clinical Pastoral Work,* Vol. I, No. 4 (Winter, 1948), p. 1.

The central thesis of this discussion is that *religion can be a con-structive, creative, healing, life-affirming force or a dark, repressive, life-crippling force,* depending on the way it is understood and used. In this chapter, I will present a list of tentative criteria for dis-tinguishing health-enhancing religion from sickness-producing re-ligion, based on experience in counseling with troubled persons. In describing criteria for a mentally healthy religion, I am not sug-gesting that there is any one monolithic, mentally healthy theology. Variations in personality needs make different religious interpreta-tions meaningful to different individuals. Respect for the unique religious needs of one's neighbor is one indication of a mentally healthy religious view.

Let me indicate the nature of some of the limitations of the ap-proach used in this chapter. In several cases, my biblical interpreta-tions are strongly influenced by *prescriptive* considerations, more than *descriptive* considerations (of what their literal meaning may have been in the thought world of century one). My assumption is that recent insights from the behavioral sciences constitute fresh reve-lations about man. These insights illuminate many of the issues dis-cussed in the New Testament, and provide us with a new perspective from which first century interpretations of the human situation can be reexamined. For example, the Sermon on the Mount passages are interpreted in this chapter in ways that seem to be constructive in the light of our knowledge concerning how personality is formed and deformed. Although my interpretations do not reflect the literal first century meanings at every point, they do represent what I be-lieve Jesus would mean (in the context of his concern for persons) were he speaking in our day.

Examining religious ideas or practices in terms of their effects on personality is one valid way of evaluating such phenomena. It is important, however, to hold this criterion in tension with other criteria—for example: What is the validity of an idea in the light of the understandings produced by that tradition's best minds? The essential task of judging the conflicting results which may accrue from the application of different criteria is a difficult one which (fortunately) is beyond the scope of this book.

All definitions reflect the hidden assumptions of the culture which produces them. Thus, current definitions of mental health may be influenced subtly by our culture in ways that make them faulty devices for evaluating religious ideas and practices. In other words, when one applies mental health criteria to religion, it is well to remember that the results will be tentative, partial, and in need of correction from other intellectual perspectives, cultures, and historical periods. All of this reminds me of the Brazilian psychiatrist in a story by Machado de Assis who decides that the disturbed people are really well-balanced and vice versa. He is committed to his own hospital, using his criteria of mental health, because he is considered by everyone to be perfectly sane.[5]

In spite of these limitations and dangers, it is important to attempt to differentiate health-stimulating from sickness-spawning religion. Both anthropological and clinical evidence support the validity of distinguishing the positive and negative effects of various religious approaches. Anthropologist Ruth Benedict has given a dramatic comparison [6] of the "adient," or love-motivated religion of the Zuni Indians of the Southwest, and the "abient," or fear-motivated religion of the Ojibwa of the Canadian-U. S. border regions. All Zuni gods are beneficent; all religious practices are interpersonal in orientation. There is no sorcery. The Ojibwa gods, in contrast, have to be bargained with and bribed. All religious practices are self-centered and there is an abundance of black magic. The Zuni are a happy people who "dance" everywhere, including their religion. The Ojibwa use dancing only for individualistic prestige, never for the joy of common participation and celebration.

The pastoral counselor encounters many examples of both the positive and negative uses of the Christian religion. I can recall many persons in whose lives Christianity was a rich source of courage, strength, and growth. It enabled them to handle personal crises of almost unbelievable dimensions. They were troubled and in need of pastoral care but they were not crushed. Their religion was obviously a very present help in time of trouble. On the other hand, the misuse of the Christian religion has also been illustrated in my counseling experience—a father who used religion as a club to force his children to conform to his puritanical distortion of Christian

[5] *The Psychiatrist and Other Stories* (Berkeley: University of California Press, 1963).
[6] *Patterns of Culture* (Boston: Houghton Mifflin Company, 1934).

ethics; a middle-aged woman living under a miasmic cloud of what she believed to be the "unforgivable sin"; a teen-ager in a frenzy of morbid guilt based in part on a literalistic self-application of certain New Testament statements regarding sexual thoughts. Those of us who have dismissed a literal belief in demons as a form of crude superstition cannot but be impressed by the "demonic" destructiveness of warped religion.

The impact of religion on mental health is usually complex. In a study of sixty-eight mental hospital patients, Wayne Oates reports that twenty percent used religious ideas to clothe their psychoses, seventeen percent showed a long-standing rebellion-submission conflict toward the religion of their early home (their religion being interwoven with unresolved conflicts with parent figures), and another ten percent seemed to be using religion as a "last straw." Surprisingly, since the study was made in the "Bible belt," fifty-one percent gave no evidence of religious interests or ideas in their illnesses. This report, contained in *Religious Factors in Mental Illness*,[7] shows that it is important not to exaggerate the role of religion in causing mental illness.

Sick religion is both cause and effect. Distorted religion is often one symptom of an underlying personality distortion. But it is more than this. The sick person's sick religion tends to reinforce his pathology! From her cross-cultural studies, Ruth Benedict concluded that a group's religion both mirrors and molds the life of that group. The egocentric, mistrust-saturated Ojibwa religion is a major factor in keeping mistrust and aggression rife in that culture. It reinforces the very factors which brought it into being. The cooperative interpersonal climate of the Zunis is both reflected and reinforced by their religious beliefs and practices. What is true in these Indian cultures is also true of individuals and groups in our culture.

SOME TESTS FOR MENTALLY HEALTHY RELIGION

Ever since William James contrasted the religion of the "healthy minded" and that of the "sick soul," [8] students of psychology of religion have wrestled with the distinguishing characteristics of health-giving and health-depleting forms of religion. Here is a list of inter-

[7] Wayne E. Oates (New York: Association Press, 1955), pp. 6-7.
[8] See *The Varieties of Religious Experience*.

dependent questions which I have found useful in separating mentally healthy from mentally unhealthy religion:

1. *Does a particular form of religious thought and practice build bridges or barriers between people?*

What religion does to interpersonal relationships is the acid test. Does it isolate one group from another, or does it draw them into a warm sense of kinship? Does it express in action the universality of God who has "made from one every nation" (Acts 17:26) and "Have we not all one father?" (Mal. 2:10)? Is it inclusive or exclusive in its conception of salvation? Those forms of Christianity which exclude non-Christians from access to God and salvation drive wedges between individuals and groups. They maintain a sense of ingroup security by keeping alive a belief in the exclusive truth of their position. But they sacrifice those mutually enriching relationships with others who differ, which could broaden their own horizons and deepen their understanding. Their arrogance and exclusivism cause jangling disharmonies in intergroup relations, and deny the spirit of the majestic conception of Christian love described in I Cor. 13.

In *Religious Factors in Mental Illness,* Oates writes: "In essence . . . healthy religion binds people together in such a way that their individuality is enabled both to be realized and to be consecrated to the total community . . . to which they belong. This is a religion of mature and responsible relatedness." [9] This particular aspect of mentally healthy religion has taken on special significance on our shrinking planet where human animosities are now armed with hydrogen bombs and worse. Norman Cousins writes:

Religion need not turn against itself to do what is now necessary. A basic unity already exists. That unity resides not in doctrine but in man himself. . . . Theology cannot survive without man. Theology therefore can transcend itself in the cause of man . . . what we can do is to try to get all to agree to the human proposition that spiritual resources are inherent in all men, that these resources, when summoned, can bring them closer to one another, and that the sacredness of life is not peculiar to any one creed.[10]

[9] p. 113.
[10] Quoted from Harvey H. Potthoff, "Theology and the Vision of Greatness," *The Iliff Review* (Winter, 1959), p. 10.

2. Does a particular form of religious thought and practice strengthen or weaken a basic sense of trust and relatedness to the universe?

As Erik Erikson has observed, a contribution which positive religion makes to mental health is that of giving people periodic experiences of the renewal of trust. To know that life is trustworthy and that one is organically related to the rest of creation produces a strengthening, healing effect on personality. Persons who have felt they had to fight the stream of life discover they can float on it. Moses expressed this in his blessing of the people of Israel: "Underneath are the everlasting arms" (Deut. 33:27). In a vital religious experience the ontological loneliness of feeling oneself to be a spiritual orphan is overcome by the awareness of one's unity with all of life.

In Protestant thought the Pauline conception that salvation (healing, reconciliation) comes "by grace . . . through faith" (Eph. 2:8) is central. Here the word "faith" has overtones of "trust," as when one says "I have faith in him." It is in a relationship of trust that the love of God can have its healing effects.

3. Does a particular form of religious thought and practice stimulate or hamper the growth of inner freedom and personal responsibility? Closely related questions are these: *Does it encourage healthy or unhealthy dependency relationships—mature or immature relationships with authority? Does it encourage growth of mature or immature consciences?*

Some psychotherapists charge that religion often fosters emotional immaturity, childish dependency, and a lack of inner freedom. Unfortunately, this is a valid accusation when applied to dogmatic theologies and authoritarian forms of church relationships. The chaplains' group, mentioned earlier, states: "One of the most common errors found in the churches is an unhealthy *authoritarianism.* Too frequently we develop fear, submissiveness, dependence, and guilt as a result of that attitude." [11] Authoritarian religious leaders, theologies, or ecclesiastical systems produce adults who are infantilized to some degree in their spiritual lives. Conformity to a theological and ethical "party line" becomes the goal. The individual is de-

[11] "American Protestantism and Mental Health," p. 1.

prived of the possibility of growth through working out his own salvation. Consequently, he cannot discover that particular religious approach that is most meaningful and satisfying to him.

The Protestant parallel of dependence on the absolute church of Roman Catholicism is dependence on an absolute book (the Bible interpreted literally) or an absolute creed. Unhealthy dependency patterns also emerge in liberal Protestant circles when clergymen (because of their insecurities and power drives) gain neurotic satisfactions from keeping their congregations dependent. In all of these cases, persons "escape from freedom," to use Erich Fromm's apt term, into the security of an authority-centered religious group. The anxieties of struggle with the complexities of adult life are avoided, but so is the growth which could result from this struggle.

The popularity of authority-centered religious groups in our society is one indication of the prevalence of emotional cripples. Many persons probably could not function were it not for the womb-like security of authoritarian religions. From the mental health standpoint these groups should be seen for what they are—immature systems for immature people. Our protest should be at the point where such religions anchor people in their immaturity. Some who have the capacity for growth toward inner freedom are trapped by a repressive system. Children who grow up in authoritarian systems (religious, familial, or political) are crippled by them. Such systems thus become self-perpetuating. They create the very neurotic needs for the absolute answers which they then supply.

A key distinction between healthy and unhealthy dependence should be made. On the interpersonal level, healthy dependence (for adults) can best be described as interdependence. Unhealthy dependence (on a religious leader, for instance) is a symbiotic (mutually parasitic) relationship in which the "true believer" gains a neurotic sense of power by identifying with the leader. The leader in turn is dependent on the sense of power derived from having others dependent on him. On a theological dimension, unhealthy dependence is involved when a person expects God to do for him what he is capable of doing for himself. Maturity-motivating religion, in contrast, encourages people to utilize their God-given inner freedom and resources to handle their life situations constructively.

Healthy dependence is based on the recognition that one is not God, and that one is, in fact, dependent on other people, nature, and God for life itself. This is the basic meaning of "humility." There is as much grandiosity in the way some "self-made" persons ignore their dependence on others as in the way some religious people try to manipulate life to their own petty ends through religious practices.

Erich Fromm's distinction between rational and irrational authority helps clarify the healthy versus unhealthy dependence issue. All of us need rational authority, the authority of competence. This was the authority with which Jesus spoke. His competence in spiritual matters was self-evident. His grasp of the truth was unmistakably authentic. This was in sharp contrast to the irrational authority of the scribes and pharisees, an authority based on status and power over others.

Religious approaches based on irrational authority breed immature (authority-centered) consciences in their adherents. Such a conscience is negative in orientation. It is saturated by neurotic guilt (fear of punishment and abandonment). The conscience of a child is formed as he internalizes the values and taboos of his culture which are screened through the praise-blame, reward-punishment systems of his parents. In healthy maturing, this childhood conscience should gradually be transcended. The mature conscience is essentially positive. It is oriented around what that individual really values. Its guilt rises not from fear of punishment but from the awareness that one has hurt what is of highest value—persons. This is rational appropriate guilt, as contrasted with neurotic guilt.

To the degree that one is burdened with neurotic guilt stemming from an authoritarian conscience, one is incapable of experiencing rational guilt. It is as though one's moral capital were exhausted in the operation of the immature conscience. The maturing religious person should experience a widening awareness of what is really worthy of pouring his life into. As psychologist Gordon W. Allport puts it, the person begins "to live in accordance with an adequate frame of value and meaning, and to enlarge and energize that frame." [12]

4. *Does a particular form of religious thought and practice pro-*

[12] *The Individual and His Religion* (New York: The Macmillan Company, 1950), p. 64.

vide effective or faulty means of helping persons move from a sense of guilt to forgiveness? Does it provide well-defined, significant, ethical guidelines, or does it emphasize ethical trivia? Is its primary concern for surface behavior or for the underlying health of the personality?

The problem of unresolved guilt feelings—neurotic and normal— is a persistent one in much mental illness. In understanding this, the distinction between *moralism* and *morality* is useful. Moralism contributes to mental illness; morality, to mental health. Moralism, concerned with controlling surface behavior, arouses neurotic guilt feelings about sex, anger, and ethical trivia, and is the product of an authoritarian conscience. Moralism is concerned with *sins;* morality, primarily with *Sin*—the condition of a person's inner life in which he is alienated from other people and God. An example of the pathetic distortion of the Christian message often produced by moralism was the sermon preached by a certain chaplain on the eve of the Normandy invasion. The men of his military group had come together for worship, knowing that many of them would not be alive by the next sunset. They were hungry for some message to give meaning to their situation. The chaplain delivered a rousing sermon to a crowded chapel, on the evils of smoking and drinking. His moralism gave them not bread but a stone!

Sound morality is concerned with both the underlying causes and the social consequences of person-hurting behavior. It seeks to provide reasonable guidelines for interpersonal relationships, fostering the kind of society where personality can mature. It recognizes that a person's capacity for genuine ethical decisions depends on the extent of his inner freedom, which in turn depends on the degree of his mental health. To the extent that a person is driven by inner compulsions and shackled by neurotic guilt-feelings, he is unfree to function ethically. He may seem to be good, because he is afraid to be bad, but there is no wholeheartedness or spontaneity in his "goodness."

A religious system which provides significant ethical norms (that is, having to do with the maximizing of personality values) gives growing individuals guidelines in developing their own value systems. The best in a tradition should be available to persons as resources in discovering their own hierarchy of values. As Erik Erikson has shown, ethical ideals are vital elements in the ego's strength. It is crucial that people come to feel guilt about significant things—that is, those misuses of one's freedom that hurt persons. The capacity to experience appropriate guilt is one of the signs of mental health. Those in whom this capacity is undeveloped are emotionally ill. In the psychiatric vocabulary they are called "sociopathic personalities."

Constructive means of reducing guilt are essential in health-promoting religion. Liberal Protestantism has often not taken guilt seriously. How guilt is handled depends on whether it is neurotic or normal. (Actually the two elements are usually blended in a given individual's psyche.) The neurotic elements can be recognized by these characteristics: (a) They do not respond to forgiveness (from God or other people). (b) They do not motivate the guilt-laden person to make constructive amends (although they may produce compulsive confessing). (c) They are the product of moralism in that they focus on surface behavior, ethical trivia, or on feelings and impulses which are taboo in one's culture. (d) They are often linked with perfectionism, an impossibly high standard which makes continual failure inevitable. Normal or rational guilt is reduced by confession (in worship or counseling) and healthy atonement (making amends). Neurotic guilt may be temporarily alleviated by such methods, but a more lasting sense of forgiveness depends on working through (in counseling) the conflicts that underly it.

Healthy religion encourages a person to accept himself as he is—imperfect, finite, sinful—and then to move ahead. Self-acceptance, based on God's acceptance, is the starting-point of spiritual growth. Perfectionism, a serious deterrent to self-acceptance, tends to paralyze growth. It is a form of self-punishment—the punishment of automatic failure. Literalistic interpretation of the biblical passage, "You, therefore, must be perfect, as your heavenly Father is perfect" (Matt. 5:48), tends to feed the perfectionistic tendencies of neurotic individuals. Charles C. Torrey's paraphrase, "Be therefore all including in your good will even as your heavenly Father includes all" is preferable, from a mental health perspective, particularly if seen as an ideal which exerts a steady pull toward widening one's circle of goodwill rather than a static, achievable goal.

As Tillich has observed, the heart of forgiveness is reconciliation.

From a mental health standpoint, the nature of the reconciliation is crucial. In certain forms of Christianity, it is similar to the groveling experience of a child who is driven back to a harsh parent by an intense fear of abandonment. To be healing, reconciliation must be like the experience of the Prodigal who comes to himself in a breakthrough of self-awareness and realizes that the parent's love has never left him, even in the far country of rebellion. Having grown through his painful far-country experience, reconciliation further enhances his personhood.

There is a consistent emphasis in Jesus' teaching on the roots or underlying causes of behavior in the "heart" of man. "For out of the abundance of the heart the mouth speaks. The good man out of his good treasure brings forth good" (Matt. 12:34-35). To the superficial moralists he was saying, "Why are you concerned only with surface behavior while ignoring the causes of this behavior in man's inner life?" His concern was for the underlying wholeness of personality.

Depth psychology has confirmed the wisdom of Jesus' focus by discovering many of the hidden (unconscious) causes of behavior. It has demonstrated the soundness of seeking to enhance total personality health rather than merely controlling surface symptoms. (Destructive symptoms—for example, Hitler's—must be controlled to protect society, of course.) Jesus' words to Nicodemus, emphasizing the necessity of rebirth (John 3:3), stress the importance of radical change at the center of a life. An error on a mimeograph stencil is repeated on every copy. Moralism's attempt to control surface behavior is comparable to correcting each copy instead of changing the stencil.

The chaplains' report, mentioned earlier, observed:

Churches have had *too little concern for understanding why people behave as they do* and have been *most relentless in their condemnation* of acts contrary to social standards with the result that many have responded with intense guilt feelings. . . . The guilty feel a sense of fear, loneliness, and rejection and the result is various degrees of emotional disturbance.[13]

[13] "American Protestantism and Mental Health," p. 1.

5. *Does a particular form of religious thought and practice increase or lessen the enjoyment of life? Does it encourage a person to appreciate or deprecate the feeling dimension of life?*

The various forms of the word "joy" are used 192 times in the Bible. Jesus' fondness for all sorts of people (including the hard-to-accept) was a scandal to his critics. His glad participation in occasions of fellowship provided his enemies with the excuse to brand him a winebibber and a glutton. He was pro-life, savoring deeply the satisfactions of communion with others and with God. His joy was directly related to his awareness that a new age of spiritual aliveness was breaking into history, making possible a new creativity in relationships. Here are the words attributed to him by the author of the fourth Gospel: "These things I have spoken to you, that my joy may be in you, and that your joy may be full" (John 15:11).

Unhealthy religion contradicts the spirit of Jesus' life by fleeing from the God-given vitalities of living into asceticism. Much of Christian history is warped at this point. Religion errs when it becomes primarily a source of controls, rules, and duties, and loses its ability to lift, inspire, and energize the totality of one's life. According to Harry Emerson Fosdick, such lopsided religion provides weights, not wings on the spirit of man. There is more than enough drabness in life without making religion into a force that further squeezes the enjoyment out of living!

One form of enjoyment that is often neglected is religious enjoyment—the uplifting, numinous, and ecstatic elements in religious experience. The spine-tingling qualities in vital religion are often missing in conventional churches. In Jungian terms, the masculine elements in religion (reason, logic, ethics, controls) are present without the balancing feminine elements (feeling, giving, accepting, nurturing). This accounts, in part, for the popularity of the sect groups which encourage their adherents to feel and enjoy their religion. When religion loses its mystical quality, many people seek a pseudoreligious experience in alcohol.[14] The prayer of Augustine in *The Confessions* has wistful overtones for modern man: "Oh! that Thou wouldst enter into my heart and inebriate it." It is a pity

---

[14] For a comprehensive discussion of the use of alcohol as a religious substitute, see "Philosophical-Religious Factors in the Etiology and Treatment of Alcoholism," by H. J. Clinebell, Jr., *Quarterly Journal of Studies on Alcohol* (Fall, 1963).

that many have found so little excitement, inspiration, and lift in their religion that they have sought these in nonreligious practices.

The full range of religious enjoyment depends on loving God with both one's mind and heart. The religion that stimulates health strives to involve the whole person in the religious quest. It brings the full scope of the intellect to bear on the pursuit of religious truth but, recognizing the importance of feelings and attitudes in personality health, it avoids top-heavy, intellectualized religious approaches. It respects the deepest freedom—the freedom to think, imagine, fantasy, and feel. Negative religion blocks this precious inner feeling by spawning neurotic guilt about asocial and antisocial feelings. Positive religion encourages appreciation of the richness which a wide spectrum of feelings brings to one's life.

Healthy religion draws a clear distinction between the right to feel and fantasy and the necessary prohibitions against acting on all one's feelings. If this key distinction is blurred, persons become so guilt-ridden and frightened about their "bad" thoughts or so destructive in their actions that their creativity is crippled. Dorothy W. Baruch declares:

No matter how we prod or pry, a child is going to go right on feeling the way he feels. If we don't let him think his feelings aloud, he'll think them under his breath. If we make him too ashamed to think them consciously, he'll feel them in his unconscious where he is unaware of them and so can do nothing about them. But we don't stop him from feeling the feelings . . . no matter how "bad" or "wicked" they are.[15]

This also applies to adults. Constructive religion views the capacity to feel, vividly and along a wide spectrum of emotions, as one of God's good gifts.

6. *Does a particular form of religious thought and practice handle the vital energies of sex and aggressiveness in constructive or repressive ways?*

There is no more revealing test of the mental health impact of a religious approach than its handling of sex and aggressiveness. Creativity-crippling repression most often occurs in these two areas.

---

[15] *New Ways in Discipline* (New York: McGraw-Hill Book Company, 1949), pp. 47-48.

When persons label these drives as "bad" in themselves, they must either deny their existence (repression) or stagger under a deadening load of guilt feelings.

Despite recent improvements, the overall record of churches in the handling of sex has been far from constructive. The doctrine of the virgin birth has at times been interpreted in ways that suggest that the normal means of procreation is tainted. Baptism has sometimes been interpreted as a cleansing of a baby from the stain felt to result from the circumstances of his conception and birth. The idea of original sin has been interpreted by some to imply that it was either the consequence or cause of sexual intercourse by the first man and woman. Such interpretations are distortions which obscure the valid meaning of these symbols.[16]

A positive Christian view of sex holds that it is God-given, to be used appropriately, as any of God's gifts. Christians (and others) should thank God that he devised such an enjoyable way of continuing the race. It may be that the human species' day-in, day-out interest in sex (as contrasted to the periodic interest of most other animal species) accounts in part, for the relative permanence of the family. Any gift of God, if misused, damages personality. Sex enhances personality when experienced in a context of love and responsibility.

The positive Christian view of sex extends the range of its appropriate functions beyond *procreation* to include the *unitive* function—that is, two persons overcoming their spiritual isolation to some extent in becoming "one flesh"—and the function of *mutual pleasure* and satisfaction. Any counselor who observes the strengthening of marriages which results from improvement in this area is impressed by the potential person-enhancing effects of mutual sexual satisfaction.

---

[16] The idea of the virgin birth of Jesus can be understood as a symbolic way of expressing the fact that deep unity is possible between God and a human being (Mary). Infant baptism should be a meaningful sacrament of thanksgiving and dedication, with none of the cleansing-from-sin overtones. The idea of original sin can be understood as a symbolic way of expressing a truth that every counselor observes repeatedly —namely the way in which neurosis (or health) is passed through the generations, In the organic matrix of interpersonal life, all men are linked psychologically to the past and to the future. The emotional problems of the fathers (and mothers) *are* visited on their children and children's children far beyond the third and fourth generations, through the orderly process of psychological transmission.

Halford Luccock once commented that he was tempted to make a list of statements which he wished Jesus hadn't made, because they lend themselves to misinterpretation.[17] High on such a list, from the mental health perspective, would be, "Every one who looks at a woman lustfully has already committed adultery with her in his heart" (Matt. 5: 28). When taken literally, this has produced a plethora of neurotic guilt-feelings by making the "wandering eye" as reprehensible as adultery. The absurdity of such an interpretation has not protected some people from misunderstanding it to mean that their desires, *per se,* are sinful. To consider the basic attraction between the sexes, which makes possible the family, as tainted, is a perversion of the spirit of Jesus' teachings. Nowhere does he condemn sexual impulse as inherently sinful. He pronounced judgment only on lust—that is, sex without mutual love which uses another as an "it." In the passage cited, he presumably was utilizing oriental hyperbole to stress the importance of considering the underlying causes of behavior rather than surface symptoms.

The puritanical approach usually does not keep people from thinking about or from engaging in the proscribed sexual behavior. It only keeps them from enjoying these activities. Moralistic approaches seem to stimulate sexual fantasies and exaggerated behavior. Sexual libertinism, at the one extreme, and the cold drabness of sex in many American marriages, at the other, are two sides to the one coin which is the price we pay for distortions in this area. The yawning chasm between standards and practice, as revealed by Kinsey's studies, is another illustration.

Psychiatrist Frieda Fromm-Reichmann once commented that, in contrast to Freud's day, hostility has become more frequently repressed than sex in our day. Christianity becomes an instrument of mental distress when biblical passages such as this are taken literally: "You have heard that it was said to the men of old, 'You shall not kill; and whoever kills shall be liable to judgment.' But I say to you that every one who is angry with his brother shall be liable to judgment" (Matt. 5:21-22). In spite of Jesus' personal example (such as responding to the Pharisees' objections to his healing on the sabbath "with anger," Mark 3:5), his words have been misinterpreted by

[17] *The Interpreter's Bible* (12 vols.; Nashville: Abingdon Press, 1951-57), VII, 693.

literalistic legalists to mean that anger as such is evil. The familiar words from the Sermon on the Mount (Matt. 5:38-42) on turning the other cheek, going the second mile, and giving one's cloak to a man who demands one's coat, also have been misused in ways that produce personality damage.

Tom, a minister's son, was taught that "good Christian boys do not fight." His normal aggressive impulses were, to his parents and eventually to him, dangerous and bad. Christian love was understood in essentially masochistic terms. His early conditioning made him incapable of living in the competitive society outside the family. In young adulthood, the whirling inner conflicts concerning his fear of his aggressiveness, his repressed anger at his parents, and the demands of his job led him to a mental hospital. Prolonged therapy eventually rescued him from his tailspin and enabled him to live in society.

The valid meaning of these passages has to do with the second-mile principle which characterizes mature relationships. A patient, being interviewed by a psychiatrist before a class, vented his rage on everyone present. Those of us who were students responded with a mixture of fear and feelings of indignation. In contrast, the psychiatrist remained calm and accepting. He was secure and experienced enough not to be threatened by the verbal lashing. He knew that the patient was sick and afraid and that his condition caused the rage. He was able to accept the patient's *need* to lash out in an effort to defend himself. In short, the doctor was able to go the second mile with that patient. By accepting what the patient could not accept in himself, he brought a healing dimension to the relationship. (The patient was free to express his anger because he knew that he would not be allowed to act out his rage. The limits provided by the psychiatrist and the attendants helped him deal with his anger, in spite of his lack of inner limits.)

When anger is pushed into the unconscious because it is unacceptable to one's self-image, it is as though dynamite were stored in the basement of a house. Eventually it will explode in such forms as a "nervous breakdown," psychosomatic illness, unreasonable fears of illusory foes, or prejudice against a minority. Repression is not the answer to the problem of handling anger constructively. The answer is to keep one's God-given assertive-aggressive energies from accumulating by directing them into socially constructive channels.

7. *Does a particular form of religious thought and practice encourage the acceptance or denial of reality? Does it foster magical or mature religious beliefs? Does it encourage intellectual honesty with respect to doubts? Does it oversimplify the human situation or face its tangled complexity?*

The words of Paul, "When I became a man, I gave up childish ways" (I Cor. 13:11), should be applied to religious attitudes and beliefs. Gordon Allport observes in *The Individual and His Religion,* "In probably no region of personality do we find so many residues of childhood as in the religious attitudes of adults." [18] Magic, another name for immature religion, is an attempt to manipulate spiritual powers to one's own ends. In contrast, mature religion is an exercise in bringing one's life into harmony with the orderly principles of spiritual reality. It sees the "will of God," not as the capricious whim of a sentimental grandfather, but as the trustworthy principles of a law-abiding universe. Jesus' Gethsemane prayer, "Not my will, but thine, be done" (Luke 22:42), is thus a magnificent example of mature prayer. Conforming his life to God's will was not abject groveling before an arbitrary, oriental potentate, but the acceptance (whatever the cost) of spiritual reality.

The law of the harvest, "for whatever a man sows, that he will also reap" (Gal. 6:7) is a description of the cause-effect nature of psychological reality. Maturity-motivating religion respects this, whereas magical religion fosters the expectation of certain immunities from reality—that is, special protection from the suffering that is a part of the fabric of existence. Such expectations produce crippling resentments ("God let me down"), when trouble inevitably strikes.

Religious beliefs that deny the reality of diseases, define evil as illusory, or encourage belief in superstitions decrease respect for reality. Mature religion is well integrated with scientific truth. It does not force one to choose between "geology or Genesis," nor to compartmentalize one's mind in "religious" and "scientific" pigeonholes. All truth is God's truth, whether discovered in the laboratory

[18] *The Individual and His Religion,* p. 52.

or in religious experience. Geology and the other sciences constitute "God's other Bible," revealing the "how" of continuing evolutionary creation, whereas the Bible tells the "who" and "why" of this process.

Religion militates against full mental health when it encourages people to ignore their honest doubts. Many congregations commit mass perjury Sunday after Sunday by repeating, parrotlike, and without awareness of the possible symbolic meanings, creeds and hymns containing ideas which many adults cannot accept literally with intellectual honesty. Such self-deception tends to stymie inner questioning and block spiritual growth. In contrast, a healthy religious climate fosters self-honesty with reference to doubts, a quality of flexibility concerning one's beliefs that leaves one open to new insights. It recognizes that there are elements of wish-fulfillment in most religions, but that healthy religion is not dominated by these elements.[19]

The cult of reassurance and positive thinking is a prevalent type of reality-denying religion. The prophets of these approaches are "modern pied pipers," [20] leading people astray with childish tunes which deny the ambiguities, complexities, and tragedies of human life. By giving oversimplified solutions to complex problems, they increase the despair of suffering people. The inadequacy of superficial answers and glib reassurances was described by "a late in-

[19] Sigmund Freud held that belief in deity represented a projection onto the universe of one's continuing wish for the presence of an ideal parent. There is no doubt in my mind that our feelings and ideas about God are influenced in deep and continuing ways by the nature and quality of our early experiences with need-satisfying adults. However, in the relatively healthy person (who continues to grow in his spiritual life) these residual elements from childhood play a gradually decreasing role. On the other hand, in a neurotic or psychotic person, distortions in childhood relationships continue to distort his relationship with God grossly. There is a chronic rigidity about such a person's "head-theology" and "heart-theology," which blocks his awareness of the living God. As Allport holds, the psychoanalytic view errs in reducing religion to wish-fulfillment, ignoring the elements of positive striving in it. As a person matures emotionally, his religious beliefs become less a product of wish-fulfillment and increasingly ways of understanding and articulating the spiritual realities experienced by that person as an adult. To accept the fact that the origins of everyone's religion are influenced by childhood experiences says nothing about the truth or falsity of these beliefs (in terms of objective reality) nor does it identify their present level of maturity. Furthermore, it is important to realize that all deep attitudes and beliefs are rooted in childhood, not just religious beliefs!

[20] I am indebted to psychoanalyst David Morgan for this apt label.

mate of Glasgow Royal Asylum for lunatics" around the year 1860. Following his recovery, he reflected: "We do not know how the waters may rise and rage, how uncontrolled may burst the fury of the storm, while *'Peace, be still,' is drowned in the maddening roar."* [21]

8. *Does a particular form of religious thought and practice emphasize love (and growth) or fear?*

Like a family, a religious group has a certain emotional climate. This is of greater importance to its mental health impact than its specific teachings. The group climate which helps personality blossom like a flower on a spring day has a central emphasis on growth, love, and grace. Those which emphasize fear make personality shrivel to protect itself from the chill. Healthy-minded religion is oriented toward the fulfillment of persons. Jesus' parables of growth (for example, leaven, mustard seed, sower) have this thrust. His emphasis on rebirth points to the need within the general pattern of growth for decisive moments of turning from less to more adequate frameworks of meaning—for surrendering smaller ways of relating in favor of more complete ones. The existentialists in psychotherapy evaluate such crises or turning points positively. As Jordan M. Scher declares, writing in the *Journal of Existential Psychiatry*, "life is a continually renewing and creating process, and one dies and is reborn many times." [22]

Grace, the instrument of healing and growth, was demonstrated in Jesus' remarkable ability to accept the rejected and to love the hard-to-love person. His words, "Neither do I condemn you," blow like a fresh breeze through the parched deserts of religious judgment. He was able to incarnate God's grace and express it in his relationships because of his amazing self-acceptance. Furthermore, Jesus' intuitive insight into the depth and darkness in human life put him in touch with another wellspring of grace. He "knew what was in man" (John 2:25). He must have sensed the sinner's inner civil war, the compulsions that truncated his freedom to choose, the tragedy which had warped his relationships. It is one of the ironies of Christian history that followers of Jesus should present the mes-

[21] *The Philosophy of Insanity* (New York: Greenberg, 1947), p. 104 (italics supplied).
[22] "The Concept of the Self in Schizophrenia" (Spring, 1960), p. 76.

45

sage not as a wonderful, fulfilling way of life, but as an escape hatch through which people flee from fears created by the misinterpreted message.

9. *Does a particular form of religious thought and practice give its adherents a "frame of orientation and object of devotion" that is adequate in handling existential anxiety constructively?*

Psychoanalyst Erich Fromm holds that everyone has a basic need for a "system of thought and action shared by a group which gives the individual a frame of orientation and an object of devotion." [23] One's "frame of orientation" is his philosophy of life. It includes his value system and his fundamental attitudes toward the universe. Viennese psychiatrist Viktor E. Frankl has built a system of therapy (called "logotherapy") on his theory that the "will to meaning" is the dominant drive in human life and the unrequited quest for meaning (producing the "value vacuum") is a major cause of personality problems.[24] Other psychotherapists have explored the role of a person's values in his psychological difficulties. Gordon W. Allport asks: "May not (at least sometimes) an acquired world outlook constitute the central motive of life and, if it is disordered, the ultimate therapeutic problem? [25] The loss of a sense of meaning is often a symptom (of depression, for example), but an inadequate "frame of orientation" sometimes is a factor in personality problems.

Every person needs an object of devotion, something to elicit his loyalty and motivate him to self-investment. Having such an object introduces what Tillich calls "the dimension of ultimate concern" into one's life. So compelling is the need for an object of devotion that those who do not find a high object will give themselves to a lower object. This is the essence of idolatry.[26] From a Christian

[23] *Psychoanalysis and Religion* (New Haven: Yale University Press, 1950), p. 21.
[24] *The Doctor and the Soul, An Introduction to Logotherapy* (New York: Alfred A. Knopf, 1962).
[25] Rollo May (ed.), *Existential Psychology* (New York: Random House, 1961), p. 98.
[26] There are various idolatrous forms of religion: *Biblicism* makes an idol of the words of the Bible, ignoring the findings of many years of dedicated scholarship. *Creedalism* makes an idol of a fossilized description of religious experience, a set of verbal symbols which, at one period of history, were used to articulate the Christian experience of certain persons and groups. *Sectarianism* makes an idol of a particular religious group. *Moralism* makes an idol of conformity to a set of ethical strictures. Each form of idolatry creates a false absolute in the name of religion. As thought-terminators, these block spiritual pioneering, allowing persons to escape the anxiety but miss the thrill of the personal struggle at the center of a maturing religious life.

standpoint, no idol, nothing short of a growing relationship with the God of the prophets and of Jesus will satisfy one's hungers for an object of ultimate devotion. This is the meaning of Augustine's familiar words, "Thou hast made us for thyself and our hearts are restless until they rest in thee." Finding an adequate frame of orientation and object of devotion depends, from the Christian perspective, on entering into what Tillich calls the "new being in Christ," a new state of consciousness and awareness. He writes: "The Christian message is the message of a new Reality in which we can participate and which gives us the power to take anxiety and despair upon ourselves." [27] Christianity can avoid the trap of arrogant exclusivism by recognizing that pathways to new qualities of awareness also exist in other religions.

Discovery of a meaningful philosophy of life and object of devotion is crucial because this is the only way of handling existential anxiety constructively. Anxiety is a response to whatever is perceived by a person as a threat to his essential well-being. Neurotic anxiety is the result of inner conflict and repression. In contrast, existential anxiety is nonpathological or normal. It is "existential" in that it inheres in human existence as a part of what Tillich calls our "heritage of finitude." The threats which arouse this anxiety are of three kinds: of fate and death, emptiness and loss of meaning, guilt and condemnation.[28]

Since this anxiety is a part of man's very existence, it cannot be done away with. Its impact can be either a paralyzing force or a stimulus to creativity, depending on how it is handled. Although psychotherapy is often helpful in reducing neurotic anxiety, it is ineffective in dealing with existential anxiety. Existential anxiety is handled constructively only by a vital religious life, including— (a) a meaningful philosophy of life, (b) a challenging object of devotion, (c) a sense of transcending the earth-boundness of life, (d) a deep experinece of trust in God and relatedness to the universe. Attempts to handle existential anxiety by pseudoreligious means (the various idolatries such as alcoholism) inevitably fail.

Living religion enables a person to confront rather than evade his

[27] Paul Tillich, *Theology of Culture* (New York: Oxford University Press, 1959), p. 208.
[28] *The Courage to Be* (New Haven: Yale University Press, 1952). See Chapter 2.

existential anxiety. As Tillich has made clear, only as such anxiety is confronted and taken into one's self-affirmation can it enhance rather than diminish one's life. When existential anxiety is not handled in this way, it helps to create neurotic problems. To quote Tillich again: "Neurosis is a way of avoiding non-being by avoiding being." [29] It is with reference to existential anxiety that religion makes its absolutely unique and indispensable contribution to mental health.

10. *Does a particular form of religious thought and practice encourage the individual to relate to his unconscious through living symbols?*

If a religious approach is to enhance personality health, it must take the deep, unconscious aspects of the mind seriously, encouraging its participants to keep open the lines of communication with this hidden world which profoundly influences everything they do. The language of the unconscious is the language of symbols—the language of myth, dreams, fairy tales, and psychoses. Healthy religion, through its symbolic rites, myths, and beliefs, helps the individual keep in contact with his unconscious. The unconscious is the wellspring of creativity (as well as a storehouse of repressed memories and primitive impulses). By keeping in touch with his unconscious, the person enriches his conscious life immeasurably. The life of the person whose unconscious is walled off from his consciousness is impoverished thereby. His psychological well-being is increasingly threatened by the forces which build up in his hidden depths, like pressure in a teakettle with its spout sealed.

The liturgical churches, with their drama of the church year and their abundance of symbolic rites and festivals, have a great deal to teach the symbol-poor Protestant groups who, in their zeal for pure religion have thrown out the baby with the bathwater. Many people are able to work through their unconscious impulses through sharing in those symbolic religious practices which are filled with profound meaning for their group. Writing out of more than a decade of experience as a mental hospital chaplain, Carroll A. Wise speaks to the importance of symbols in religion:

[29] *Ibid.,* p. 66.

The function of religious thought is that of penetrating beneath the level of appearance and sense experience to discover fundamental meanings and relationships. Such thought uses its symbols for the purpose of apprehending and expressing insight or understanding of the nature and aim of life as experienced by the individual and group.[30]

11. *Does a particular form of religious belief and practice accommodate itself to the neurotic patterns of the society or endeavor to change them?*

One mark of a maturity-motivating religious approach is that it is concerned with the redemption of society as well as of individuals. Healthy religion has a vigorous concern for the growth of individuals, but alongside this is an equally vigorous interest in changing the factors in society which produce personality damage on a mass scale. Rather than preaching "peace of mind" or "adjustment" to society it challenges persons to creative discontent and nonconformity to the sick side of our culture.[31] It helps to counteract the forces which provide the matrix within which personality problems are spawned like mosquitoes in a stagnant pool. It stands in judgment on the neurotic aspects of our culture. More about this in Chap. 5.

12. *Does a particular form of religious thought and practice strengthen or weaken self-esteem?*

The late David Roberts once observed that if parents had to choose one thing which alone they could give their children, it should be a sturdy sense of their own worth. Without a solid sense of self-worth, a person is limited in his ability to live fully, to relate in a mutually fulfilling way, and to find a religious life with real depth. In Jean Anouilh's play "The Lark," the inquisitor declares in effect that the thing which made Joan of Arc dangerous was not that she had visions, but that *she had dared to trust in herself as a human being.*[32]

The point at which a particular form of religion influences self-esteem most directly is its *doctrine of man.* Three strands of Christian thought, when emphasized, tend to strengthen self-esteem—the doc-

[30] *Religion in Illness and Health* (New York: Harper & Brothers, 1942), p. 137.

[31] In *The Undiscovered Self,* Carl G. Jung makes a case for the importance of religion as the counterbalance to the mass-mindedness which characterizes our society. (Boston: Little, Brown and Company, 1957), pp. 19-31.

[32] *The Lark* (New York: Random House, 1955), p. 113.

trines of the goodness of creation (Gen. 1:31), the image of God in man (Gen. 1:27), and the incarnation (John 1:14). If man is created in the image of God then he must be a creature of inherent worth. If the "Word became flesh"—that is, if God could use a fully human personality to express himself in history—then human nature cannot be fundamentally depraved. There is no doubt that the essential worth of man is solidly grounded in the Christian faith. Being aware of this, the eighteenth-century French thinker Fénelon could write, "We should be in charity with ourselves as with our neighbors."

In spite of these three doctrines, a considerable slice of Christian theology through the centuries has pictured man as groveling in depravity, total or partial. The Genesis story of the fall of man has been interpreted to mean that man's original goodness and the *imago dei* in him were completely corrupted by his disobedience to God. According to this view, man in his present condition is fundamentally bad and lost.

Negative views of man sometimes produce detrimental effects on self-esteem, particularly in children and youth. Claude, a young adult from an ultraconservative Protestant group, reports that the theme song of his early religious life might have been the hymn line, "For such a worm as I." As a result of obtaining psychotherapy in his early twenties, he gradually achieved a sense of his worth as a person. He realized that he wasn't a worm. Commenting on this, he said: "I saw that I had much more to give to life as a *person* than I had ever hoped when I felt like a *worm*." Basically Claude's low self-esteem was the result of his parents' lack of self-esteem. But the negative climate of the family was reinforced by their negative theology.

Liberalism in theology (of the nineteenth and early twentieth century variety) held to a naïvely optimistic view of man. The "Fall" was rejected as an outmoded fragment of primitive folklore. Man was seen as essentially rational and good. Evil in society was attributed to "social lag." Education would cause the escalator of social progress to continue upward with alacrity. The grim facts of recent history have produced widespread disillusionment and reaction to this facile optimism. Negative theological views of human nature have proliferated, emphasizing man's inner corruption and impotency to do anything to save himself. Even his good works are, to quote Luther, "filthy rags" before God. Some recent theologians have agreed with Calvin that as Christians we ought to despise "everything that may be supposed as excellence in us." Only an act of divine intervention can save man.

Fortunately, depth psychology provides an alternative way of understanding the grim record of man's inhumanity to man. By employing new tools for exploring the depths of man's psyche such approaches have thrown new light on the nature of human nature. Depth psychology, for the most part, does not support the easy optimism of the early theological liberals which ignored the depth and darkness in man. Anyone who has struggled in the hidden recesses of a tangled human life, who has seen there the demonic intensity of human destructiveness, cannot take a rosy view of the human situation. Neither do the depth psychologists accept the view of theological pessimism. If they were to communicate with such theologians, the depth psychologists might say: "From our perspective, your *description* of the dark distortions in human life are essentially accurate, but your diagnosis of their causes is woefully inadequate. Your prescription for the cure of these distortions is almost as bad as the illness."

In spite of their extensive firsthand knowledge of the destructiveness in men, many contemporary depth psychologists (in contrast to Freud) hold a kind of cautious optimism regarding human potentialities. They can do this because of two factors in their experience: (a) They see the tragic distortions of personality as being caused by cruel inner conflicts, severe emotional malnutrition and blocked growth, not by some inherent corruption in the soul of man. (b) They know from experience that constructive changes can occur through psychotherapy. In many cases, the "demonic" rage can be drained off, the emotional hungers and conflicts lessened, the trapped potentialities for creative relationships released. Counselors and psychotherapists who are religiously oriented see all of this as the way God works, using a therapeutic relationship as the channel of his grace by which psychological healing and growth can occur.

Theologians who are open to the evidence from depth psychology see many traditional theological ideas as meaningful symbols. The

"Fall" is seen as a mythological or poetic way of describing the birth of self-awareness and conscience. The Garden of Eden represents the psychological unity of a child with the mother, and of man with mother-nature. In eating the fruit of "the tree of the knowledge of good and evil" (Gen. 2:17), the eyes of conscience were opened for the symbolic parents of the human race. They were separated from the unity of the other animals with mother-nature, and thrust into the world of self-awareness and choice. The gradual dawning of conscience and self-awareness in the evolutionary struggle of the race is recapitulated in the early experience of every child. The slow struggle of the race toward developing its moral and spiritual potential is far from complete. Because of man's tremendous creative potentialities, he is capable of terrible destructiveness when his creativity is blocked or distorted.

Traditional theology has held that all men are sinners. Depth psychology has a parallel insight—namely, that all men have primitive, asocial impulses which are dangerous unless, through the normal process of socialization, the individual has acquired inner controls based on his natural desire to be accepted by his group. The individual who has not acquired these inner controls is sick; his sickness is potentially treatable.

The dynamics of pride as it relates to self-esteem have also been illuminated by the findings of the depth psychologists. Traditional theology (and its various "neo-" forms) regards pride as a deadly sin. Reinhold Niebuhr, for example, holds that man's "original sin" is his basic self-love, pretension, and the grasping after self-realization.[33] Based on his experience as a psychotherapist for a quarter of a century, Carl R. Rogers rejects Niebuhr's view and declares: "If I were to search for the central core of difficulty in people as I have come to know them, it is that in the great majority of cases they despise themselves, regarding themselves as worthless and unlovable."[34]

Any view of man which regards pride, selfishness, self-love, or self-idolatry as the major cause of man's problems misses the crucial fact that these are often symptoms of deeper causes—anxiety, self-hatred, inner conflict, and blocked growth. Pride is a symptom-level defense

---

[33] *The Self and the Dramas of History* (New York: Charles Scribner's Sons, 1955).
[34] "Reinhold Niebuhr's *The Self and the Dramas of History*: A Criticism," by Carl Rogers in *Pastoral Psychology* (June, 1958), p. 17.

against these unbearably painful feelings. It is a frantic defense against the agony of feelings of weakness, vulnerability, and despair. Ultimately pride is a regressive defense against existential anxiety. The person makes an idol of himself and his own powers because he cannot trust anything else. Lacking a trustful relationship with God and others, he has no defense against his fear of death and meaninglessness. He retreats to the primitive defense of narcissism which only increases his anxieties. For an adult, narcissism (a normal response for a very small child) is like a suit of medieval armor in a modern battle. As a defense, it cuts the person off from the only sources of genuine help—meaningful relationships with others and with God. Narcissistic pride arises from anxiety and self-rejection but it becomes a malignant symptom which produces greater anxiety and self-rejection. A vicious cycle is thus established.

To prescribe self-flagellation and self-depreciation as a treatment for pride is to prescribe the very poison which caused the sickness. True, the person must relinquish the ineffective defense of narcissism, but he can do this only within a relationship of trust. To develop trust, he must experience unearned acceptance which, according to Tillich, will allow him to "accept himself as being accepted." This acceptance is present in every good family, in every effective counseling relationship, and wherever else genuine love is found in relationships. In theological terms, this is the essence of the experience of salvation by grace through faith (see Eph. 2:8), the Pauline idea that became central in Reformation thought.

It is significant that this key doctrine, like many others, can be interpreted in a way that strengthens or in a way that weakens self-esteem. It has often been understood in a negative light—namely, that man isn't worth saving, but God chooses to save him anyway. This view is like a guilt-stimulating parent who condescendingly accepts his child, even though the child in no way deserves acceptance. In contrast, the doctrine can be understood as an affirmation of man's inherent value in God's sight. This view is like a healthy parent-child relationship in which the parent naturally accepts the child because he is his child and he loves him. The child knows that he has the parent's love, that there is no need to earn it. He grows within the sunshine of this love, doing good as a spontaneous response to the love. A parent-child or a man-God relationship of this quality stimulates the growth of persons toward robust self-esteem. Valuing themselves, they are able to value others.

SUMMARY

In summary, a particular form of religious belief and practice enhances mental health when it builds bridges between people, strengthens the sense of trust, stimulates inner freedom, encourages the acceptance of reality, builds respect for both the emotional and intellectual levels of life, increases the enjoyment of life, handles sex and aggressiveness constructively, is concerned for the health of personality (rather than surface symptoms), provides effective means of handling guilt, emphasizes growth and love, provides an adequate frame of reference and object of devotion, relates persons with their unconscious minds, endeavors to change the neurotic patterns of society, and enhances self-esteem.

CHAPTER 3
The Worship Service and Mental Health

Worship is "return" from a far country where one lives estranged. Worship is encounter with the personal which awakens powers and transcendence within us. It is reverently "entering into" a life other than one's own. It is transaction—an actual interchange of energy which involves openness on the part of the pray-er.[1]—Ross Snyder

THE CHURCH'S CENTRAL GROUP EXPERIENCE

Each Sunday millions of Americans participate in services of worship. Each year hundreds of millions of person-hours are invested in this experience. The Sunday worship service brings a larger percentage of a church's members together with some degree of regularity than any other activity. Corporate worship is a unique function of the church in our society. It is the local church's central group experience and a major means of communicating the Christian message.

As the focal point of a congregation's life the worship service should make major contributions to the growth and wholeness of persons. Unfortunately, for many Protestants corporate worship has relatively little meaning. It does not excite them or feed their heart-hungers. Instead of being an uplifting experience, it registers with them as a mechanical routine. They have been immunized by years of dull worship services and the power of authentic worship to "reach" and energize them has been lost. The purpose of this chapter

[1] "Prayer and Worship Re-examined," *Pastoral Psychology*, XI (March, 1960), 48.

is to describe how this power can be recovered through the release of the potentialities for healing and growth which are present in any experience of corporate worship. What are the mental health values which can come from genuine worship within a church service?

CORPORATE WORSHIP AS A CENTERING EXPERIENCE

A living worship service is a centering experience for a particular religious community, simultaneously expressing and strengthening its unity. To the extent that worshipers enter into the experience with their "being," their psychological fields overlap and they become a genuine group. The religious nature of this activity gives the group a strong vertical dimension—a sense of transcendence. The blending of horizontal (person-to-person) and vertical (person-to-God) interaction gives worship its unique ability to enhance mental health. In effect, the living organism of a worshiping congregation symbolizes and incarnates the church's reason for being—love of God and neighbor.

Sharing in a meaningful worship service gives one an experience of what Cyril Richardson calls "the mystical unity which underlies all human life." He observes that recent research in the field of extra-sensory perception reinforces a truth of which the church has had a perennial awareness (in its emphasis on intercessory prayer, for example) —that we are not isolated units of consciousness. On deeper levels of the psyche there is a kind of mystical participation in one another. Carl Jung's idea of the "collective unconscious" is one way of conceptualizing this.

The practical effect of the centering-sharing experience of worship can be that of helping individuals overcome feelings of insularity and isolation. Through the sharing of mutually meaningful symbols, hymns, prayers, and liturgies, a congregation experiences a drawn-togetherness which helps to overcome the shadow of loneliness which haunts sensitive people in our society. Feeling "cut off" from others is one of the major elements in the inner world of the mentally ill. The group of hospital chaplains quoted in Chap. 2 had this to say of worship:

Effective services of worship, whatever more they may be, are good instruments of group therapy. In the group which is thinking and feeling together about the same common ideas, the emotional response is heightened . . . music, pageantry, sermon, prayer and response are used to focus the attention of the group upon what is believed to be the Highest Good and the Most Real, manifested in the person of Christ. Twenty centuries witness to the effectiveness of such worship in changing men's lives for the better, in bringing release from guilt and freedom from fear, in giving direction and purpose to their striving, and in lifting them out of neurotic self-concern into healthful and creative relationships to their fellows.[2]

Ross Snyder has articulated a world view which provides a conceptual foundation for understanding worship. He starts with a "field theory" of the universe—that is, one in which everything is interpenetrating: "Man exists only in a field of the personal. He who is aware of and remains open to this field quality will live most vividly and in greater dimension." [3]

Worship is seen as an effort to return to the state of openness to the personal field in which the individual has a small but creatively significant part. God is conceived, not as another localized, individual consciousness, but as the personal ground out of which we emerge and by means of which we grow and find renewal. God is best known through concrete personal life and through transactions of the spirit with the people around oneself, including those present symbolically and in memory. Entering into life other than one's own awakens powers within us through an actual interchange of energy. Worship is relating. It is finding God in personal encounter. It is a return from the far country of estrangement both from other people and from the "ground of personal spirit that is hidden deep within us (and the universe) ."

The energizing effects of corporate worship become understandable within this world view. Ross Snyder writes:

I am present with people whose lives interpenetrate mine, and it is this living network that is at worship. Also as a worshiper I reverently enter into the lives of people who have lived with greatest passion and integrity. . . . There is this sense of the numinous actually being present as the ground of our life together and of my own personal life. Therefore corporate worship . . . has distinctive quality and power.[4]

---

[2] "American Protestantism and Mental Health," p. 4.
[3] "Prayer and Worship Re-examined," p. 47.
[4] *Ibid.*, p. 48.

Snyder's approach is complemented by Reuel L. Howe's conception of prayer as the practice of relationship. Howe points out that the five types of prayer describe five kinds of relationships:

Adoration is giving ourselves to another in love and honest admiration. Confession is the acceptance and acknowledgment of our words and acts of alienation. Petition is an acknowledgment of our dependence on one another. Intercession is the expression of our responsibility to live for and to help one another. And thanksgiving is the expression of our gratitude for fellowship and all other blessings.[5]

Prayer, the heart of worship, is an act of love which results from choosing to respond to God's love. It means letting go of one's egocentric isolation and becoming able to live in the mystery of relatedness.

There must be a genuine warmth (with dignity) in a worship service if personal isolation is to be overcome. The minister sets the tone for this climate, but the congregation determines whether it will be actualized. Harvey H. Potthoff tells a story about a woman in a certain church who was asked, after the service, whether she was a stranger there. She responded, "Why, yes, I've been a stranger here for forty years." [6]

There are, however, many people who need the church who are threatened by close relationships. Some of these attend the worship service because they expect it to involve only a limited degree of social interaction. They can gain genuine help from the service, if their need for social distance is respected. An overemphasis on "fellowship" can overwhelm such persons. Those churches which ask strangers to stand during the service or which exert heavy pressure on fringe-participants to interact following the service tend to drive such persons away.

Increasing general congregational participation in the worship service strengthens its centering function without threatening the fringe-type person. Familiar, singable (and theologically valid) hymns are important. Studies in the psychology of music show that group singing is an effective way of creating group solidarity. The

[5] *Man's Need and God's Action* (New York: Seabury Press, 1953), p. 152.
[6] "The Church as a Saving Fellowship," *Iliff Review*, Vol. XVII, No. 1 (Winter, 1960), 39.

imaginative minister will find a variety of ways to increase meaningful congregational participation. (The Episcopal practice of the congregation saying "Amen" frequently during prayers and rituals is an example of a participation-enhancing worship form.)

There is a growing awareness in the field of pastoral counseling that many who turn to the church cannot utilize insight-oriented approaches to help. Because of weakness or rigidity in their personalities, they can be helped most by a sustaining relationship of dependence within which they can handle their life situations more constructively. The church fellowship offers a major resource for helping millions of such persons in our society to live closer to their own unique potentialities.

Because of his symbolic role as a religious authority figure, the minister naturally attracts a circle of dependent persons who gain strength by identifying with him and with the group which he leads. These people feel safer and stronger (and better able to function) because they are related to a leader and a fellowship which have strengths they lack as individuals. The need for dependency relationships obviously is not limited to those who are emotional cripples. All of us, to some degree, need supportive relationships with groups and their leaders. We function better when we have such relationships and falter when uprooted from them. In this light, consider the following statement about the value of corporate worship:

The weekly experience of corporate worship is supportive to many persons, including those who cannot identify with other group experiences demanding more intimate participation. The fact that life-transforming insights do not flash on the psychic landscape of a very large percentage of a congregation on a given Sunday does not mean that the service is of little value. Everyone—weak and strong egos alike—needs meaningful, supportive experiences. The fact that such a supportive group experience is available week in, week out, year after year, is of tremendous importance to people, quite apart from the new insights they achieve.[7]

The worshiper, aware of his minister, his fellow-worshipers, and his part in the "endless line of splendor" which is the church through

[7] H. J. Clinebell, Jr., "Ego Psychology and Pastoral Counseling," *Pastoral Psychology*, XIV (February, 1963), 36.

the centuries, is released to some degree from his loneliness and empowered by the awareness of belonging.

WORSHIP AS AN EXPERIENCE OF PERSONAL INTEGRATION

I recall a game from my childhood played with an old-fashioned spring driven phonograph. We would wind it until the record table whirled as fast as possible. Then we would drop small objects on the spinning surface and respond with delight as they flew off in all directions. That childhood game is a reasonable fascimile of modern life as many experience it. Many of us go around so fast we are constantly threatened by centrifugal forces. These have deleterious effects on both our inner serenity and the health of our relationships.

For many people the worship hour is the only time during the week when they sit quietly and "collect" themselves. Worship involves what Hocking calls "the principle of alternation," of gaining inner strength by alternating from one kind of activity to another. During his most active period, Albert Schweitzer's daily schedule was a classic illustration of the use of this principle. On a given day he might move from conducting a worship service, to making medical rounds in his hospital, to doing construction work on a new leprosy-treatment center, to practicing the organ, to working on a manuscript. In our hyperactivist culture, worship is a radical and essential form of alternation for most of us. In an effective worship service, the participants have an existential awareness of the meaning of the words of the Lord to Isaiah: "In quietness and trust shall be your strength" (Isa. 30:15).

There is healing power in quietness and rest. After an exhausting week, many worshipers respond with gratitude when their minister repeats the ancient invitation, "Come to me, all who labor and are heavy-laden, and I will give you rest" (Matt. 11:28).

Worship is integrating because it encourages persons to center down while looking up. Edward Bok had inscribed on the mantle over the fireplace in his mountain cabin, "I Come Here to Find Myself. It's So Easy to Get Lost in the World." Centering down, finding oneself, taking a long look at one's life—these are healing experiences, particularly in the context of a unifying faith and an accepting fellowship. Samuel H. Miller writes: "Worship, as Hocking points out, is the pursuit of the 'whole.' . . . It presses beyond every detail, and affirms in faith God who holds all things in his hands. . . . All the brokenness of life comes together in a great *Te Deum*." [8]

As a time-exposure to what is regarded by the person and the group to be the most important aspects of reality, worship gives the individual an opportunity to separate the wheat from the chaff in his values and activities. Harry Emerson Fosdick writes "In worship we are reminded of the values that the world makes us forget." [9]

In planning a worship service, the minister should provide generous opportunities for quietness. He should be aware of the pace of the service, seeking to establish a quiet rhythm and a mood of serenity. There should be a balance between quietness and challenge in the total service. It is within the milieu of a reviving worship experience that the challenge of the sermon can best be received. In addition to these considerations, it is well to remember that the inner condition of the minister will be felt by his congregation. When the woman touched Jesus she sensed the serenity and vitality of one who was open to himself, to others, and to the universe. This inner openness is extremely difficult to maintain in our frantic kind of world, but it is the prerequisite for effective leadership in worship.

WORSHIP AS AN EXPERIENCE OF TRANSCENDENCE

Another value of worship is that of providing a rich experience of the numinous and the transcendent. This is of particular importance to mental health in our period of history. Technological cleverness has dulled our awareness of the wisdom of wonder. In a searching analysis of our society's need for spiritual renewal,[10] Douglas V. Steere has pointed to Carl Jung's diagnosis of our inward poverty:

Whether from an intellectual, moral or aesthetic point of view, the undercurrents of the psychic life of the West are an uninviting picture. We have built a monumental world around us. . . . But it is so imposing because we have spent upon the outside all that is imposing in our

[8] Samuel H. Miller, "Worship and Work in the Industrial Age," *Pastoral Psychology*, XI (March, 1960), 26.

[9] Quoted by Charles F. Kemp in *Life Situation Preaching* (St. Louis: Bethany Press, 1956), p. 208.

[10] "Spiritual Renewal in Our Time," *Union Seminary Quarterly Review*, XVII (November, 1961), 33-56.

natures—and what we find when we look within must necessarily be as it is, shabby and insufficient.[11]

Steere then draws on the insights of Arnold Toynbee to identify the historical roots of our present impoverishment. Toynbee has shown how the genius and creativity of the West has been poured into technical pursuits since the beginning of the seventeenth century, largely to the neglect of man's inner life. He holds that our civilization will perish unless we invest a larger proportion of our "liquid spiritual capital" in the cultivation of educational resources and deep religious insights.[12]

Experiencing awe and wonder can revive and stretch the spirit of a man. But this requires the interruption of the infatuation with our own cleverness. The experience of wonder flourishes when one becomes aware of the mysteries and revelations of God in four areas— the inner life of man, interpersonal relationships, science, and nature. Reviving wonder requires relinquishing what Toynbee calls "the idolization of the invincible technician." It requires interrupting our worship of the golden calf whose face is an electronic computer. Somehow we must give up our obsession with manipulating nature and our fellows. Only thus can we recapture the wonder and mystery of the world revealed by our experience. What is needed is something of that openness to experience suggested by Jesus' words: "Whoever does not receive the kingdom of God like a child shall not enter it" (Mark 10:15). In his description of the psychologically healthy ("self-actualizing") person, psychologist Abraham Maslow includes the "oceanic feeling" among the characteristics of such a person.[13] This is very close to the mystical sense of organic relatedness to others and the universe. Albert Einstein once declared:

The fairest thing we can experience is the mysterious. It is the fundamental emotion which stands at the cradle of true art and true science. He who knows it not, and can no longer wonder, no longer feel amazement, is as good as dead, a snuffed-out candle. It was the experience of

[11] *Modern Man in Search of a Soul* (New York: Harcourt, Brace, and World, 1933), p. 214.
[12] *An Historian's Approach to Religion* (New York: Oxford University Press, 1956).
[13] "Self-Actualizing People," by A. H. Maslow in *The Self,* edited by Clark E. Moustakas (New York: Harper & Row, 1956), p. 178.

mystery . . . that engendered religion. A knowledge of the existence of something we cannot penetrate, our perceptions of the profoundest reason and the most radiant beauty, which our minds seem to reach only in their most elementary forms;—it is this knowledge and this emotion that constitute the truly religious attitude.[14]

Much of what is healing and growth-stimulating in worship is on a nonverbal level. There are deep feeling-level responses in genuine worship which help keep us in touch with neglected areas of our inner lives. Feelings from our early experiences which continue as important, though hidden influences in our lives as adults are activated and dealt with in worship. When one's heart is "strangely warmed" in worship, experiential values are actualized which touch the whole personality. This is much more than just an experience of certain feelings. William James observed that mystical states, although similar to states of feeling, are also states of knowledge to those who experience them. "They are states of insight into depths of truth unplumbed by the discursive intellect." [15]

In other words, worship at its best takes seriously all levels of the psyche. Because the deeper, nonverbal levels tend to be impoverished in our culture, worship should concentrate special attention on these levels through the use of symbolic and artistic expressions. It should attempt to involve the whole person in a total experience. Because it can touch the depths as well as the heights of human experience, it has tremendous health and growth potentialities.

As a strange blend of "animal and angel," to use Nietzsche's phrase, a man grows weary of being chained to the world of nature, subject to its drives and its tragedy. Worship is a way of renewing one's awareness of the eternal in the crowded dailyness of time. In her cross-cultural studies, anthropologist Ruth Benedict noted the ubiquitous presence of a belief in what she called "wonderful power." This sense of the vertical dimension in man's life—of the God "in whom we live and move and have our being"—is the ever-flowing wellspring of worship.

How can increasing numbers of worshipers come alive to the reality of the vertical dimension? Many factors play a part. The

[14] Albert Einstein quoted in *Living Prayerfully* by Kirby Page (New York: Farrar and Rinehart, 1941), p. 132.
[15] *Varieties of Religious Experience*, p. 371.

scriptures, the sermon, prayers, sacraments, music, lighting, heating (or air conditioning) , church architecture, and visual symbols which communicate an awareness of the mystery and majesty of God are all instruments to this end. The crucial factor, however, is the attitude of those who lead the service. They set the tone. Their sense of awe and reverence will be communicated to the congregation. The minister's sense of reverence will be transmitted to his people by the way he handles each facet of the worship service. A congregation will sense to whom the pastoral prayer is addressed. They will be aware of whether or not the minister experiences the Bible as containing the living Word when he reads from its pages. They will know if he has a mystical sense of encountering the personhood of the author of a particular passage, and if, through that encounter, he meets the living God. The minister has a responsibility to teach the choir, ushers, custodian, and congregation to grasp the uniqueness of worship, as contrasted with other gatherings of people.

WORSHIP AS A SPIRITUAL FEEDING EXPERIENCE

One of the major mental health values of worship is as a feeding experience. Every person needs periodic replenishing of his inner resources. Regular intake experiences are required to balance the outgo. Intake experiences are those in which one feels loved, cared for, esteemed, and fed through the stimulation of ideas, music, inspiration, relationships, and the pleasures of the senses. Worship is a major means of overcoming inner emptiness through the rich experience of psychological-spiritual feeding.

The amount of spiritual hunger in our society is immense, but it would be even larger were it not for the churches. "Mother Church" is a source of nurture for millions. Some people feel too angry and/or guilty about their intense, unconscious dependency needs to be able to come to the great spiritual breast of the church. But many others can accept feeding from the minister and the church. They come to the worship service and are fed (hopefully) the "bread of life." They "hunger and thirst after righteousness" but also after acceptance, love, and serenity. If they are fortunate, their spirits are nourished by the familiar flow of the service, by the hymns and anthems, by the uplift of the church's architecture, by the well-known liturgies and rituals, by the inspiration of great passages from the Bible, by the challenge to their minds of a thoughtful sermon, and by the supportive presence of many friends.

The sacrament of Holy Communion is the symbol, par excellence, of the giving, feeding function of the church. It is an action-symbol of the nurturing love of God. It is a celebration of the givingness of life. (The theme of gratitude is expressed in the word "Eucharist" by which the sacrament is known in the Eastern Orthodox churches.) Participation in this sacrament is a deeply moving and renewing experience for those who have discovered its vital symbolism. It is a way of renewing one's "good parent" within and thus enabling one to experience an inner source of giving and love.

The profound effect of Holy Communion on the lives of many worshipers is an example of the healing power of symbols. The sacrament is meaningful on many levels. For example, one of the deeper levels has to do with the desire to consume and become like one who is both feared and admired. The sacramental meal practiced by the primitive tribes of Australia illustrates this level of meaning. They periodically kill and eat a representative of the sacred totem animal of the tribe. The attributes of the totem animal (for instance, the speed and strength of the kangaroo) , are thought to be acquired by the person consuming this animal in the sacramental feast. The symbolism of sharing common food and drink and thus becoming united on a deep level appears in many cultures. This theme is also embodied in the communion service.

There is little doubt that, on a profound level, communion is a reenactment of certain impulses and conflicts which occurred during the "oral" stage of infancy, when food was love and the lack of it, death. This is the level of intrapsychic conflicts which, if unresolved, produce mental illness. The significance for mental health of the orality of the worship service in general and the communion sacrament in particular can be understood in this context. Unacceptable impulses are transformed through symbolic, ritual practices into socially constructive feelings and motivation. Thus, the continuing inner conflicts from the first years of life are rechanneled and their intensity drained off through group religious practices.

In planning and leading worship, the minister should concentrate on enhancing its feeding function by enriching the service in every way possible. In his selection of materials, he should use a variety of resources from the spiritual riches of the ages and from contemporary sources. He can help to feed the minds of his people by presenting great ideas, their senses through visual symbols and the beauty of fine music, their hearts through sacraments and prayers which touch them with emotional power. Most important of all is the giving of himself in and through the service. A minister who is self-aware knows when he has poured his God-given inner resources into a worship experience. His people know it too and respond with gratitude.

WORSHIP AS A TRUST-ENHANCING EXPERIENCE

Erik Erikson, a leading psychoanalytic thinker, holds that a baby develops a sense of "basic trust" or "basic distrust" during the first year of life. If, due to the quality of his relationship with the mothering-one, he comes to feel that life can be trusted to satisfy his basic needs, he develops a core feeling of trust. This is "basic" in that it becomes the basis for all subsequent relationships of trust. An adult's foundational attitudes about himself, others, and the world in general are colored by these powerful feelings from his earliest experiences.

But what about those whose ability to feel inner trust is limited as a result of early experiences of emotional malnutrition? (This, of course, means everyone, to some degree.) In an article entitled "On the Sense of Inner Identity," Erikson speaks to this crucial question: "There can be no question that it is organized religion which systematizes and socializes the first conflict of life. . . . It is *religion which by way of ritual methods offers man a periodic collective restitution of basic trust* which in adults ripens to a continuation of faith and realism." [16]

Dynamic worship is a wellspring for the renewal of trust. Across the centuries men and women have found a renaissance of trustful feelings—in themselves, in others, in God, and in the future—through corporate worship. This fresh baptism of trust allows many people to handle psychological loads of crushing dimensions. A beautiful symbol of the presence of basic trust is the Quaker idea of the "inner light." Ross Snyder used the editorial "I" in commenting on the effect of this idea: "I have a depth of spirit and mystery. To some

[16] *Psychoanalytic Psychiatry and Psychology*, edited by Robert Knight and Cyrus R. Friedman (New York: International Universities Press, 1954), I, 353 (italics supplied).

degree I am of the image of God. . . . I too am freedom—a transcendence over what I already am, and from the impersonal order of the universe." [17] The effect of such an experience is to reinforce and undergird self-esteem.

The renewal of basic trust gives a person the ability to face the abyss of ultimate or existential anxiety (see Chap. 2). When a person can feel with the psalmist,

> Lord, thou hast been our dwelling place
> in all generations. . . .
> from everlasting to everlasting
> thou art God (Ps. 90:1-2),

he is strengthened in facing the fragility and brevity of his life on this planet. He can incorporate into his self-identity the awareness of the transitoriness and tragedies of his existence. Studies of the reactions of concentration camp prisoners have shown that the acute stresses did not produce the expected degree of physical and psychological deterioration in persons who had one or both of these attributes—dedication to the good of their buddies or a strong sense of the glory of God. Worship, as an experience of relating and rediscovering trust is like a cool, clear spring in a parched land beside which an exhausted traveler can renew his strength.

DIMINISHING ONE'S LOAD OF NARCISSISM

Authentic worship helps a person get himself out of the center, relinquishing the burden of self-worship. The effect of worship should be something like absorbing the significance of the findings of modern astronomy. For instance, the light which will allow one to see the great nebula in the constellation Andromeda tonight started coming through the frigid reaches of space before the first man walked on the earth. It has been traveling at 186,000 miles per second for a million and a half years. And yet the Andromeda nebula is one of the nearest star cities to our star city, the Milky Way. Wrestling to comprehend an incomprehensible fact such as this can help one get out of the center. Worship should have a similar effect. It should help us chuckle at the absurdity of our many forms of strutting self-

[17] "Prayer and Worship Re-examined," p. 48.

idolatry. The man who, with a smile, commented to his friend, "I just resigned as general manager of the universe," had good reason to feel better. He had relinquished the feeling of having to be responsible for many things completely beyond his control.

The phenomenon of "surrender," as the pivotal point in recovery from alcoholism has been explored by psychiatrist Harry Tiebout. Anyone who has dealt perceptively with recovering alcoholics has observed surrender. The alcoholic's narcissism is an ineffective defense which feeds both his grandiosity and his isolation from help. This must be surrendered if he is to recover. The person who has shed his narcissism is like one who has a gigantic weight removed from his back. Narcissism is the alcoholic's curse. It prevents him from accepting outside help and from growing genuine self-esteem based on humility. The effects of narcissism are less obvious but equally real in nonalcoholics. As indicated in Chap. 2, narcissism is a self-damaging effort to cope with gigantic feelings and fantasies from one's early life. It reactivates the feelings of overwhelming anxiety which caused it originally and stands like a high wall between the person and the help which he desperately needs.

In planning and leading worship, the minister should keep the problem of narcissism—his own and his congregation's—clearly in focus. Narcissism blocks a person from those experiences which rejuvenate trust. The Christian emphasis on the sinfulness of all men is actually a recognition of narcissism's prevalence. Worship can help to facilitate surrender by using confrontation within the context of grace and trust. Effective confrontation in which the worshiper becomes aware of his narcissism and his essential dependence on God and others is a difficult art because it so easily becomes moralizing. If a minister can experience the Lord, "high and lifted up," he can then lead his people in worship before the same God. This experience is a narcissism-reducer. Unfortunately, the severely narcissistic person usually turns the worship into self-worship, making it a narcissistic orgy. In many cases a major crisis in the life of such a person is required to shatter his self-damaging defense and open him to other people and God.

WORSHIP AS A WAY OF RESOLVING GUILT

Guilt often stands like a hard cold lump between persons and between man and God. Out of his personal struggles with psychosis and many years' experience as a hospital chaplain, Anton Boisen concluded that the most damaging feelings in mental illness are the sense of awful isolation and the feeling of unpardonable guilt. Guilt also plays a crucial role in less intense forms of human unhappiness. Keeping guilt within constructive bounds is one of the major contributions of dynamic worship to mental health. A valid test of the effectiveness of worship is its ability to help persons find that experience of reconciliation which is the essence of forgiveness.

The way in which unconfessed guilt corrodes the spirit and erodes the physical health of a man was described vividly by the psalmist:

> When I declared not my sin, my body wasted away
>   through my groaning all day long.
> For day and night thy hand was heavy upon me;
>   my strength dried up as by the heat of summer (Ps. 32:3-4).

> Blessed is he whose transgression is forgiven, . . .
> Blessed is the man to whom the Lord imputes no iniquity,
>   and in whose spirit there is no deceit (Ps. 32:1-2).

Guilt-reduction often occurs in a sequence of stages during the worship service. The first stage is the sharpening of the awareness of one's guilt. Hidden guilt feelings are brought into consciousness by being in the setting which represents the highest ideals of one's group. This leads spontaneously to the second stage, confession of guilt. The young Isaiah's experience (often taken as a prototype of the sequence of worship) was described in this way: ". . . I saw the Lord sitting upon a throne, high and lifted up . . . And I said, 'Woe is me! For I am lost; for I am a man of unclean lips, and I dwell in the midst of a people of unclean lips; for my eyes have seen the King, the Lord of hosts!" (Isa. 6:1, 5).

Opportunities should be provided in a worship service for a quiet period of guided self-examination in which the minister suggests areas of introspection. Firm, loving confrontation by the minister should be a part of this. Following such self-searching, a great prayer such as the "General Confession" of the Anglican service, can be a deeply moving experience: "We have erred, and strayed from thy ways like lost sheep. . . . We have left undone those things which we ought to have done; And we have done those things which we ought not to have done."

Such a process can lead to emotional catharsis (as in counseling) —the pouring out of infected feelings, whereby the poison is drained from the wounds of one's spirit. As Tillich has indicated, the ability to confess deeply requires a relationship and an atmosphere in which *forgiveness is already present.* The forgiving, healing, reconciling love of God should be the foundation of any worship service that takes guilt seriously. This is the good news of the gospel. It should saturate every dimension of the worship service. An accepting, non-judgmental spirit on the minister's part sets the tone for a worship service in which grace becomes a living experience.

The third and fourth stages of the guilt-to-reconciliation path are the powerful awareness of cleansing and forgiveness leading to the spontaneous response of seeking to meet the needs of others. In Isaiah's vision, a seraphim touched his lips with a burning coal from the altar and said, "Behold . . . your guilt is taken away, and your sin forgiven" (Isa. 6:6-7). When the burden of guilt was lifted, Isaiah's response was expressed in action. Hearing the voice of the Lord asking, "Whom shall I send?" he responded, "Here I am! Send me" (Isa. 6:8).

The action phase of forgiveness should certainly include making restitution for one's mistakes and sins. Jesus' emphasis on being reconciled to one's brother before offering one's gift at the altar (Matt. 5:23-24) points in this direction. It is not that God withholds his acceptance, but that the orderly laws of the psychological life makes it impossible to experience forgiveness fully until we have done everything possible to repair the damage caused by our sins.

If guilt feelings do not respond to the normal process of confession-reconciliation it may be because they are neurotic (or irrational) feelings (see Chap. 2). If so, counseling or psychotherapy is needed to resolve the inner conflict at the root of the feelings.

In their reaction to the guilt-creating, manipulative techniques of the rigid fundamentalist approach, many nonfundamentalist Protestants have overlooked the seriousness and prevalence of the problems of guilt. Millions of persons suffer from severe guilt feelings which are below the conscious level. Some of these feelings, given the necessary setting and stimuli, are capable of being brought into awareness. Since awareness of guilt feelings is the first step toward their transformation, this is the place where efforts in worship should be concentrated initially. Focusing on the fact that sin is the condition of being alienated from God helps to avoid the pitfall of moralizing.

WORSHIP AS A CHALLENGE TO FACE REALITY

Worship should bring the mystical and the ethical elements in religion into union. Albert Schweitzer's "deed mysticism" (in contrast to a mysticism which regards contemplation as an end in itself) is an illustration of the needed balance. Persons should be challenged to invest the new understanding and power they derive from worship experiences in helping others and improving society. Through the scriptures and the sermon, the minister can help the worshiper discover what will be required to "give up childish ways" in various areas of his life. Growth toward more mature meanings and relationships in one's life should result from such exploration. Carroll A. Wise says, in relation to worship that:

Participation in the religious group, involving a strong sense of fellowship, should stimulate the individual to a discovery of the realities of his own personal experience. It should be a source of strength and stimulation to his ego, especially at times when forces working against the discovery of reality are strong within the personality. When the symbols of the group are living and vital, they serve also as a powerful means for the development of cultural patterns on the basis of personal values.[18]

The theology of the prayers, hymns, and sermon should call individuals away from immature, reality-manipulating styles of life. Ross Snyder gives this pointed example of the form immature religion would take were it expressed in prayer: " 'O God, protect and save me from the consequences of my living. Do thou, O Lord, take away the consequences of my constant violation of the truth; allow me to go on hating my neighbor; allow me to live irresponsibly— But thou O Lord canst prevent the results of all this living.' " [19]

[18] *Religion in Illness and Health*, pp. 178-79.
[19] "Prayer and Worship Re-examined," p. 45.

Mental health enhancing worship should "speak the truth in love," confronting the worshiper with the ethical demands of the Christian way, and helping him develop those energizing relationships with persons and God which will enable him to respond creatively to these demands.

WORSHIP AS AN EXPERIENCE OF SELF-INVESTMENT

Worship, at its best, is much more than a feeding experience. As in any relationship, it is the blend of receiving and giving that strengthens mental health. Participation in both the give and take of relationships contributes to personality growth. (The therapeutic value of helping other alcoholics, a cardinal principle of A.A., is a case in point.) Worship brings the awareness that it is in self-giving that one receives the finest satisfactions of life. The giving aspects of a worship service include the outpouring of adoration to God, intercessory prayers (symbolizing outreaching concern for others), the offering (which is a symbolic giving of a portion of one's working life), and the acts of personal dedication, usually at the close of the service.

The most significant forms of giving should, of course, occur in one's daily life between worship experiences. The "lay renaissance," (see Chap. 12) with its emphasis on the layman's ministry to the world, gives both worship and Christian education a fresh, practical relevancy. The worship experience should be a power station which motivates Christian action. Education (including the educational dimension of worship) should be a lighthouse to guide this action into channels that are of real significance in the Christian view of existence under God.

There is a danger that the giving which results from worship will be the product of one's guilt. Such giving is recognized by its strained and grudging quality. The great mystic, Von Ogden Vogt once described worship as "celebration of life." When it is this, the self-giving which results is characterized by spontaneity. It resembles the way a person in love gives to his beloved—naturally and gladly. As both Paul and Luther recognized, the experience of being cleansed, forgiven, and restored to relationship is so profoundly moving that the good life follows as a natural flowing of gratitude.

WORSHIP AS A WAY OF HANDLING THE CRISES OF LIFE

Anton Boisen has declared that "the function of Christian worship is to help men to face their actual problems and difficulties in the light of the Christian faith and to find insight and courage to deal with them constructively." [20] The week-in, week-out experiences of many people support this view. They take their inner struggles, fears, and burdens with them to the worship service. Many find a new perspective for viewing their life situations (which may transform their self-defeating responses to those situations) and fresh energy for problem-handling and load-carrying.

The festivals of the church year and the sacraments have special usefulness in assisting people in structuring the rapidly passing years and in handling the inevitable crises of living. One of the significant ecumenical developments in Protestant worship during the last fifteen years has been a growing appreciation for the liturgical year. The successive seasons and festivals encourage the reliving of the moving historical drama of the Christian story [21]—with its many parallels in the life of the individual and the family. The *Advent* season symbolizes psychologically the expectancy of continuing renewal and renaissance in one's life. *Christmas* touches deep, universal feelings about the miracle of birth and family life. *Epiphanytide* centers on spontaneous adoration and outreach in response to the miracle of new life. *Lent,* a period of alternation with particular importance in our activist culture, is a time of reflection on one's inner condition. *Holy Week* encourages the enhancing of one's awareness of the tragic dimension of life, and *Easter* (followed by Eastertide) depicts the Christian response to this tragic dimension. *Pentecost* celebrates the birth of the Christian fellowship which plays so important a part in a dedicated churchman's life. *Trinitytide* offers an opportunity for worshipers to grow in their relationship with God as he is known in the three major forms of his self-revelation—through his creation (Father), through human relationship (Son), and directly in the experience of prayer (Holy Spirit). *Kingdomtide* emphasizes the Christian's concern for social problems and the redemption of society.

[20] "The Consultation Clinic," *Pastoral Psychology,* XI (March, 1960), 50-51.
[21] For a discussion of the traditional meanings of the liturgical seasons, see W. F. Dunkle, Jr., *Values in the Church Year* (Nashville: Abingdon Press, 1959).

As this traditional cycle of the church year becomes increasingly familiar to Protestant worshipers, its value will be enhanced. To the extent that the seasons and festivals of the church year are living symbols to the individual, they help him feel related to his historical roots. This sense of rootage helps to undergird one's sense of personal identity. Following the traditional pattern of the church year helps to rescue the worship service from being mainly the product of the subjective interests and tastes of a particular clergyman.

The sacraments (holy communion and baptism for most Protestants), as well as sacred rites such as marriage, confirmation, healing practices, and funeral services are symbolic ways of dealing with the major stress-points and crises of living. The services of marriage and infant baptism (or dedication) are family-centered rites, ways of dealing with the anxieties and mystery surrounding sex and love, birth and growth. They symbolize the vertical dimension in these experiences and express the undergirdingness of the Christian fellowship. Current awareness of the importance to the health of a family's relationships with the extended family (including the church) accents the significance of these ancient practices of the religious community.

Confirmation is the contemporary equivalent of ancient tribal puberty rites. Unfortunately many confirmation experiences lack significance for the participants. There is a pressing need for revitalizing this "rite of passage," as a way of helping the adolescent make the transition from childhood to adulthood. Pastoral services and religious practices related to sickness have a special importance for mental health. Serious illness usually produces a substantial emotional crisis. Practices such as prayers for the sick and the laying on of hands remind the patient of the healing forces of God that are available to him. They also help to remove the blocks (guilt, anxiety, hopelessness, and so forth) which may hinder the flow of the healing forces within the person. During my experience as a hospital chaplain I was impressed by the powerful influence which a person's attitudes and feelings exert on his recovery from illness and surgery. Strengthening the will to live, weaning oneself from self-pity, finding release from irrational fears and discovering the surrounding concern of God—these factors can have a decisive effect on the return of health.

The mystery of death is a part of the larger mystery of life itself. The threat of nonbeing which accompanies the thought of one's own death or that of loved ones is a threat that can be handled constructively only by religious means. Funeral rituals within a context of a continuing ministry to the bereaved play a role in facilitating "grief work" (the normal process by which the person copes with loss) and thus aiding the recovery process. The significance of the corporate worship aspect of the funeral should be emphasized since it is within the context of a supporting fellowship that one can best confront ultimate anxiety.

Sacred rites and sacraments can be misused as forms of magic. The reaction against a magical, mechanical form of penance was a key factor in precipitating the Reformation. Unfortunately, in the vigorous rejection of anything that smacked of magical sacramentalism many Protestants have lost the awareness of the valid role of sacraments and sacred ceremonies as living symbols (that is, communicators of meanings) . Symbols can be doors through which worshipers can enter into the hidden meanings of experience. Education for creative worship should help people discover the power of the symbols from both their own tradition and the traditions of others.

SUMMARY

It has been shown that corporate worship contributes to positive mental health to the degree that it helps the individual experience a sense of belonging, personal integration, diminishing of his guilt and narcissism, reestablishment of a sense of trust, worthy self-investment, and strength for handling his problems constructively. Let me recommend that those who are responsible for planning worship services, test their services against these potential contributions to personality growth and health. If this is done, it is safe to predict that certain changes in form, content, and emphasis will follow. Of course, finding ways to make worship come alive in a very personal way for increasing numbers of persons is not an easy goal. In planning worship, it is important to take into account the variety of backgrounds, needs, and spiritual hungers of any given congregation. A great deal depends on one's particular tradition. In general, a certain variety in the contents of worship within a familiar structure would seem to be a desirable approach. The training of a congregation in the meaning and purpose of each aspect of the worship service is an important function of the minister and the worship committee. Encouraging feedback from sensitive laymen is highly useful (assuming that the minister's self-esteem is sturdy enough to take it). If such laymen feel free enough to speak with candor, their evaluation and suggestions can be of major help in strengthening the mental health impact of the service of worship.

In discussing worship, philosopher William Ernest Hocking, after speaking of the high values in life including beauty, recreation, friendship, and love, declared: "Worship is the whole which includes them all."[22] When worship even approximates this exalted inclusiveness of values it helps mental health to flourish.

[22] Quoted in Charles Kemp's discussion of the relations of worship and the sermon in *Life Situation Preaching*, p. 207.

CHAPTER 4
Preaching and Mental Health

But of course preaching, for me, has, in a sense,
been personal counseling. I mean to say my definition
of preaching is personal counseling on a group scale.[1]
——*Harry Emerson Fosdick*

Each Sunday more than 200,000 sermons are preached. How many of these make a distinguishable difference in the lives of the hearers? How many have an energizing and renewing effect? Do the majority of these sermons stimulate the growth of persons? Do they motivate at least a few persons to throw off the shell of their smaller selves, stretch their spiritual muscles, and begin to live in larger dimensions of the Kingdom? Do they lighten the load, strengthen the arm, and feed the hungers of the world-weary folks who come seeking help? Do they open inner windows through which new understanding of life in God's world can enter? Do they communicate the "good news"? Are they channels for the healing, cleansing stream of God's grace?

The sermon offers a minister one of his most valuable opportunities to enhance the mental and spiritual health of his people. Like group counseling, effective preaching offers an efficient means of helping a number of individuals simultaneously. From a mental health viewpoint, the sermon has both preventive and therapeutic potentialities. For relatively healthy persons it can stimulate personality growth and raise the general level of their creativity. It can release strength within those who are struggling with a personal crisis.

[1] Interview on NBC-TV on May 10, 1959.

It can support those whose personality foundations are weak, and motivate some who are burdened to seek professional help.

That many sermons do not enhance personality health is obvious. A cartoon depicting a woman shaking hands with a minister as she left the church, had this caption: "Thank you for your sermon! It was just like water to a drowning man." The woman's confused compliment loses its humor when applied to many sermons. How can a preacher avoid doing harm to persons? How can he maximize the contributions of his sermons to personality wholeness?

PREACHING AS AN ACT OF WORSHIP

The sermon is an integral part of a worship service. The effective sermon is itself an act of worship—of loving God with one's mind and heart. The mental health values of worship, discussed in Chap. 3, apply with particular force to the preaching dimension of worship. As a shared experience of meaning, the sermon stimulates the development of a sense of community. Many people gain ego support by identifying with the preacher as he proclaims the great themes of wisdom and faith, courage and hope as understood in the group's tradition. Hearing a sermon is a feeding experience, the food being more or less nourishing depending on the sermon's quality. An effective sermon facilitates the renewal of trust by communicating the eternal verities of the faith within the supportive matrix of a religious community. The sermon should be a channel of guilt-reducing grace. It should reduce narcissism by accepting confrontation of the hearer with the futility of the many and alluring varieties of self-worship and the warm attractiveness of the life of trust. Person-centered preaching shares insights concerning common human problems and explores alternative ways of handling them. Certainly, the sermon is the strategic part of the worship service for challenging persons to creative self-investment. Effective preaching is an invaluable instrument of pastoral care—a "perspective-giving, appreciation-perceiving and insight-creating discipline of the human spirit." [2]

PREACHING THAT BLOCKS AND BINDS

From the mental health standpoint, preaching is a hazardous activity. When a sermon communicates a distortion of the Christian

[2] Edgar N. Jackson, *A Psychology for Preaching* (Des Moines, Iowa: Meredith Press, 1961), p. 94.

message (see Chap. 2), it becomes a growth-stunting influence. Preaching is a way of relating. The preacher-listener relationship is, in a sense, one-to-one—that is, one preacher listened to by a group listening as individuals. On a deeper level, there exists a web of relationships wherein individual listeners respond to the nonverbal communication of their fellow listeners and the minister is influenced by the response of his congregation. The constructive or destructive factors in a sermon relationship are the same factors which make any relationship helpful or harmful.

The first negative factor in some preaching is *authoritarianism*. To be effective, a sermon must possess a degree of "rational authority"—the authority of competence. If his message lacks this self-validating quality, a minister may try to compensate by using the pseudo strength of irrational authority (authoritarianism). The coercive element in such preaching is thinly disguised. The spirit of mutual spiritual search is missing. The *ex cathedra* tone of the sermon tends to activate the hearer's immature responses—compliance or defiance—rather than stimulate his spiritual creativity.

A second negative factor which sometimes appears in preaching is *moralizing* (see Chap. 2). This harms mental health by creating neurotic guilt and/or self-righteousness, both inimical to robust morality. A minister who specializes in such preaching creates a guilt-laden atmosphere. Or, as a defense against guilt-feelings, parishioners may develop self-images which suffer from what one wag termed "halo-tosis." That young man who ate with publicans and sinners in first-century Palestine would probably feel very uncomfortable in such a church (in spite of the fact that his name is prominently displayed). The clergyman who majors in moralistic sermons is often a very angry person. He may also be very "successful" since there are so many adults in our society whose "Child" needs to be punished by the "Parent" of an authority figure.[3] Regular verbal spankings help keep their neurotic guilt-feelings diminished.

A third destructive factor in some sermons is the arousal of *irrational fear*. Fear and guilt are effective "softeners" by which homi-

___

[3] Eric Berne, author of *Transactional Analysis in Psychotherapy* (New York: Grove Press, 1961), holds that each person has three "ego states," which are in constant interaction with the ego states of others—Parent, Child, and Adult.

letical manipulators weaken the hearers' resistance to being manipulated. Studies of brainwashing have shown that if a person can be made to feel frightened or guilty enough, he becomes putty in an authority figure's hands.

A fourth negative factor is *exhibitionism*. Homiletical ego display is sometimes rationalized by the label "confessional." To the perceptive listener, such a minister is confessing his own intense hunger to be given attention, approval, or punishment. He is too busy feeding himself to hear the Lord's injunction, "Feed my sheep."

It is important to remember that all four of these forms of destructiveness operate, to some extent, outside a minister's awareness. They are projections of his personality problems. Most of us who preach occasionally fall into one of these negative patterns. The person who does so persistently needs therapy, not condemnation.

In addition to these destructive factors, there are two factors which make for irrelevance in preaching: *oversimplification* and *theologizing*. Sermons composed of easy generalizations about either the nature of human problems or their solutions are popular precisely because they ignore the ambiguities, paradoxes, and complexities of existence. They are agents of comfortable illusion. The comfort ends, however, when the comforted confronts the stubborn facts of everyday reality. When the simple message has a head-on collision with a snarled human problem, the irrelevance of such sermons is evident. The pampering sermon is one form of oversimplification. Grace is cheap. Goodness brings inevitable success. Challenge and confrontation are conspicuously absent.

As Fosdick has observed, a minister who is preaching a certain theological system usually misses the target of a sermon—live persons with live problems.[4] Precisely the same is true of preaching a psychological system. A minister's conceptual systems must be related to the world where people live and hope, cry and die. The late Halford E. Luccock once told of a young minister to whom a parishioner commented: "Brother Conway, you seem to be preaching to the moon." [5] Relevance is not easy to achieve, but it is

---

[4] Simon Doniger (ed.), *The Application of Psychology to Preaching* (Great Neck, N. Y.: Pastoral Psychology Press, 1952), p. 61.
[5] *Ibid.*

essential to genuine pastoral preaching. Translating one's ideas into understanding language is also essential. We ministers have an arsenal of specialized jargon which unwittingly can be used to dominate an audience, making them feel stupid, angry, or both. Some ministers become charmed with their verbal style. Well-articulated words become ends in themselves, not vehicles of communication. In this connection, Charles Goff once observed that some sermons are too smooth—like a player piano.

To summarize, all of these six factors harm persons because they diminish the self-esteem of the man in the pew, treating him as an object rather than a subject. In Martin's Buber's terms, they create "I-It" relationships. They increase the sense of "nobodyness," to use Martin Luther King's phrase.

SOME POSITIVE EFFECTS OF PREACHING ON MENTAL HEALTH

Just what is "good preaching"? Too often this phrase refers primarily to fluency in the use of the religious vocabulary and/or saying the things laymen like to hear. In contrast, a valid test for preaching is this—*How well does it communicate the basic meaning and experience of the Christian message?* The heart of the gospel is the "good news" of God's accepting love. To know the meaning of the gospel requires experiencing reconciliation (with oneself, others, and God). Growth occurs as a result of preaching when people experience the gospel message as a present reality. This experience releases the blocked inner strivings toward wholeness which are the gift of God. A minister would do well to test his sermons by questions such as these: To what extent did I communicate ideas that are true to the best in the Christian tradition? Did the quality of the relationships which were established help to bring these ideas alive in the experience of the listener? Were these relationships rich in acceptance and reconciliation?

The sermon offers a superb opportunity to communicate the Christian message in a supportive, life-affirming, growth-stimulating way. As Wayne Oates suggests, helpful messages of comfort, reassurance, inspiration, and teaching can frequently be communicated more effectively through preaching than through counseling.[6] A minister has a unique advantage among the helping professions, in having a

[6] *The Christian Pastor* (rev. ed.; Philadelphia: Westminster Press, 1964).

81

weekly opportunity to undergird his work with individuals by a message to his assembled flock. Recent developments in "milieu therapy" and the "therapeutic community" approach indicate that therapeutic goals can be achieved in much larger groups than had been thought possible in orthodox group therapy theory.[7]

It is wise for the minister to check his sermons frequently against mental health criteria (such as are described in Chap. 2). What he selects and emphasizes from the total biblical record and how he interprets it should be guided by his knowledge of what produces the gospel experiences of reconciliation and growth. From every possible source (including art, literature, theological thought, drama, the behavioral sciences, and his experiences with human relationships), he needs to widen and deepen his understanding of human nature and the human situation. He needs to know both *what is in man and what man is in.*

The message from the Bible can best come alive for individuals if the minister relates that message to their past experience, felt needs, and daily problems. John Dewey and others have demonstrated that learning is need-oriented. Learning occurs when certain ideas or attitudes are perceived by individuals as meeting their needs in some way. Whether a sermon deals with a biblical theme, a social problem, a Christian doctrine, the world mission of the church, Christian family life, or a personal problem such as doubt, it will have meaning for the individual only if it touches one of his many areas of inner need. A sermon will speak to him only if it "speaks to his condition." Somehow, in preaching, the magnificent insights of the Christian way must intersect the world of frustration, hope, and fear where most of us live. Preaching is proclaiming the good news of transforming love, but the proclamation can be heard only if it is directly related to the dilemmas, problems, and decisions which people face in their daily lives. A minister's most intimate awareness of his people's inner worlds comes from his face-to-face relationships with them in pastoral care and counseling.

There is some validity in the familiar charge that sermons frequently "answer questions nobody is asking." Many people, of course,

---

[7] Maxwell Jones, *The Therapeutic Community* (New York: Basic Books, Inc., 1953).

are asking the wrong questions.[8] They do not ask certain highly significant questions because they are unaware of those inner needs which would cause them to be asked. A sermon relationship, like a counseling relationship, should start with the question people are asking, but it should help them learn to ask new questions which can lead toward spiritual growth.

Some people ask, "How can I be *comforted?*" when they need to ask, "How can I be *confronted?*" (by the demands of reality). The common, erroneous assumption that there is an inevitable conflict between the pastoral and the prophetic, between counseling and preaching, results from a false dichotomy—acceptance versus confrontation. Confronting a person with reality can be, in certain circumstances, the most accepting way of relating to him. This is equally true in preaching and in counseling. I can recall marital counseling experiences in which the turning toward a healthier relationship occurred when the counselor stated, in effect, "It seems to me that you both need to do some growing up in your relationship." Certainly preaching should include confrontation. Jesus' preaching and counseling offer striking examples of creative confrontation.

The key to the effectiveness of confrontation is contained in the words, "speaking the truth in love" (Eph. 4:15). Confrontation is creative only when the truth is spoken in love—that is, within a relationship of acceptance. A congregation which knows that their minister cares about them as persons will accept confrontation from him which they would automatically reject from another source. The same is true in a strong counseling relationship. The truth is spoken in love only when the minister applies the truth to himself as well as to his congregation. If he speaks of the sins of his people and his community as though he were exempt from the failings of the rest of humanity, he will, in effect, be speaking down to his people. Confrontation is most likely to be accepted if the confronter makes it clear he is aware of his involvement in the sin and sickness which are the lot of men in general.

I recall the anxiety-laden questions that crossed my mind during

[8] For example, a person suffering from neurosis often asks, "Why don't others give me the love for which I am so hungry?" This question leads to a dead-end, psychologically. The productive question which leads toward inner freedom and personal growth is this—"Why do I relate to others in ways that keep me at a distance and prevent me from participating in the give and take of loving relationships?"

my first experience of preaching to a mental hospital congregation—
"What are they feeling and experiencing?" "Will my message have
a positive, negative, or no effect on their illness?" "Do I dare speak
as though I have answers to their enormous problems?" I am convinced that queries such as these are also worth raising when one
preaches to a "normal" congregation.

The feeling-tone of a sermon often has more to do with its mental
health impact than does content. Two clergymen in a given town
preach on "Forgiveness." Both sermons are biblically sound and
adequately preached. They are similar in content. And yet, when
the worshipers leave the service of pastor A, their inner condition is
very different from those leaving pastor B's service. A's parishioner's
have a dull we've-heard-that-before feeling, whereas B's people feel a
sense of having experienced the new life of forgiveness. The difference in the reaction which occurs is in the spirit of the man doing the
preaching.

The kind of preaching that enhances mental health has been
called by various names. Henry Sloane Coffin and Charles Kemp have
described it as "Pastoral Preaching." [9] Wayne Oates used the term
"Therapeutic Preaching," [10] and Edgar Jackson, "Person-centered
Preaching." [11]

TRUTH THROUGH RELATIONSHIP

The minister's own mental health deeply influences the impact
of his sermon on the mental health of others. For better or for
worse, who he is as a person inevitably comes through with force.
The spirit of the service is a direct reflection of the personality of
the minister. Phillips Brooks's classical definition of preaching as
"truth through personality," in contemporary terms could be put as
"truth through relationship" (emphasizing the interaction between
preaching and listener). Recent studies in communication theory
and group dynamics have confirmed Brooks's insight concerning the
importance in preaching of the personality of the preacher. Roy
Pearson declares: "If it is essential that the preacher understand the

---

[9] Henry Sloane Coffin, *What to Preach* (Cleveland: Church World Press, 1926); and
Charles F. Kemp, *Pastoral Preaching* (St. Louis: Bethany Press, 1963).
[10] *The Christian Pastor.*
[11] *A Psychology for Preaching.*

people to whom the sermon is delivered, it is equally important that he understand the person who delivers it." [12]

To some degree, every sermon is autobiographical—an act of self-revelation. The more the preacher is lacking in self-awareness, the more he will project unconscious feelings and images through the sermon, with distorting effects on the Christian message. Since the most difficult secret to keep is one's opinion of oneself, the minister's self-image will inevitably appear in his sermons.

The unexpected responses to sermons, which ministers frequently receive, may be due to the hearers having "tuned in," without the minister's awareness, on feelings and attitudes transmitted between the lines of a sermon. "The sermon I didn't intend to preach"— describes the feeling-level messages which are transmitted between the lines of a sermon. To paraphrase Emerson, what one makes his parishioners feel speaks so loudly they cannot hear what he says. The goal of preaching is to make the feeling-message undergird and reinforce the verbal message.

Most ministers who take counseling seriously find that it deepens their preaching. Not that one should ever violate a confidence by using case material in a sermon. Rather it is the experience of walking with troubled persons on their inner journey that deepens preaching by enhancing the minister's "feel" for human problems.

Realizing that depth preaching can only come from depth encounters with persons (especially the depths of their own personhood) some ministers are increasing their self-awareness through personal psychotherapy. The Rev. Harry B. Scholefield describes the impact of an educative analysis on his preaching:

In arriving at a higher degree of self-acceptance and self-knowledge, . . . I became aware that many of the uses I was making of sermons were at variance with my conscious intents. I lived through a good many conflicts which at first I denied had anything to do with sermon composition or preaching. As I lived them through . . . I began to put a fresh and higher value on the pulpit and its varied meanings.[13]

[12] *The Ministry of Preaching* (New York: Harper & Brothers, 1959), p. 70.
[13] "The Significance of an Educative Analysis for the Parish Ministry," in *The Minister's Own Mental Health*, Wayne Oates (ed.) (Des Moines, Iowa: Meredith Press, 1961), p. 325.

A thoughtful Christian layman has adapted an article from *Printer's Ink* entitled "Your Copy Is You" (by substituting "sermon" for "copy") :

Your sermon will be only as good and no better than you yourself as a thinking, analytical, understanding and sympathetic human being. If you are shallow, your sermon will be shallow: if you are blatant, your sermon will be blatant; if you are sincere, reasonable and persuasive, your sermon will be sincere, reasonable and persuasive. Because your sermon, more than you will ever realize, is you.[14]

A minister becomes a transmitter of the grace of God only if he has had a firsthand experience of that grace in his own inner life. His heart having been "strangely warmed," he is able to communicate this warmth to others. The openness and integrity of his own relationship with God will determine his effectiveness as a facilitator of healthy relationships with God.

PREACHING AS PRECOUNSELING

As a typical congregation listens to a sermon, there are always several persons who are sizing up the minister, attempting to decide whether or not to seek his help with a problem. Silently, they are asking themselves: "If I expose my painful problem to him will he be judgmental or accepting? Will he listen? Will he be shocked? Does he know enough about real life to understand? Can I trust him with my secret? Is he too busy to have time for me? Does he care about people?" How these silent questions are answered may determine whether these persons take the difficult step of crossing the threshold of the minister's study for help. The relationships established through the worship service and the sermon constitute either bridges or barriers between the minister and those who need his help.

One criterion for judging the effectiveness of a sermon is the number of troubled persons who seek help during the following week.[15] Any minister who is skilled in the art of pastoral preaching has heard words such as, "I haven't known where to turn with this problem. But last Sunday, as you were speaking, I felt I should talk to

---

[14] The original article by Walter Weir in *Printer's Ink* (May 5, 1960) was adapted by W. W. Reid in *The Pastor's Journal* (July-August, 1960 issue), p. 10.

[15] On the other hand, the sermon is of direct help to many people, some of whom may not come for counseling because they have been sustained and strengthened by it.

you about it." A sermon can help an individual overcome his inner resistances to seeking help by strengthening his sense of need and by awakening hope that something can be done about his dilemma.

In his autobiography, Fosdick describes the focus of effective preaching: "Every sermon should have for its main business the head-on constructive meeting of some problem which was puzzling minds, burdening consciences, distracting lives, and no sermon which so met a real human difficulty, with light to throw on it and help to win a victory over it, could possibly be futile." [16] This kind of "life situational" preaching will bring burdened people out of hiding to seek the minister's help.

What are some of the elements in preaching that help build bridges of rapport between minister and laymen? The warm feeling-tone of the minister's manner, his contact with his audience, his awareness of the tangled complexities of ordinary life, and his attitude toward his own weaknesses are all key factors. Charles Goff, a superb pastoral preacher, once told a group of young ministers of which I was a part, "Talk as you think you'd like to have someone talk to you when things were going badly." In a similar vein, Harry Emerson Fosdick has said, "I preach as a personal counselor . . . that is, I endeavor to address a congregation as though I were talking with an individual." [17]

Personal warmth and the evidence of competence are essential ingredients in a sermon that open doors for troubled people to seek help. Genuine warmth, in contrast to "pulpit radiance," comes from only one source—liking people. Warmth is, of course, no substitute for competence. A minister who characteristically preaches intellectually vacuous sermons will have few "takers" for counseling appointments, no matter how torrid his heart. It is the communication of these two feelings—"He cares about people" and "He knows what he is doing"—which attracts counseling opportunities.

A technique for testing the relevance and empathic qualities of one's preaching is to listen to a tape of last Sunday's sermon while imagining that one is a despairing person with whom one has counseled recently. This can be shaking. That sermon on "Christian

[16] *Living of These Days* (New York: Harper & Row, 1956), p. 94.
[17] J. R. Spann (ed.), *Pastoral Care* (Nashville: Abingdon-Cokesbury Press, 1951), p. 53.

Hope" which drew an abundance of ego-feeding plaudits may seem like twenty minutes of pious platitudes when viewed from the dark chaos of an alcoholic's inner world.

PREACHING AS GROUP COUNSELING

In their volume on mental health and the community, T. A. Rennie and L. E. Woodward discuss the positive function of preaching:

If the preacher has acquired a thorough understanding of personality development and habitually sees people as individuals with distinctly personal histories, if he accepts their present habits and characteristics in the light of their earlier conditioning experience, he can develop a manner and method in preaching that give people the feeling they are understood. . . . If the preacher will talk in terms of everyday feelings, habits and aspirations, commonplace life situations, and familiar Biblical scenes and sayings rather than in technical formulations of a theological or psychological nature, he can accomplish a great deal to help his people to better understanding of themselves and better adjustment to each other.[18]

The same factors which cause a sermon to create counseling opportunities are also vital in making it personal counseling on a group scale. Insight into life, nonjudgmentalism, warmth, and competence all contribute to a healing-growth milieu in the worship experience. A group-counseling sermon has a cutting edge and a spirit of urgency. At the University of Wisconsin various professors are asked by the student body to give a "last lecture" incorporating what they would say if it were their last opportunity to communicate what is most important to them. The results are so impressive that these lectures always draw overflow audiences. Perhaps a minister who is bogged down in the "weekliness" of his preaching role could apply the spirit of the "last lecture" to the topic he has chosen for next Sunday. There is no reason why a chill ought not to go down the spines of the members of the congregation occasionally as a sermon comes vividly alive for them. Stories pregnant with the drama of life, striking incidents from biographies, and dynamic interpretations of scripture have the ability to reach listeners in powerful ways.

[18] Thomas A. C. Rennie and Luther E. Woodward, *Mental Health in Modern Society* (New York: The Commonwealth Fund, 1948), pp. 262-63.

To transmit vitality a sermon must possess involvement on the minister's part. The danger of exhibitionism should not cause one to miss the real communicative power of personal witness. Think of the motivating influence of personal testimonies in Alcoholics Anonymous. The central focus of a healthy sermon should be Christian insights as they relate to concrete problems of living. In moderation, the subjective experiences of the minister in his own struggle to live the Christian life can enhance the communication of the gospel experience.

Sermons can be individual counseling on a group scale if they help people discover the living Word through the words of the Bible. It is true, unfortunately, that the historical-critical approach to the Bible has hardly touched most laymen. If the majority of churchmen are to discover the relevance of the life-changing ideas of the Bible, they must be helped to grow beyond naïve literalism. The sermon can help them understand the historical-developmental approach to the Bible as a friend that opens new windows in their spiritual lives. This requires what Paul Tillich calls "deliteralization"—in other words, moving beyond the symbolic stories (such as the creation myth and Jonah) to discover the glowing, self-authenticating truths-for-living which are visible only when one escapes from wooden literalism. Deliteralization (or "demythologizing," to use Rudolf Bultmann's term) should not deprive a congregation of the opportunity to participate in the universal symbols of our religious tradition. Deliteralizing does not mean debunking, but means moving beyond literalism to find a deeper level of meaning in the traditional symbols such as the Lord's supper, baptism, the cross, the Christmas story, and so forth. Symbols have an important place in preaching.

In an article on "The Impact of Pastoral Psychology on Theological Thought," Tillich emphasizes this point: "Intellectual and moral preaching fails to reach those levels of the personal life which can, however, be opened by authentic symbols—symbols which themselves have roots in the unconscious depths of individuals and groups." [19] He points out that "living symbols" (those which are alive with meaning for the person) are instruments of grace, vehicles for the impact of the divine presence on the unconscious as well as

[19] *Pastoral Psychology*, XI (February, 1960), 20.

the conscious life of persons. Liturgical, sacramental, biblical, and artistic symbols often have an impact on the totality of a person's life, grasping dimensions of his inner world which are missed by nonsymbolic expressions. As Tillich indicates, living symbols have both revealing and healing power.

To be a form of group counseling, a sermon must involve participation and response on the hearer's part. Experiments in learning have shown that unless there is emotional involvement, relatively little is learned and that is readily forgotten. One-way communication is notoriously inefficient as a teaching method. Participation is the key means of eliciting personal involvement.

Active listening is, of course, a form of participation. It would be a salutary (though perhaps disconcerting) experience for a preacher if he could turn a switch and listen to the thoughts of his congregation during the sermon. Various listeners might be thinking: "How can you be so sure?" "Oh, yea?" "So what?" "I'd like to believe that, but I can't." "What in the world does 'eschatological' mean?" "I wonder if I turned off the stove?" "You said it, reverend!" "That's a real doll in the second row!" "I've never thought of that." "Stop shouting!" "But I've just lost my job!" "But why did God let Bill die of cancer?" "I shouldn't have cheated on my income tax." "Amen." "You make it sound so easy." "This seat feels like a rock!" "I'll have to try that this week." "This is agony trying to stay awake." "But how do I go about loving *my* lousy neighbor?" "He's certainly wound up today!" "O God, help me find a way out." "That idea gets to me!"

In *The Miracle of Dialogue*, Reuel L. Howe speaks of the "monological illusion"—the erroneous belief that communication occurs when people are told what they ought to know. From his experiences at the Institute for Advanced Pastoral Studies, he observes that many younger ministers are disillusioned with preaching because they are not aware of alternatives to the ineffective, homiletical monologue.[20] Dialogic preaching, in which the preaching-listening relationship is taken seriously, breathes new life into this pastoral function. Fosdick holds that a sermon should be a "co-operative dialogue in which the congregation's objections, questions, doubts and confirmations are

[20] *The Miracle of Dialogue* (New York: Seabury Press, 1963), p. 32.

fairly stated and dealt with." [21] In his Yale lectures on preaching, Gene Bartlett stated that "the pastor-preacher joins a conversation already going on within every man." [22] Training in counseling is directly relevant to this kind of preaching. For example, the preacher may reflect and deal fairly with feelings, attitudes and doubts which he knows people frequently have in certain problem areas. This technique is used in counseling to help the counselee know that the counselor has empathetic understanding of his feelings. It is even more important in preaching because the listener has little opportunity to express his own objections, doubts, feelings, and reactions openly.

Preaching can learn from counseling (and creative education) at another point—that it is far less help to people, in the long run, to give them answers than it is to provide them with resources for finding their own answers. From the mental health standpoint, the spirit of preaching should be—"Here are rich resources from many sources including our religious tradition. I invite and challenge you to use them in your search for meaning." Offering alternative ways of understanding doctrinal matters (the resurrection, for example) and then leaving the decision to the individual (who will make it in the final analysis, in any case) is consistent with this approach. The same principle applies to complex ethical issues. The preacher should share his own convictions in this spirit—"This is the way I see it through the glass of my experience—perhaps darkly. I invite you to consider this, but I respect your responsibility to find your own position." If a sermon is to stimulate personal struggle with the complexities of existence, it must always raise more questions than it answers.

Many ministers have experimented with techniques for creating homiletical dialogue, direct feed back, and grass-roots congregational involvement. For a number of years, Leslie Weatherhead had a question-and-answer period following his Sunday evening sermon. Post-sermon discussion groups immediately following the service or during the week are devices frequently used. During series of sermons on Christian beliefs, I found it useful to have a five-minute period for question-writing immediately after the sermon. Questions sub-

[21] *Living of These Days,* p. 97.
[22] *The Audacity of Preaching* (New York: Harper & Row, 1962), pp. 84 ff.

mitted one Sunday were answered at the beginning of the following Sunday's sermon. Unfortunately, most congregations are so steeped in sermonic "spectatoritis" that they respond slowly to such inter-action stimulators.

The presermon "clinic" in its various forms is a procedure with rich possibilities. Dietrich Ritschl suggests that the minister take part with a select group of laymen in the study of the scripture passage from which the sermon will be preached the following Sunday. This tends to make the sermon a function of the congrega-tion. Another approach is for the minister to share his key ideas on a topic with a lay group several days or weeks before a sermon is preached. Their criticisms, suggestions, and discussion serve as im-portant grist for his homiletical mill. These approaches not only increase the relevance of sermons but give laymen a sense of genuine partnership in their preparation.[23]

From a mental health standpoint, a sermon should stimulate action as well as interaction. Halford Luccock calls attention to the fact that the response to the sermon at Pentecost was "What shall we do?" Let me suggest a two-step approach to the action phase of the response to preaching: (a) *Motivation*—Healthy motivation moves people, not primarily by guilt but by the warm, wonderful experi-ence of reconciliation. It challenges them to live in the kingdom which embryonically is present among us, and to work for its permeation into the fabric of interpersonal relationships and the structures of society. All this is a glad response to the gift of God's accepting love. (b) *Modus operandi*—Having succeeded in inspir-ing people to change their behavior, serve those in need, or join in social action, the next step is to help people discover a way of im-plementing their new intentions. The impact of many sermons is wasted because they do not include a closing section in which ques-tions such as "So what?" and "What can *I* do about it, now?" are answered in terms of realistic "next steps" which the hearers can take. Some ministers prepare a study-work sheet for distribution at the close of a sermon, with headings such as "Will you Help?" "What

[23] For a discussion of a variety of ways of stimulating dialogue, see Clyde H. Reid, "Preaching and the Nature of Communication," *Pastoral Psychology*, XIV (October, 1963); also see Gene E. Bartlett, *The Audacity of Preaching*, for suggestions concerning ways of including the congregation in sermon preparation.

I Can Do About Racial Segregation" or "Study and Action Suggestions." As Gene Bartlett puts it, sermons should end with R.S.V.P., not Q.E.D. There is sound mental health wisdom in the familiar line, "Inspiration is to be enjoyed, then employed."

A sermon is group counseling when it communicates within a supportive religious group the healthy values of the tradition. Many people who have unreliable inner controls need this periodic reinforcement of their value-structure to help them maintain constructive limits in their behavior. This underlines the importance of the minister's standing for something, firmly and dependably, and not simply being permissive and accepting. It is crucial that what he stands for be not moralistic trivia but the central principles of the Hebrew-Christian tradition—justice, respect for people, trust, love, and brotherhood under God. Being a transmitter of the important values of the culture is more than a way of shoring up weak inner controls on antisocial behavior. It is one of the minister's essential roles in society.

PITFALLS AND POSSIBILITIES OF "PSYCHOLOGICAL SERMONS"

Even a cursory inspection of the church service announcements in Saturday's newspaper shows that some ministers are taking Fosdick's group-scale counseling idea seriously but presumably are ignoring his warning against becoming "amateur pulpit psychiatrists." Topics such as "Three Secrets for Overcoming Inferiority Feelings" and "Master Your Fears Through Faith" are not uncommon. The hallmark of a psychological sermon is its focus on an emotional problem and its use of psychological concepts in discussing a solution. Like many clergymen who are impressed with the value of insights from depth psychology and psychotherapy, I have frequently preached such sermons. It is my impression that whatever benefits resulted could have been achieved in other ways without the negative effects frequently produced by such sermons.

The fallacy in such preaching is the assumption that intellectual knowledge about an emotional problem is helpful to a troubled person. The minister trained in counseling knows that intellectual understanding is not the same as "insight," that insight involves deep self-awarenesses (reliving blocked feelings) which raise self-esteem and rectify distorted relationships. Intelligent, literate indi-

93

viduals often use their ability to conceptualize as a resistance to self-awareness and a defense against accepting the deeper help they need. Sermons which encourage psychological conceptualization without a therapeutic experience tend to encourage the listener to build higher walls around himself. What he needs is not theories (however valid) about love but the experience of love. If the spirit of any sermon (including a psychological sermon) communicates this experience, it will tend to enhance mental health.

Unfortunately, the thing that often unconsciously motivates the preaching of the "how to" psychological sermon is hidden moralism. The language is different; the dynamics are the same. Such a sermon may be a disguised way of spanking people for their guilts, fears, inferiority feelings, and so forth, in the name of helping them. It is moralistic in that it encourages the psychological equivalent of works-righteousness approaches to salvation—that is, it encourages the attempt to pull oneself up by one's own rational bootstraps rather than opening oneself to the healing-growth resources in good relationships. The person who tries the bootstrap approach and fails has added another layer of suffering to his already heavy load. He may now feel guilty about his guilts or afraid of his fears.

I recall a psychological sermon on "Let not the sun go down on your wrath." It had these major points: Unwarranted anger is a sign of immaturity; anger is bad for your mental and physical health; don't let your anger smolder but replace it with love and forgiveness. The minister obviously had read widely in the popular religio-psychological literature. Many of his comments about the roots of anger were valid. Yet I suspect that the results of the sermon, in addition to transmitting certain head-level ideas about anger, were to make his congregation feel guilty about their unresolved hostility and to arouse hidden anger toward the minister himself. The minister was inaccurate in his belief that anger as such is bad for health. Only chronic anger or anger which is pushed out of awareness to fester in a pool of guilt in the unconscious has a deleterious influence on health. The minister's oversimplified remedy for anger showed the superficiality of the sermon. Replacing anger (especially inappropriate, immature anger) with love and forgiveness is a worthy goal, but it can be done only by personal maturing.

94

There is no reason to exclude from preaching, insights about human life from any source, certainly not from the sciences of man.[24] Relatively healthy people possess sufficient inner freedom to utilize such insights constructively. Here are some guidelines for reducing the dangers in the use of psychological concepts in preaching:

(1) *Double-check the accuracy of one's facts.* Seward Hiltner recommends that ministers who have professional psychotherapists in their congregation interact with them before preaching on a psychological topic.[25] A brief consultation over lunch with a clinically trained chaplain, a psychiatrist, a social worker, a psychologist, or a minister with advanced training in counseling is an excellent way of confirming one's facts.

(2) *Translate psychological terms into understandable English and, if possible, into the religious vocabulary.* Except with an unusually sophisticated audience, psychological terms tend to block rather than facilitate communications. Many such terms elicit fear-laden associations. Psychological concepts should be employed sparingly and presented in juxtaposition with the parallel ideas from the Bible or the Christian tradition. For example, a quote from Erich Fromm stressing the importance of mature "self-love" could well be followed by indicating that the same insight is implicit in the words of Jesus "You shall love your neighbor as yourself" (Matt. 19:19). Or, this statement from Søren Kierkegaard might be cited: "If anyone, therefore, will not learn from Christianity to love *himself* in the right way, then neither can he love his neighbor . . . To love one's self in the right way and to love one's neighbor . . . are at bottom one and the same . . . Hence the law is: 'You shall love yourself as you love your neighbor when you love him as yourself.' "[26]

(3) *Avoid anything that might be taken as an easy answer.* It is wise, in fact, to go beyond this by frankly stating that most human problems are complicated, that some require professional therapy,

[24] Here are some of the titles of Fosdick's great sermons on personal problems, which made use of psychological insights: "The High Uses of Trouble," "When Life Goes All to Pieces," "How to Stand Up and Take It," "The Conquest of Fear."

[25] "Editorial," *Pastoral Psychology*, IX (March, 1958).

[26] Robert Bretall (ed.), *A Kierkegaard Anthology* (Princeton: Princeton University Press, 1946), p. 289.

that many cannot be solved fully, and that often the best we can do is change our attitudes toward them.

(4) *Balance introspective elements in preaching with those which look upward and outward.* As Viktor Frankl has observed, many people intensify their problems by "hyperreflection." The more they concentrate on introspection, the more anxious they become about their anxieties. They become psychological pulse-takers. Rather than encouraging further introspection, it often is healthier to help such persons find a challenging center of self-investment outside themselves.

In general, it is much better to include psychological insights in every sermon than to preach sermons which are mainly psychological. It is the correlation of the wisdom of our religious tradition with more recent insights from the psychological sciences that gives preaching vitality and the power to reach persons in this "age of psychology."

(5) *Always stress the importance of seeking professional help when problems do not respond to self-help procedures.* Regular mention in sermons of the community resources which are available helps people to implement this recommendation.

(6) *Create channels for evaluative feedback.* The importance of this cannot be overestimated. Several perceptive laymen should be asked by the minister to listen with a keen ear and report on the strengths and weaknesses of a particular sermon. "P.S.E. Sheets" (Post-Sermon Evaluation) encourage candor by asking specific questions about content, delivery, congregational reaction, and suggestions for strengthening future sermons on the topic. The privilege of serving as "sermon evaluators" should be rotated among the mature laymen of a church. This procedure should be handled informally and casually, without publicity or fanfare.

ALLIES: PREACHING AND PASTORAL COUNSELING

In his Yale lectures on preaching some ninety years ago, Phillips Brooks declared, "The work of the preacher and the pastor really belong together, and ought not to be separated." [27] Several facets of the complementary nature of counseling and preaching have been

[27] Phillips Brooks, *Lectures on Preaching* (New York: E. P. Dutton and Company, 1877), p. 75.

discussed—the way in which effective preaching brings troubled persons to counseling, the function of counseling experiences in helping to keep preaching relevant to real human problems, and the ways in which training in counseling can be used in preaching.

A final point at which preaching and counseling need each other is when the preacher unwittingly threatens or does harm to an individual's mental health. A woman in her middle years was unable to remarry following the tragic death of her husband, in spite of several opportunities to do so. Something beyond her control would cause her to withdraw from every relationship which began to move toward marriage. Her problem was rooted in repressed hostile feelings toward her deceased husband concerning which feelings she felt intense unconscious guilt. To atone for her guilt feelings, she denied herself the satisfaction of remarriage. After a number of years, she was able to partially overcome this block and was about to remarry. Then, one Sunday in his sermon, her minister used a sermon illustration which plunged the woman back into her guilt. The illustration was a story which praised a lighthouse keeper's widow who did not remarry but, instead, continued faithfully to tend the light for many years. When asked how she found strength to carry on, she replied that she looked across the water to the green hills where her husband was buried and heard him say, "Mind the light, Mary." Fortunately, the woman who was about to remarry was able to make an appointment with her minister to talk about her distress. The wedding was postponed and through depth counseling she discovered and worked through her underlying ambivalance toward her first husband. Fortunately, the sermon illustration had brought her problem into the open where it could be dealt with by means of counseling. However, if the woman had not felt free to seek such counseling, she might have retreated permanently into her self-punishing pattern, making remarriage impossible.

Every sermon involves risks of this type. An inept, inaccurate or misconstrued statement can have serious negative effects on the mental well-being of someone who is present. For this as well as other reasons, it is imperative that a congregation feel that their minister is highly approachable for individual counseling. His availability for counseling should be publicized regularly in the church bulletin. In addition, he should let it be known that he welcomes the opportunity to talk individually with anyone who wishes to discuss any issue raised by his sermons. This will contribute to the dialogic atmosphere of a congregation and will also help transform the unintentional negative effects of preaching into counseling opportunities. Informed by such experiences, the minister can move toward deepening the levels of communication which occur during his sermons.

In his autobiography, Fosdick recalls the decisive turning-point in his preaching. He had known for some time that counseling could achieve results. He writes: "It was a great day when I began to feel that a sermon could be immediately creative and transforming." [28] It is no wonder that after this occurred, preaching became exhilarating for him and an experience of group counseling for his congregation.

[28] *Living of These Days,* p. 99.

CHAPTER 5
The Prophetic Ministry and Mental Health

*We are moving toward the close of the 20th century
with a religious community largely adjusted to the
status quo—a taillight behind other community
agencies rather than a headlight leading men to
higher levels of justice. . . .*

*There was a time when the church was very power-
ful . . . the early Christians rejoiced at being deemed
worthy to suffer for what they believed. In those days
the Church was not merely a thermometer that re-
corded the ideas and principles of popular opinion;
it was a thermostat that transformed the mores of
society. Whenever the early Christians entered a town
the power structure got disturbed and immediately
sought to convict them for being "disturbers of the
peace" and "outside agitators." But the Christians
pressed on, in the conviction that they were "a colony
of heaven," called to obey God rather than man.
Small in number, they were big in commitment . . .
they brought an end to such ancient evils as infanti-
cide and gladiatorial contest. . . .*

*Things are different now. So often the con-
temporary church is a weak, ineffectual voice with
an uncertain sound. So often it is the archdefender
of the status quo. Far from being disturbed by the
presence of the church, the power structure of the
average community is consoled by the church's silent
—and often even vocal—sanction of things as they
are.*[1]*—Martin Luther King, Jr.*

[1] "Letter from Birmingham Jail," *Christian Century*, LXXX (June 12, 1963), 772.

THE NATURE OF THE PROPHETIC MINISTRY

What does a church's concern for a just society and a warless world have to do with mental health? Everything! The prophetic ministry constitutes an essential part of any church's mental health opportunity. A dynamic concern for the problems of individuals should not cause a neglect of the social matrix which spawns individual problems. A church should work "like a miner under a landslide" to eliminate the social causes of mental illness and to create a growth-enhancing society in which positive mental health will bloom like a rose.

It is a church's business to be a leavening influence in its community—to work as well as pray, for the kingdom's coming "on earth as it is heaven." Its "community" is composed of concentric circles which eventually widen to include the world community. John Wesley's familiar words, "The world is my parish," have a breathless urgency in our day when no point on the planet is more than one-half hour from ICBM obliteration. A church's prophetic ministry is a contemporary expression of the passion for social justice of the Old Testament prophets. It reflects the spirit of Jesus' cleansing of the temple—an incident in which he "disturbed the peace" in challenging an exploitative system. The prophetic ministry is a vital part of "diakonia," the New Testament word for the church's ministry to the community, through which it becomes the continuing incarnation of Christ in the world. This ministry is as much the responsibility of laymen as of clergymen. In fact, since the layman is often in a strategic position to implement a "marketplace ministry," his prophetic opportunity frequently surpasses that of the clergyman.

THE INTERDEPENDENCE OF INDIVIDUAL AND SOCIAL PROBLEMS

There are various handy escape routes available for avoiding one's Christian responsibility to change institutionalized forms of evil. One is the other-worldly thrust of some contemporary theologies which affirm a radical discontinuity between this world and God's kingdom. Such theologies cut the nerve of social concern and action. Fortunately, their influence on American ministers has been relatively small and even less on laymen. A more popular escape route consists of a lop-sided emphasis on helping individuals. This general

47946.

route has several alternates. The revivalist road is one of these with its one-sided emphasis on the salvation of individuals. Interestingly enough, an alternate of this same route is the one followed by some who are so overly invested in pastoral counseling and/or spiritual healing as to virtually ignore social problems. This is a revival of individualistic pietism in psychological garb. From a mental health perspective, it is shortsighted and out of balance.

A church should have a balanced concern for both the individual roots of social problems and the social roots of individual problems. Obviously it is essential to work simultaneously on both ends of the human situation.

The circular relationship between individual and social problems becomes increasingly clear as the research findings of the behavioral scientists accumulate. A study was made of the outlook and attitudes of persons living in two middle income housing projects. The only major difference between the two projects was that one was integrated and the other was not. It was found that Negroes living in the racially integrated facility showed a more positive attitude toward life and seemed better adjusted in general than those in the nonintegrated housing.[2] Segregation per se has a damaging effect on the self-esteem and therefore the mental health of those segregated. A psychiatrist who studied the effects of the school desegregation conflict on children in the Deep South reports: "I have been struck by how clearly young Negro children foresee the bleak future of their lives. With crayons, a medium of quiet eloquence . . . they draw a world of fear and foreboding, of worthlessness, of anticipated uselessness." [3] All of his young Negro subjects expressed intense feelings of loneliness and vulnerability.

Studies by social psychiatrists emphasize the role played by environmental pressures on the development of personality illnesses. Slum areas subject those who are trapped there (usually because they are members of a ghettoed minority group) to severe stresses which erode their self-esteem and spawn all manner of social prob-

[2] *Social Action in Review* (May-June, 1957). Published by the Commission on Social Action of the Union of American Hebrew Congregations.

[3] Robert Coles, "Racial Identity in School Children," *The Saturday Review* (October 19, 1963), p. 57. See also M. M. Grossack (ed.) *Mental Health and Segregation* (New York: Springer Publishing Co., 1963).

lems. Try to imagine, for instance, the interpersonal friction and lack of privacy which results from cramming two parents and six children into one, cockroach-infested room with a primitive kitchen and a toilet shared with three other families.

Recent studies have discovered that the poor are much more vulnerable to the severe forms of mental illness, than are middle class groups. Thomas S. Langner and Stanley T. Michael, in a monumental study of midtown Manhattan residents, found that socioeconomic status is more closely associated with rates of mental illness, than any other demographic factor. (See *Life Stress and Mental Illness*. New York: Basic Books, 1963.) The increased vulnerability was found not to be simply the result of greater stresses on security and self-esteem (*e.g.* broken homes, poor health, job insecurity). Lower class persons with the same number of stress factors as middle class counterparts develop more personality illness. A major reason for this is the fact that chronically impoverished persons respond to stress in ways that tend to be ineffective, leading to increased psychiatric impairment. For example, many become passive, depressed and withdrawn, thus moving away from the very qualities (initiative and imagination, for instance) which would allow them to take advantage of chance opportunities to improve their lot. Having tasted the bitter dregs of repeated failure, planning ahead and working for a better future (typical middle-class responses) seem utterly futile to them.

Some poverty-crippled persons respond to painful frustrations with anti-social behavior which starts a negative chain reaction with the law. The underprivileged respond to stress by moving toward alcoholism, drug addiction, and with schizophrenic and paranoid ways of relieving the stress, far more often than do those who are undergirded with middle-class securities. The tragedy of all this is compounded by the fact that most community mental health facilities are oriented to middle-class goals, vocabularies, patterns of problem solving and models of healing. Traditional introspective psychotherapy is ineffective with the vast majority of persons from the impoverished classes. Fortunately, several experimental programs in psychiatry are gradually developing action-oriented alternatives which have therapeutic promise for such groups. For example, informal therapy groups in which members take active roles in helping each other handle concrete problems in living, seem to be more effective. Obviously, the alleviation of our country's huge "pockets of poverty" is an essential means of preventing a vast amount of mental illness.[4]

A dedicated psychotherapist who had spent his professional life treating sick individuals observed this sobering fact: "We therapists are treating disturbed persons on a retail basis while our society is creating personality disturbances in wholesale fashion." The late Japanese Christian leader, Kagawa, once used a figure of speech which aptly applies to any church which ignores social problems: It is maintaining a rescue station at the bottom of a cliff to help those who have fallen while neglecting to work at the top to keep others from falling.

SOCIAL FACTORS WHICH CONTRIBUTE TO MENTAL ILL HEALTH

A Los Angeles news commentator, after scanning the Monday morning headlines of mayhem and chaos, began his newscast with the phrase: "This is what happened over the weekend in this craziest of all possible worlds." Any condition of social injustice, economic deprivation, political tyranny, or racial discrimination has a deleterious effect on the self-esteem of the victims. Anything that raises the anxiety level or lowers the self-esteem of parents diminishes their ability to be sensitive and responsive to the heart-hungers of their children.

Among the many social problems our society faces, three problems stand like volcanoes threatening to engulf our society—thermonuclear war, racial injustice, and the population explosion. The impact of this terrible trio on mental health defies imagination.

Near the close of 1962, Aldous Huxley added some grim variations on his "Brave New World" theme. He predicted that the next decade will produce a situation in which one-third of the world, with its military-oriented, highly developed technology, will perpetually "descend into the steel and concrete dungeons of total civil de-

---

[4] I am indebted in this discussion to an illuminating article on the special mental health needs of the underprivileged by Dale White—"Mental Health and the Poor," *Concern,* October 15, 1964, pp. 4-7. For a study of factors involved in social disintegration and their negative impact on mental health, see *People of Cove and Woodlot,* by Charles C. Hughes *et al* (New York: Basic Books, Inc., 1960).

fense." [5] The other two-thirds will be caught in the population explosion producing extreme hunger, poverty, social unrest, and the constant danger of totalitarian political control.

The psychological destruction that has resulted from recent wars and their aftermath of disease, famine, and hopelessness is well known. Now the world lives under the dark, malignant cloud of World War III that will, if it comes, make the others seem puny by comparison. Commenting on the threat of a thermo-nuclear holocaust, Stuart Chase writes:

Military experts can discuss "first strike," "second strike," and "counter-strike-with bonus"; but beyond these semantic exercises, it is obvious to the careful inquirer that both the U.S. and the USSR are now equipped to eliminate each other as viable societies by exploding a few large hydrogen bombs high in the stratosphere, generating firestorms of metereological dimensions. These can incinerate every combustible object, natural or man-made, over vast areas, including occupants of all but the deepest oxygen-equipped shelters. [6]

The psychological and social problems created by the "baby A-bombs" dropped on Japan are minor compared to the aftermath of a hydrogen Armageddon with an estimated 93 million Americans and at least that many Russians destroyed and much of the earth poisoned by radioactivity. Unimaginative people, he holds, will continue to "hope for the best," taking refuge in what psychologists term "denial of reality." Chase continues: "People with reflective minds know that when the button is pushed, accidentally or otherwise, the country they love will, in a matter of minutes, cease to exist as a going concern. The fact that the enemy also ceases to exist is scant consolation. Our freedom will be buried in the same trench with his tyrannies." [7]

Nightmare thermonuclear weapons are poised in underground ICBM silos on both sides of the cold war. In the light of this, the game of prenuclear age power politics which the leaders of nations continue to play is preposterous, suicidal nonsense. The nuclear sword of Damocles which hangs over our civilization is, even for the

[5] *Los Angeles Times* (December 1, 1962), p. 8.
[6] "Bombs, Babies, and Bulldozers," *The Saturday Review* (January 26, 1963), p. 22.
[7] *Ibid.*

semiaware, a realistic source of constant anxieties of major proportions. Let me emphasize that we *should* feel anxious and should be motivated by this anxiety to change the situation. The salutary effects on the mental health of mankind would be beyond estimate if this horrible cloud could be removed through the achievement of permanent nuclear disarmament and an international police force under a strengthened United Nations.

The circular relationship between social and psychological problems is well-illustrated by the peace issue. We will not have stable peace unless we are able to master some of the gigantic inner problems of man—his pent-up rage, his fears, his "escape from freedom" into authoritarian systems, his over-identification with nationalistic groups. Psychiatrists William C. Menninger and Jerome Frank have both pointed out that the behavior among nations displays many of the symptoms of psychologically sick individuals—paranoid mistrust, tension, pettiness, extreme self-centeredness, and the need to see one's enemies as all bad and oneself as all good. In an address entitled "The Psychiatry of Enduring Peace and Social Progress," psychiatrist Brock Chisholm, Director-General of WHO, from 1948-1953 declared: "So far in the history of the world there have never been enough mature people in the right places." [8]

Fifteen years ago a group of psychiatrists, including Harry Stack Sullivan, Daniel T. Bain, and George S. Stevenson, made this significant statement in a preparatory report from the International Congress on Mental Health:

Principles of mental health cannot be successfully furthered in any society unless there is progressive acceptance of the concept of world citizenship. World citizenship can be widely extended among all people through the application of the principles of mental health . . . the problem of world citizenship in relation to human survival needs to be formulated afresh in the light of new knowledge about aggressiveness in man, group tensions and resentments, race prejudices and nationalist sentiments and stereotypes. [9]

Knowledge from the sciences of man can help us achieve world citizenship, which, in turn will contribute mightily to mental health.

[8] *Psychiatry*, Vol. 9, No. 1 (February, 1946), p. 6.
[9] *Preparatory Report* (London: International Congress on Mental Health, 1948).

We in the church need a spirit like that of John Wesley who, in a sermon on the Beatitudes described the man of love as a "citizen of the world." This is our first loyalty as Christians!

The real threat to man's existence is not the A, H, or C bombs, but *man*. The unique factor about the present situation is that the vast human potentiality for destructiveness (in blocked creativity) is now armed with fiendish instruments of mass annihilation. This makes it imperative that we learn to understand and control the destructive forces within man, individually and collectively. Otherwise the recurring fratricidal conflicts of the past will be supplanted by a monstrous genocidal conflagration.

Shortly before his death, Carl Gustav Jung wrote a sobering article pointing out that relatively few people take seriously the fact that man has an unconscious mind which influences everything he does. The potentialities in the unconscious represent almost unimaginable destructive or creative forces. The importance of whether they are used destructively or creatively has been magnified a thousandfold by what Jung referred to as "that peculiar flower of human ingenuity, the hydrogen bomb." [10] Looking to the foreboding future, his words should have an authentic ring to the ear of a Christian: "Virtually everything depends on the human soul and its functions. It should be worthy of all the attention we can give it. . . ." [11]

Racial Justice and Mental Health

The late Dorothy W. Baruch once described a child who kicked her when he came to her office because he was angry with his mother. She commented that she was glad that he could learn, through psychotherapy, how to handle his angry feelings constructively. She said that she preferred having a temporary shin bruise to having him kick Negroes, Mexicans, or Jews when he grew up. [12] A study of the psychology of prejudice, reported in *The Authoritarian Personality*, [13] showed that prejudice is often associated with personality

[10] "God, the Devil and the Human Soul," *The Atlantic Monthly* (November, 1957), p. 61.

[11] *Ibid.*, p. 57.

[12] Dorothy W. Baruch discusses the roots of prejudice in *New Ways in Discipline*, pp. 38, 57, 140, 230.

[13] T. W. Adorno, *et al.* (New York: Harper & Row, 1950).

distortions. A person who is frightened by life and unable to accept his own negative impulses may project these onto minority groups. This is the underlying cause of scapegoatism. A comprehensive survey of the research studies on prejudice [14] showed that some prejudice is a result of culturally conditioned attitudes and is not the result of deep personality illness. The sickness is societal rather than individual, although disturbed individuals often rise to leadership roles in such situations.

Discrimination is prejudice in action. The negative effect on the mental health of those segregated was basic in the supreme court's milestone decision on public school desegregation in 1954. Separate facilities are inherently unequal because of the psychological effects on the excluded group. The psychological damage to those doing the segregating is more subtle and insidious. James Weldon Johnson once said that the race issue is really a struggle "to save black America's body and white America's soul."

The churches can never become the healing forces which they should be in the area of mental health until they heal the sickness of segregation within their corporate life. As Fred D. Wentzel put it: "The church must continue to be weak and self-defeating in its efforts to create the brotherly society until it begins to represent in its own attitude and practice an all-inclusive fellowship. It is now a very sick man telling everybody how to be well." [15] The responses of the predominantly Caucasian churches to the brotherhood revolution that is currently sweeping this country has been, with some notable exceptions, a disappointing page in Christian history. When we cut the roots of prejudice and provincialism in the churches a giant step will have been taken toward releasing their spiritual integrity and healing power.

The Population Explosion and Mental Health

The population explosion is a world-wide threat to mental as well as physical health. Each week some two million babies join the world population, the majority of them in areas already overpopulated and underfed. The hungry two-thirds of the world is growing twice as

[14] Gordon W. Allport, *The Nature of Prejudice* (Garden City: Doubleday & Company, 1958).

[15] *Epistle to White Christians* (Philadelphia: The Christian Education Press, 1948), p. 56.

rapidly as the affluent one-third. Two-thirds of the economic progress made by underdeveloped nations since 1950 has been wiped out by the population explosion. The basic cause is not an increased birth rate but the radically decreased death rate, resulting largely from antibiotics and disinfectants developed during World War II. To illustrate, in a generation life expectancy in India has risen from twenty-three to forty-eight years.

The world population did not reach one billion until 1830, but it took only another hundred years to reach two billion, and another thirty years to reach three billion (in 1961). If the present rate continues, over six billion persons will huddle together on the globe by the year 2000, and in another six hundred years each inhabitant will have only one square yard on which to live.[16] Sir Julian Huxley, former UNESCO director, regards birth control as the only real hope in the problem and terms it "a prerequisite for anything that you can call progress and advance in human evolution." He holds that the population explosion is "the gravest problem of our time," more serious than war or peace, in the long perspective. It is obvious that unless the explosion is checked, it will produce a nightmarish spiraling of all manner of personality-damaging social problems.

What can churchmen do? Individual couples can practice responsible family planning. Denominations can take a forthright stand (as several have done) holding that responsible family planning through the use of the most effective contraceptives is not only ethically permissible, but is the only Christian approach to parenthood in the face of the population explosion. There is need for continuing exploration of possible ways of obtaining Roman Catholic cooperation on this issue. Whether or not such ways are found, nonCatholics have an obligation to give moral support to birth control education programs beamed at all parts of the world. The goal, as an American State Department official has put it, is "a world in which every birth is accompanied by a birthright."

Inexpensive, easily used contraceptive methods are now available. Whether or not they are used widely enough to interrupt the geometric progression of the population increase depends on the motiva-

[16] The figures cited and the quotations are from "How Many Babies Is Too Many?" *Newsweek* (July 23, 1962), pp. 27-30.

tion of parents. This is an area needing much additional research. Commenting on the situation in his country, a Pakistani leader declared: "Sex is the only poetry known to the poor man. He procreates when he is happy, procreates when he is unhappy, procreates when he is indifferent." Theological as well as medical issues are involved. In New Delhi, a woman said, as she sat in the doorway of her mud hut nursing her fourteenth baby, "These are all God-given children." [17]

Neurotic Aspects of Our Culture

Those who have explored the social factors in personality growth have found that there are certain characteristics of our society which stunt such growth. These factors make it difficult for adults and children to maintain mutually satisfying, growth-nurturing relationships. Penetrating analyses of these factors have been made by Karen Horney,[18] by Erich Fromm,[19] and by David Riesman.[20]

A basic factor which makes it difficult to maintain warm, intimate, need-satisfying relationships is the extreme competitiveness and pressure to "succeed" in terms of power, property, and prestige. Closely linked with this are the prevalent feelings of isolation, alienation, and depersonalization. Rollo May has described our times as the "schizoid age"—our age of unrelatedness.[21] T. S. Eliot expresses the aching loneliness of modern man through one of his characters in *The Cocktail Party:*

> Do you know—
> It no longer seems worthwhile to *speak* to anyone.
>
> .   .   .   .
>
> No . . . it isn't that I *want* to be alone,
> But that everyone's alone . . .
> They make noises, and think they are talking to each other;
> They make faces, and think they understand each other.
> And I'm sure they don't.[22]

[17] *Ibid.*
[18] *The Neurotic Personality of Our Time* (New York: W. W. Norton & Company, 1937).
[19] *The Sane Society* (New York: Holt, Rinehart & Winston, 1955).
[20] *The Lonely Crowd* (New Haven: Yale University Press, 1950).
[21] *Pastoral Psychology* (November, 1954), p. 6.
[22] *The Cocktail Party* (New York: Harcourt, Brace and Co., 1950), p. 134.

There are many reasons for the unrelatedness of our times. Prominent among them is the mass migration to the anonymity of the city. Moving from a small town where one was surrounded by friends and clan to a large city where "people are lonesome together" is a "detribalizing," shaking experience. Alan Walker has noted that the Wise Men lost sight of the star when they reached the big city. Modern city man often loses sight of the star of his own worth and meaning. He rapidly becomes mass man—feeling lost in the subway herd, a cypher in the census statistics, a punch card in his company's computer. He feels helplessly caught in the swirling vortex of economic, political, and population forces over which he has little, if any, control.

The competitiveness of our society with its ruthless drive to "get ahead" is in part a result of the lack of mutually satisfying relationships. People who do not have deep relatedness often substitute competitiveness and its rewards. But competitiveness is also a cause of this lack of relatedness. Here again the cause-effect factors are circular and self-perpetuating. The child who grows up in a highly competitive family feels that he is valued only as he can bring success to his parents. His deep need to be loved for his own sake is thwarted, and he comes to value himself and other human beings only as he or they are instruments of success. His self-worth is based entirely on what Fromm calls the "marketing orientation"—that is his ability to "sell himself." He depersonalizes others, seeing them as things to be used as he claws his way upward.

Ironically, as Fromm has put it, our society has produced machines which act like men and men who act like machines.[23] The director of the Carnegie Tech Computation Center has suggested that western civilization has renounced man as an ideal and, in his place, has substituted the supercomputer. The rise of a machine civilization has depleted interest in the humanities and in artistic creativity. Graduates of engineering and technical schools emerge, he says, with no idea what man really is but with "a very clear and loving idea— or ideal—of what a computer is." [24]

Another cultural reason for the prevalence of anxiety and in-

[23] *The Sane Society,* p. 360.
[24] "Mathematician Says Computer Is Menace," *Los Angeles Times* (June 16, 1963).

security is that the contemporary individual is no longer sustained by what Jung called the power of the *"consensus Omnium."* [25] Gone are many of the supports which men found, in a more comfortable day, in widely accepted religious and philosophical certainties. Revolutionary changes in science and history have shaken the foundations of man's spiritual certainties. The current religious boom occurring simultaneously with declining ethical vitality probably is more a symptom of loneliness, anxiety, and searching for identity, than of faith.

What a church can do about all of this is the subject of this volume. Briefly, a church should become an island of sanity in our neurotic society, avoiding thing-centeredness and keeping persons at its heart. It should seek new, creative ways of bringing people suffering from "mass-itis" into small groups where they can experience depth relationships. Somehow the church will have to repent of its own scramble for quantitative success so that it will be capable of exposing the dog-eat-dog aspects of our culture for what they are—sick. It must resist the temptation to peddle success-oriented religion to people who grasp it because they are too hungry to know the difference between a stone and bread. Most important of all, it must work to help people find a relevant, intellectually respectable faith and an experience of values so alive that "when you cut them they bleed."

MENTAL ILLNESS AND THE PROPHETIC MINISTRY

The social problem which has the most direct pernicious effect on mental health is the inadequate provision which our society makes for the treatment of the major mental illnesses. Jesus' concern for the mentally ill was clearly evident in his healing ministry. As his followers, Christians should share this concern.

In 1955, Congress appointed a "Joint Commission on Mental Illness and Health" to make the first nationwide study of treatment resources and needs. The commission, composed of seventy leaders in the mental health field, reported in 1961. Its conclusion should touch the nerve of every Christian's conscience: "A large proportion of mental patients at present, as in the past, are not treated in accordance with democratic, humanitarian, scientific, and therapeutic

[25] *The Undiscovered Self.*

111

principles. We have substantially failed the majority of them on all counts." [26]

The most shocking fact revealed by the Joint Commission's report was that "More than half of the patients in most State hospitals receive no active treatment." [27] This is due mainly to the shortage of trained treatment personnel. Many patients are placed in what is euphemistically called "continued treatment" (which, in more honest language means "discontinued treatment"). Many are on these chronic wards because treatment was not given in the earlier stages before their illnesses became treatment-resistant. Some of these could still be reached with the newer treatment techniques if adequate staff were available.

If a member of one's family is hospitalized for mental illness, his chances of being released as improved or recovered are linked directly with the adequacy of treatment in that particular hospital. When a board from the American Psychiatric Association recently inspected 273 private, state, and federal mental hospitals, only 75 were approved as meeting minimal standards. Another 74 were conditionally approved. Of the 181 state hospitals included in this inspection, only 28 were placed on the approved list.[28] Of all state and local government mental hospitals in our country, only 29 percent are approved by the Joint Commission on Accreditation of Hospitals.[29]

Recent experience has demonstrated that many persons who are hospitalized for psychiatric disturbances would not need to be hospitalized if outpatient mental health clinics were available in their communities. At least 3,600 full-time clinics would be required to provide one such facility for every 50,000 persons which is the ratio recommended by the American Psychiatric Association. Only 1,400 now exist—most of them part-time and with long waiting lists. (A study in Los Angeles County found that the average waiting period was twenty-six weeks.) [30] The existing clinics are unevenly distributed, fifty percent being in northeastern cities.

In discussing the condition of our nation's mental hospitals with

[26] *Action for Mental Health* (New York: Basic Books, Inc., 1961), p. 56.
[27] *Ibid.,* p. 23. About eighty percent of all psychiatric patients are in state hospitals.
[28] "Facts About Mental Illness" (The National Association for Mental Health, 1962).
[29] *Action for Mental Health,* p. 19.
[30] "The Mental Health Survey of Los Angeles County, 1957-59" (Welfare Planning Council of the Los Angeles Region, 1960), pp. 129 ff.

a mental health group on the West Coast, psychiatrist William Menninger declared:

As we sit here, 750,000 souls are in human warehouses across America where they don't have enough doctors to shake a stick at, where 60 per cent are just sitting, rocking out their lives. I am convinced that the great majority of these 750,000 people could get well—if enough folks cared. If enough of us did something about it, they would be out of the hospitals and contributing to our communities.[31]

He went on to tell the story of the dramatic mental hospital renaissance in Kansas. Before the drastic upgrading of the hospitals, eighty percent of mental patients were hospitalized for life. Now the situation is reversed. More than eighty percent of first admissions go home within a year, *seventy percent within ninety days*. Admissions are continuing high, but people are getting well and going home because they are receiving intensive treatment immediately. More people are seeking treatment voluntarily because mental hospitals in Kansas are now places of hope.

Today, in some states, only forty-five percent of mental patients are discharged from mental hospitals. With good treatment, at least eight out of ten could return to their communities totally or partially recovered. What a tragic waste of human beings!

In spite of the continuing inadequacies in the current treatment of the mentally ill, remarkable progress has been made during the past few years. The year 1956 was a major milestone, when, for the first time since state hospital records had been kept, there was a decline in the total number of patients at that year's end. This decline has continued in subsequent years, despite the rise in the number of mental patients admitted each year and the country's growing population. Obviously, genuine progress has been made in treatment methods. The old "snake pit" atmosphere no longer exists in the vast majority of state hospitals and the locks are coming off many wards.

There are a number of factors which account for the speedier release of patients. *Tranquilizing drugs* play the major role, drastically reducing the need for physical restraints, rendering many patients amenable to treatment, and often allowing them to leave the hospital

[31] "Mental Health, Everybody's Business," *Town Hall* (June, 1961), p. 20.

much sooner than would otherwise be feasible. *Intensive treatment units,* where an all-out therapeutic effort is made immediately after admission, have produced impressive results. The *therapeutic community* approach, pioneered by psychiatrist Maxwell Jones of England, aims at making the entire experience of living together on a ward therapeutic in its effects. Every staff member down to the ward attendant shares responsibility for the therapeutic climate of the ward. The patients are encouraged to share in the responsibility for the total welfare of the group. *Family therapy* for the close relatives of the mentally ill is still another factor which helps the recovery of the patient. *Remotivation therapy* is a new method which has succeeded in reaching many long-regressed, "hopeless" patients.

The modern treatment approaches aim at keeping a patient in the hospital fulltime for the briefest period possible, since the longer he stays the more difficult the readjustment to the community. As a patient improves, he spends more and more time at home. He may become a "night patient" or a "day patient," spending only part of each day in the institution. Recent improvements in community mental health facilities are making it possible to treat many at home who formerly would have been institutionalized. The thousand plus psychiatric units in general hospitals contrast sharply with the situation fifteen years ago when only a few existed. Such units are ideal for short-term and part-time treatment. Their general hospital location encourages earlier treatment, since a sense of stigma is less apt to be attached to going there. Day care centers, night hospitals, walk-in clinics (where persons in crisis can go for help without appointments), halfway houses, and foster home programs for recovering mental patients who cannot return to their families are examples of the types of new facilities that are beginning to appear in various parts of the country.

There is an exciting stir of hope in the air. Never before in the dark history of mental illness treatment has there been anything like the present surge of imaginative experiments in new treatment modalities. True, the majority of mental hospital doors are still locked and new facilities such as "day hospitals" are scarce, but the pace of progress is accelerating each year. The tide is turning in this long-neglected area.

Another sign of progress is the advance in the average amount spent daily per mental patient. These figures are encouraging in comparison with expenditures a decade ago. They are still absurdly low. Shortages of treatment personnel have gradually become somewhat less acute over the last few years. However, the number of registered nurses, trained social workers, and qualified psychiatrists working in mental hospitals is still far below an adequate level.

Because of the overall gains in treatment, the chances of recovery are improving steadily. For example, the likelihood of total or partial recovery from the largest mental crippler, schizophrenia, has climbed from twenty to seventy percent in the past forty years. Psychoses due to syphilis, pellagra, and lead poisoning have been practically eliminated through medical progress.

One of the major signs of hope in the treatment of the mentally ill is the active role that the federal government is now playing. Long-range improvement in both the prevention and treatment of mental illness depends on two factors—training of mental health workers and research. The National Institute of Mental Health has the major research and training-grant program in the country. Progress is clearly evident in the rise in congressional appropriations for this center from $18,000,000 in 1956 to over $100,000,000 in 1960.

The development of more adequate treatment facilities received a powerful boost in 1963 with the passage of federal legislation providing for the development of a pilot community mental health center in each state. The impetus which led to this legislation came from President Kennedy not long before his death. In the first presidential message to Congress dealing solely with mental illness and retardation, he gave this ringing challenge: "Shabby treatment of the many millions of the mentally disabled" he said, "has gone on too long. We can procrastinate no more." [32] In response to his call for "a broad new mental health program," Congress appropriated funds to stimulate state and local action in creating intensive treatment centers and to encourage research on mental retardation. State and local governments will form a partnership with the federal government in what will become a step toward more adequate care of the mentally ill and retarded.

[32] *Time* (February 15, 1963), p. 44.

A PLAN OF ACTION FOR THE LOCAL CHURCH

Here is a practical plan by which a church can exert its maximum influence on a community's efforts to provide better treatment for the mentally ill. As in all community problems, a church should be involved in two ways—through its organizational life (for example, a social action committee) and through the mental health witness of individual church members in the community. Here are some of the ways in which a church can help in the fight to conquer the scourge of mental illness:

(1) *The church should help to build a broad foundation of enlightened heart-understanding of mental illness.*

Churches can play a strategic educational role in constructing a foundation for mental health action in the community by developing increased understanding of the problems of mental illness. The educational opportunity created by the churches' direct face-to-face contact with 120 million adults and youth is immense! The crucial goal of such education is to change negative attitudes toward mental illness and to dispel the miasmic cloud of fear, stigma, and mystery that still surrounds it. In his autobiography, Harry Emerson Fosdick tells with complete candor of the nervous breakdowns suffered by his mother, his father, and later himself. This matter-of-fact, relaxed objectivity demonstrated by one of the most creative religious leaders of our century is a refreshing illustration of the goal of mental health education.

Why is it that we still reject, stigmatize, and provide only half-hearted treatment for the mentally ill in spite of the millions of words that have been written and spoken to promote an enlightened approach to the problem? The report of the Joint Commission is brutally frank on this issue:

One reason the public does not react desirably is that the mentally ill lack appeal. They eventually become a nuisance to other people and are generally treated as such. . . . People do seem to feel sorry for them; but in the balance, *they do not feel as sorry as they do relieved to have out of the way persons whose behavior disturbs and offends them.*[33]

The basis of the stigma is fear—fear of what the irrational person might do, fear that we might suffer a similar fate. In addition to fear,

[33] *Action for Mental Health,* p. 58.

there is the suspicion in some minds that the person really brought the problem on himself. In guilt-ridden people this leads to the urge to punish—an urge that is obvious in relationship to illnesses such as alcoholism and sexual perversions. It is also present in other forms of personality illness. Remember that many mentally ill persons were still chained to the walls of jails and almshouses a little more than a century ago in America (see Chap. 12) .

A church's approach to mental illness education should emphasize the fact that, with a few exceptions, mental illnesses are treatable illnesses. It should communicate the kind of realistic new hope for the mentally ill which now exists. William Menninger has declared that contrary to the widespread opinion that mentally ill persons seldom get well, mental illnesses have the highest recovery rates of any group of illnesses. If patients are given a fair chance, from seventy to ninety percent can recover! [34]

Education on mental illness always should be integrated with an emphasis on positive mental health. It is educationally valid to present them together. The cold chill which the subject of mental illness elicits in many people needs to be offset by the warm sunlight of an emphasis on positive mental health. Prevention and treatment together constitute the whole picture of mental health which people need to see and understand.

Mental health education should acquaint learners with rigorously accurate information concerning the size and seriousness of the problems. It should communicate an understanding of the nature of mental illness that will help to erase the inaccurate stereotypes about it (that is, it should include facts showing that the proportion of mentally ill persons who are wild and destructive is about the same as the proportion of planes that crash as compared with the total number of planes that fly.) Ideally, mental health education should take place in small groups in which the distorted attitudes and feelings of the participants can be worked through. Even more effective as an attitude-changing experience is firsthand contact with recovering patients in a progressive mental hospital.

(2) *A church should cooperate with other groups to improve treatment facilities in its area.*

[34] See "Mental Health, Everybody's Business."

There are now forty-seven state associations of mental health and over eight hundred local chapters affiliated with the National Association for Mental Health, 10 Columbus Circle, New York, N. Y. These citizens groups are working to improve care of the mentally ill. Such groups can be highly effective instruments for stimulating and coordinating community mental health activities. A local church's social-action or mental health committee should support such an association vigorously. Where no Mental Health Association exists, churchmen should consider spearheading the formation of such a group. Paul B. Maves tells of a minister who was one of the key persons in establishing a mental hygiene society in New Jersey. Another clergyman took a similar role in Ohio.[35] State or local mental health associations can provide church social-action groups with current information concerning the problems and needs of their area, including mental health legislation which needs citizen support.

Patient care can be improved through volunteer service in clinics and hospitals. At a large mental hospital on Long Island, women from nearby churches established the "Protestant Service Organization," through which they give thousands of hours of volunteer service each year. They assist the chaplain in the religious program, organize parties and picnics, and in a variety of other ways show the patients that the church and the outside world have not forgotten them. Monthly birthday celebrations are held for patients, including the some six hundred who have no families or whose families have rejected them. At a mental hospital in Minnesota, young people, mainly from the churches, volunteer to lead folk dances, songfests, softball games, and parties. The girls among the volunteers administer home permanents during "Toni Time." These programs have had a striking effect on the morale of the institution they serve.

For over a decade Oberlin College students have had a volunteer program at a nearby mental hospital. A study of the patients visited regularly by the students (compared with a matched control group of other patients) showed that the program had made a significant difference in the general improvement and discharge rate of those visited. Not everyone is suited to work with mental patients, but other important work can be found by the chaplain or the hospital's

---

[35] *The Church and Mental Health,* p. 224.

Director of Volunteers. "Wanted—Your Magic" is the title of a useful pamphlet for enlisting volunteers.[36]

Church leaders and church groups can help to identify the major gaps in their community's mental health service and work with others to fill them. A large suburban area in New York was, until recently, utterly lacking in mental health facilities for children. It happens that a relatively small service group within that community became aware of this need and took the initiative. After gathering data from the schools, police, and social agencies that would confirm the existence of the need, this group succeeded in rallying the community to establish a child guidance clinic. Approval of the project was obtained from the county medical and psychiatric societies. Throughout the project there was a close working relationship between citizen committees and the mental health professionals. Educational meetings open to the public were held regularly. Memberships in a child guidance association were solicited throughout the community. Contributions began to come from various sources. As funds became available, a professional personnel committee began to interview prospective staff members and a facilities committee found housing for the clinic. Finally, after two years of hard work by scores of persons, including many of the religious leaders of the community, a new child guidance clinic opened its doors. Because of the grass-roots interest generated during its formation, community support continued at a high level. After a year of successful operation, the clinic was able to qualify for matching funds from the state to expand its services.

For the first time in the history of our country, a concrete, comprehensive plan is available for developing adequate treatment facilities for the mentally ill. It is contained in *Action for Mental Health,* the final report of the Joint Commission on Mental Illness and Health. A church's mental health committee profitably could study this plan and use it as a basis for action. These facilities are called for by the plan: (a) *Community mental health clinics* serving both adults and children are the main line of defense in reducing the need for prolonged or repeated hospitalization. One clinic should be avail-

[36] New York State Society for Mental Health, 105 East 22nd Street, New York, New York.

able for every fifty thousand persons. (b) *Every community general hospital of one hundred beds or more should have psychiatric beds* to provide short-term and emergency treatment. (c) *Intensive treatment centers,* never larger than one thousand beds, are recommended to replace present state hospitals. They would be located regionally and would have a well-trained staff at least as large as the patient population. They would concentrate on treating those in the acute stages of a mental illness. (d) According to the plan, all existing state hospitals of more than one thousand beds should be gradually converted into centers for the care of chronically ill persons, both physically and mentally ill. Special therapies for helping chronic patients have been developed and are applicable to both types. (e) *Aftercare and rehabilitation services* are essential since the goal of this program is to keep hospitalization at a minimum. Such services include night hospitals, day hospitals, nursing homes, foster family care, work services, rehabilitation centers, half-way houses, and ex-patient groups. (f) *Resident schools for the reeducation of emotionally disturbed children* were also recommended by the plan.

Other services which a community should have in order to meet its mental health needs are: psychological services in the schools and social agencies, services for the mentally retarded, psychiatric treatment for juvenile and adult offenders, a suicide prevention center, a clinic serving alcoholics and, very important, Alcoholics Anonymous, Alanon, and Alateen groups. Ideally, most of these services should be located and/or coordinated in a community's mental health center (with the exception of A. A., Alanon, and Alateens). This should become the nerve center of the total mental health thrust of a local community.

(3) *A church should encourage the recruitment and training of persons for the mental health professions.*

In spite of recent gains, the critical shortage of trained personnel is still the crucial factor retarding the improvement of treatment programs. In most mental hospitals there are shortages in all the mental health professions: psychiatrists, clinical psychologists, social workers, psychiatric nurses, occupational therapists, and clinically trained chaplains. At present there is one chaplain for every 1,600 mental patients. These chaplains represent the church's most significant direct ministry to the mentally ill. The denominations should do everything possible to recruit and train additional chaplains so that the chaplain/patient ratio could be reduced to 1/600.[37]

Each local church should encourage some of its most able young people to enter the mental health professions, regarding them as Christian vocations in the most significant sense. Attractive representatives of these professions may be invited to speak at youth meetings and Christian vocations conferences on topics such as "Psychiatric Nursing as a Christian Calling." Service in mental hospitals as volunteers helps stimulate interest in these careers. Several of the students from the Oberlin project have subsequently chosen mental health careers as a result of their experiences as volunteers. The National Institute of Mental Health has produced an excellent booklet on "Careers in Mental Health," [38] which should be among the vocational guidance resources of a church.

(4) *Churchmen should give active support to legislative efforts designed to provide increased mental health education, research, and treatment.*

The problems of mental health are too gigantic to be handled, in the long run, on any except a total community basis. Chances for a major breakthrough improve as local, state, and federal levels of government each play increasingly responsible roles in mental health. As indicated above, this process is gaining momentum. The rising tide of hopeful programs confronts churchmen with an opportunity to exercise their ballots and use their influence to support constructive mental health measures. The anti-mental health letters which every legislator receives must be offset by communications from pro-mental health persons. When key mental health legislation is before state or municipal governments, it is essential that enlightened Christians exercise the power of the pen. Opponents are often well-organized and vociferous. Mental health is everyone's business but not everyone will accept his responsibility. In most cases, the decision of a municipal government concerning whether or not to implement

[37] Richard V. McCann in *The Churches and Mental Health*, p. 39, suggests a 1/800 ratio.
[38] Public Health Service Publication #23 (National Institute of Mental Health, Bethesda 14, Maryland).

state or federal legislation by establishing a local mental health center is the result of the work of a small minority of citizens who cared enough to express their views pro and con.

In addition to backing every sound effort to provide better treatment for the mentally ill, churchmen should throw their weight behind legislative efforts to prevent mental illness. In practical terms this means more education and research. About one percent of the twelve billion dollars spent annually on research in our country is spent studying people and their problems. The amount invested in research on mental illness and health in a recent year was about the same as the cost of the Triton nuclear submarine. One hundred million dollars were spent on the research that resulted in the polio vaccine. Certainly no one regrets this expenditure. The same perspective should apply to mental illness. Even greater sums doubtless will be necessary to produce the research discoveries in the hidden causes of mental illness, which are essential both to more effective treatment and to prevention.

A local church should take its place on the front lines in the battle to conquer the scourge of mental illness. One of the subtle but valuable contributions which participation of religiously-motivated persons brings to the mental health activities of a community is a spirit of dedication and quiet enthusiasm. Lawrence K. Frank, a leader in the mental health movement, has observed that if a community's mental health program is to draw on the strengths of our culture and to have meaning for the majority of people, it must be presented as more than a psychiatric proposal. It must succeed in enlisting much of what people mean by their religion.

When Christians are religiously concerned there is a vitality to their dedication which becomes a subtle leavening influence in everything they touch. This spirit is very much needed to help overcome the stolid apathy that so frequently retards community mental health efforts.

IMPLEMENTING THE PROPHETIC MINISTRY

There are at least four channels through which the prophetic ministry can be implemented: (a) prophetic preaching, (b) study-discussion groups (and other educational programs), (c) social action groups, and (d) action by individual members through community social action projects. These four methods can be applied effectively to the many social problems which plague local, national, and world communities. In sermons and lectures on prophetic issues, it is particularly important that concrete suggestions be made concerning what the hearer can do. Small, practical "next steps" at the close of such a presentation help to motivate action and to put to work the concern that has been aroused. Since most social problems are vastly more complicated than the uninformed person even suspects, disciplined study in small groups, focusing on a particularly urgent social issue, can prepare people to act wisely.

Unfortunately, many churches today seem to have replaced militancy on social issues by a bland irrelevance.[39] In our era of the "soft sell," the danger of a church becoming a chameleon without knowing it is great. The discovery of one's personal prophetic ministry as a Christian is a very good thing for one's mental health, as well as for one's church and community. Finding an "object of devotion" that really matters brings a new aliveness to an individual. The same is true for a church group. I recall the awakening of a social action committee which decided to launch a community effort to deal more constructively with the problems of a slum-ghetto. A year before her death at seventy-nine, the greathearted humanitarian Eleanor Roosevelt wrote: "There is so much to do, so many engrossing challenges, so many heartbreaking and pressing needs."[40] If a church catches something of this spirit of urgency and challenge, if it comes alive to the problems of its community and world, the cause of mental health will prosper.

[39] For a searching article on this problem, see Ronald E. Osburn, "U. S. A.: The Need for Renewal," *The Christian Century* (April 4, 1962), p. 420.
[40] Brochure of the Eleanor Roosevelt Memorial Foundation, 1963.

CHAPTER 6

The Church School's Contribution to Mental Health

You can use your classroom program, your curriculum, yourself and your relationships to give empty youngsters massive doses—big servings, tremendous helpings—of whatever they are seeking: love . . . achievement . . . belonging . . . praise . . . acceptance independence. The specific medicine these children need is something you have: "A good life." [1]—*J. L. Hymes*

Every eight seconds a baby is born in the United States. This amounts to more than four million per year—four million new opportunities for the transmission of the best in our heritage. The primary responsibility for transmitting the religious and ethical dimension of this heritage rests with the parents of these children and with the education programs of churches and synagogues. Some forty-four million children, youth, and adults currently participate in 287,642 Sunday schools and other religious education programs. Over three and one-half million individuals, most of them volunteers, teach in these programs.

The church school [2] should be a powerful influence for mental health. During a child's most impressionable years, his "church" is actually the Sunday school classes to which he belongs. If they are dull, then his earliest and deepest feelings about the church will be

---

[1] *Behavior and Misbehavior* (New York: Prentice-Hall, 1955), p. 5.

[2] I am using the term "church school" to mean the entire formal educational ministry of the church involving a wide spectrum of age and interest groups at various times during the week.

those of dullness. If these classes open windows of adventure, then his first associations will be ones of lift and excitement.

From its very birth, the Christian church has been a teaching-learning community. Jesus was often called "teacher" by his hearers. He gathered around him a group of learners (disciples). He then appointed them to teach others. (Luke 9:1-6.) The early church put increasing emphasis on teaching the Christian message. The Gospels of Mark, Matthew, and Luke grew out of the teaching activities of these early communities of believers.[3] This teaching-learning tradition has continued through Christian history. Stimulated by new insights from the fields of education and group dynamics, it is acquiring fresh vitality in the contemporary church.

In a real sense, of course, Christian education is the church. There should be educational dimensions and goals in everything it does.[4] The focus of this chapter will be on the church school—the instrument by which the church carries on its formal educational ministry. The key question is this—*How can the church school maximize its contribution to personal growth and spiritual health?*

THE GOALS OF RELIGIOUS EDUCATION

In no area of the life of the churches on a national level have mental hygiene insight and principles made a greater contribution than in the field of religious education. For the past quarter of a century, leaders in religious education have been applying these dynamic resources to their field. Harrison S. Elliott, a pioneer in the modern approach to religious education, once commented that "mental hygiene contributes to religious education both a point of view and a methodology." [5] Mental hygiene gives a view of the nature of persons, how they learn, and the kinds of experiences which help them grow. It also guides the choice of educational methods, emphasizing those which provide growth-stimulating experiences.

In the final analysis, the choice of the goals of religious education is dependent on one's views of the nature of man and of religious

[3] See *Foundations of Christian Teaching in Methodist Churches* (The Board of Education of The Methodist Church, 1960), pp. 13-15.

[4] See Wesner Fallaw's *Christian Education for Tomorrow* (Philadelphia: Westminster Press, 1960).

[5] "Mental Hygiene and Religious Education," *Pastoral Psychology,* Vol. III, no. 27. October, 1952, p. 16.

truth. One of the most salutary developments in religious education circles in recent years is widespread participation in the growing rapprochement between theology and psychodynamic theory. As one religious educator points out, "If we take our tradition seriously, we discover that much that mental hygiene has dramatized for us is inherently within the Judaic-Christian tradition." [6] Increasingly the goals of religious education are being formulated as a result of the dialogue between the behavioral sciences and the biblical-theological disciplines.

Here is a succinct formulation of the basic purpose of Christian education which I see as consistent with mental health principles:

> Through Christian education the fellowship of believers (the church) seeks to help persons become aware of God's seeking love as shown especially in Jesus Christ and to respond in faith and love to the end that they may develop self-understanding, self-acceptance, and self-fulfillment under God; increasingly identify themselves as sons of God and members of the Christian community; live as Christian disciples in all relations in human society; and abide in the Christian hope.[7]

The following are some of the specific goals of Christian education which serve to implement this basic purpose and thereby to enhance personality health:

(1) *Mastery of the salient facts and concepts of one's religious heritage.* Knowledge about the Bible, the history of Christianity, and contemporary expressions of the faith serve as both raw materials and tools with which the individual can develop his personal faith-for-living. Until he has some understanding of his tradition, he is unable to appropriate those particular aspects of the religious environment into which he was born which satisfy his individual religious needs. From a mental health standpoint, it strengthens one's sense of personal and family identity to know where one stands religiously—that is, to have a secure grounding in one's tradition.

In emphasizing mastery of facts and ideas, I am not advocating a return to the sterile procedures of rote memorization of extensive creedal or biblical material. Rather, I am siding with the post-World

[6] A communication from Paul Irwin, professor of Christian Education, School of Theology at Claremont, California.
[7] "Foundations of Christian Teaching," p. 31.

War II thrust in Christian education which holds that there is a faith to be communicated as well as encountered in experience.[8] Such communication by a teacher who has a deep feeling for a religious tradition often leads students to an encounter with the meanings which speak to human needs from that tradition.

If one is to have a degree of objectivity concerning his own tradition, he must be cognizant and appreciative of the other great religious heritages. This has become what, in the light of the demands of our shrinking globe, Norman Cousins calls "survival knowledge." Experiences which give our children an awareness of the values in other religions are no longer "elective" items in sound religious education. All of us should enrich our spiritual lives by appropriating insights from various streams of religious discovery.

(2) *The acquisition of religious values and attitudes toward oneself, others, God, and existence.* Commenting on Richard Niebuhr's view of revelation, Ross Snyder declares: "Christian revelation is revelation to you to the degree that it enables you to penetrate more deeply into the events and issues of life. That is, it actually enables you to see things differently than you would without it, and unless it does, it has not really been 'learning.' " [9] The transmission of concepts in religious education is a means to the end that a person will acquire religious attitudes and values which will guide his living. The Christian ideas of God as loving father and the oneness of all men under him have an effect on one's life only if they become essential ingredients in one's convictions, at the nucleus of one's being, about the meaning of existence. When life-attitudes are molded by such religious values they make a constructive difference in one's response to the purchase of a home by a family of color in one's previously all-white block.

There is growing agreement within the mental health field on the importance of possessing a viable philosophy of life. Helping individuals develop such a personal philosophy is, of course, a central concern of the church school. Teaching in the area of values should draw on the best in the Hebrew-Christian tradition—

[8] Martin Buber's use of the figures of the funnel and the pump in his discussion of education is relevant at this point. See *Between Man and Man* (London: Kegan Paul, 1947), p. 89.

[9] "The Developmental View of Life and Christian Teaching," Writers' Conference, November 15-22, 1957, p. 7.

tested, undergirded, illuminated, and implemented by the insights of the psychological sciences. The church should welcome the attempt of persons such as Erich Fromm to move beyond relativism, to base ethical norms on those qualities in persons and relationships which allow men to grow toward fulfillment of their God-given potentialities. If God made men in his image, then an ethical approach founded on man's inherent growth-qualities cannot but be a valid form of revelation.[10]

(3) *Experiencing interpersonal relationships in which God and the good life come alive for the individual.* Creative church schools work hard to make everything that occurs in the classroom (worship, problems in interpersonal relationships, teaching-learning, and so forth), laboratories in which religious truths can be brought to life and experienced. The emotional climate of the classroom is all-important in the achievement of this goal. Ross Snyder maintains that "the major matter learned in any class is 'belonging.' Not the ideas (significant as they are) but the rooted feeling, 'There is something going on in the world that I am a part of. I have a place in some circle of acceptance and in some enterprise of history-making.' " [11] Grace that is seen and felt in relationships makes a decisive difference in the lives of persons.

(4) *Experiencing the struggle and challenge of working out one's own salvation.* Creative religious education aims not at the inculcation of a rigid system of ideas but at the acquisition by the learner of a searching, experimental approach toward religious truth. The challenge should be an invitation to embark on a lifelong journey toward an increasingly meaningful spiritual life. This involves avoiding closure in one's thinking about religious meanings. It requires the willingness to tolerate the anxiety of living with question marks. It means experiencing the agony of relinquishing cherished "certainties" when, in the light of larger experiences, they prove to be partial or inaccurate views. It may be that many of our present interpretations of "Christian truths" will prove to be inadequate to understand what scientist Loren Eiseley calls "those multitudinous

---

[10] See, for example, Erich Fromm, *Man for Himself, An Inquiry Into the Psychology of Ethics* (New York: Rinehart and Company, 1947).

[11] "The Developmental View of Life and Christian Teaching," p. 4.

universes that inhabit the minds of men.[12] Our interpretations may prove to need radical revisions in order to be relevant in coping with the unforeseeable world of our grandchildren.

The challenge of this kind of learning is a challenge to wrestle and struggle with truths as they apply to one's life. The model is not one of gentle, placid growing but of crisis—leaps and falls, perhaps of struggling up a precipitous mountain face. This, in fact, is the way that growth occurs. Here is Ross Snyder's forceful statement of the matter: "Development is the emergence of new centers out of which hot energies pour, new qualities, a new level of organization and control. And, therefore, it is not 'more of the same' even though it cannot occur apart from all that already is." [13] Learning in this framework is filled with surprises. It makes for a life of invitation and excitement.

This kind of learning, however, has a great lot of agony in it. The Christian doctrine that suffering is a part of creativity is taken seriously. Things are not always clear or orderly at the beginning. The realities of life come right into the class; we do not conduct a nice, soft, safe discussion where everybody knows what the answers are going to be before we start.[14]

Jacques Barzun, Dean of Faculties at Columbia University, has suggested that the test of a man's education is whether he finds pleasure in the exercise of his mind. In this vein, one of the major goals of religious education is helping persons to find zest and lift in the religious life. It is through the struggle of grappling with baffling problems, of confronting complex truth and mind-stretching mysteries that one finds deep satisfactions from his religious life.

The total number of hours of formal religious education is limited. Therefore, the emphasis should be on the motivation to learn and on learning how to learn. The writer who has most influenced my thinking about teaching-learning is Nathaniel Cantor. In his penetrating volume, *Dynamics of Learning*, he makes this point convincingly: "The student must be helped to want to learn, to learn how to learn, and to want to learn as long as he

[12] "The Glory and Agony of Teaching," *Think* (October, 1962), p. 23.
[13] "The Developmental View of Life and Christian Teaching," p. 1.
[14] *Ibid.*, p. 2.

lives." [15] If religious education achieves this goal with children, it has given them a priceless asset for living.

Religious growth, the *raison d'être* of the church school, has several dimensions: moving toward maturity in one's understanding of religious concepts, in one's life-attitudes, and in the quality of one's relatedness to other persons and to God. Religious maturity commensurate with one's chronological age is an essential aspect of positive mental health. The most difficult blocks to such maturing result from the transfer of negative feelings derived from childhood experiences with adults to one's relationship with God. Such experiences can constitute formidable logjams in the river of one's religious creativity. Psychotherapy may be required to remove such blocks.

THE IMPORTANCE OF THE STUDENT-TEACHER RELATIONSHIP

Teaching is the fine art of helping persons to learn. The degree to which the goals of religious education are achieved depends, to a large extent, on the quality of the student-teacher relationship. Carroll A. Wise sharpens the issue when he points out that although religious symbols can be transmitted by formal, academic means, the inner meanings of these symbols cannot. These meanings have to be achieved by the individual for himself. The fact that this occurs largely as a result of identification with an admired person makes the personality of the teacher a crucial consideration.[16] The teacher-student and student-student relationships are transmission lines along which attitudes and values are communicated. Depth education involves identification with the teacher and/or with the learning group. Cold, mechanical teachers may present significant facts in abundance, but the truths will seldom influence or inspire the students. On the other hand, warm, enthusiastic, dedicated teachers who pour themselves into their teaching often have a lifelong impact on students.

In discussing college teaching, Nathan M. Pusey has stressed the essence of any teacher's job: "The teacher's task is not to implant facts but to place the subject to be learned in front of the learner

[15] Nathaniel Cantor, *Dynamics of Learning*, (3rd ed. Buffalo, N. Y.: Henry Stewart, 1956), p. xii.

[16] Carroll A. Wise, *Religion in Illness and Health* (New York: Harper & Brothers, 1942), p. 236.

and, through sympathy, emotion, imagination, and patience, to awaken in the learner the restless drive for answers and insights which enlarge the personal life and give it meaning." [17] The teacher who is "open" to his students will often sense their needs for reassurance, confrontation, appreciation, challenge, or affection.

Church school teachers should be chosen from among the adults in a church who are obviously growing spiritually and interpersonally. Several years ago, the National Education Association reported that about twenty percent of our public school teachers could profit from psychotherapeutic help because of minor emotional difficulties.[18] At least this high a percentage would be found among church school teachers. I recall one church in which an elderly woman with obvious senility-related mental problems was superintendent of the pre-schoolers department. She had been in this unfortunate condition for several years. Because no one wanted to hurt her feelings, the most impressionable children in that church school were being exposed each Sunday to her declining mental health. Finally the minister mustered his courage and, with the backing of the commission on education, asked her to relinquish her post. A well-deserved "appreciation party" for the woman poured oil on her wounds. But what about the children's wounds?

Teachers of younger children should be selected with special attention to the robustness of their emotional health. Children of the impressionable ages often take their Sunday school teacher very seriously and are highly sensitive to the emotional nuances of their teacher's responses.

One of the minister's two key roles in the church school is helping the superintendents to locate and motivate growing teachers who will both present and represent the gospel in a healthy manner. What is essential is not freedom from neurotic conflicts, but a core of inner strength "upon or against which the pupil may begin to build his own firm attitudes." [19] In her book, *The Unconscious in Action, Its Influence on Education,* Barbara Low states:

[17] Wesley Allinsmith and George Goethals, *The Role of Schools in Mental Health* (New York: Basic Books, Inc., 1962), p. 138.

[18] N. L. Kelly, "The Teacher's Role in the Prevention of Alcoholism," *Inventory* September-October, 1957, p. 22.

[19] *The Role of Schools in Mental Health,* p. 137.

What does psychoanalysis suggest as the fundamental requirements for the most favorable relationship between teacher and taught? . . . the educator has need of knowledge of his own psyche, in order to know and deal with his special tendencies and complexes. . . . "Only the person who is educated and inwardly free can educate others properly." [20]

MENTAL HEALTH CRITERIA FOR TEACHER SELECTION

Here are some questions which should be asked in screening volunteers and in ascertaining who should be recruited for teaching: (a) Does the person have a relatively mature religious faith, uncluttered by the vestigial remains of childhood magic and fears? It is essential that a church school teacher have a growing relationship with God, though not necessarily "God" in the conventional or orthodox mode. (b) Will he be able to present and represent the Christian way in a constructive, attractive, life-affirming way? (c) Why does he want to teach, if he is a volunteer? Does he have an ax to grind? Or is he motivated by a wish to help others find a meaningful religious life? (d) Does he respect and like children, youth, or adults? The quality of his relationships with his own children is often the best clue. (e) Does he have a reasonably sturdy sense of self-esteem? His ability to esteem others will depend on this. (f) Are his interpersonal relationships generally constructive? The heart of the teaching-learning process is an interpersonal relationship. Does he manipulate others or does he respect their freedom to grow toward their unique personhood? (g) Is he growing and teachable? The direction of his life may be more important than its current location. Is he open to new ideas and methods? Does he have an authority problem which will make it difficult for him to accept on-the-job supervision from a person with more training? His ability to accept constructive criticism without being unduly threatened is an indication of the adequacy of his self-esteem.

TRAINING FOR CREATIVE TEACHING

After reading the foregoing list of criteria, most church school teachers or potential teachers will probably feel, "I'm not up to that! Count me out." To reduce the danger of precipitating a mass lemming-like exodus of Sunday school teachers, let me hasten to say

[20] (London: University of London Press, 1928), p. 52.

the criteria are statements of ideal qualities which even the most effective teachers only approximate. Nearly everyone has a self-esteem problem to some degree. Most of us have difficulties at times relating to our own children. All of us have some vestigial remnants of childhood fantasies and feelings in our religious life. Very little Sunday school teaching would be done if only those who rate high as judged by all these criteria were eligible to teach. In short, as finite beings, possessing a combination of personality assets and liabilities, all of us fall short of these ideals.

However, if one's life is not dominated by one's liabilities it is possible to be an effective teacher in spite of them. If one is open to relationships, then teaching itself can be a growth experience for the teacher. With the help of a creative lead-teacher, superintendent, or pastor, a teacher can find both satisfaction and invitation to personal growth through teaching. The teacher becomes a co-learner. Christian education occurs within the milieu of a group struggling to be a redemptive community. The teacher has unusual opportunities to participate in experiences at the live centers of growth in that community.

An ongoing program of teacher-training is essential if teaching is to be a satisfying experience and if religious education is to move decisively toward the goals described earlier. Active involvement in teacher-training is the second vital aspect of the minister's church school role. To be a "teacher of teachers" is one of the most vital functions of the pastor's total ministry. Any major positive changes in the quality of a church's educational program presupposes the minister's or director of Christian education's active leadership.

Unfortunately, many of us in the ministry are not well-equipped to be "teachers of teachers" in the sense of being knowledgeable concerning recent developments or even basic principles of Christian education. To meet this need, the Central Pennsylvania Conference of The Methodist Church has devised a study-action seminar in Christian education for ministers. Twelve carefully selected ministers are invited each year. After an initial orientation day at Lycoming College, the seminar meets once a month to study training methods relevant to the teachers of a particular church school department. Between seminars each minister spends some ten hours in training sessions with those teachers in his church school. In one year, nine ministers who previously had virtually ignored their nursery departments held fifty-one training sessions for nursery teachers and, in the process, acquired sixteen additional teachers. In the seminars the ministers experienced the small-group process. They discovered that they could apply this method in teacher-training and in other small group activities.[21]

There are several effective approaches to teacher training such as working under an experienced teacher as an apprentice teacher, regular workers conferences, and personal conferences with an experienced superintendent. "Laboratory schools" are a highly useful form of training. These are usually held for five consecutive days with a minimum of thirty hours of guided experiences. Certified instructors conduct sessions with children of a particular age group. The student teachers observe the instructors in action and also work under supervision with the children themselves. Instructors and student-teachers plan, experiment, and measure results. Demonstration teaching, with adults taking the roles of children, is another device which is used. This reality practice helps adults grasp the inner world of children. Skilled public school teachers can be used as instructors in church school teacher-training programs.

To enhance mental health values, teacher-training should help teachers grasp the meaning and method of dialogic teaching. *Miracle of Dialogue* [22] is a useful resource. Understanding the "developmental task" of the age group with which they are working is also essential. Erik Erikson's *Identity and the Life Cycle* [23] and Lewis J. Sherrill's writings,[24] are valuable books in this area. Understanding of the teaching-learning process can be enhanced by systematic study of Nathaniel Cantor's volumes, *Dynamics of Learning* and *The Teaching-Learning Process*.[25] Contact with Cantor's germinal mind will cause a teacher to begin preparation by asking, "Who am I

---

[21] For a description of this project see L. Paul Neufer, "Our Pastors Went to Sunday School," *The Christian Advocate* (October 13, 1960), p. 17.

[22] Reuel L. Howe (New York: Seabury Press, 1963).

[23] (New York: International Universities Press, 1959).

[24] *Guilt and Redemption*, rev. ed. (Richmond: John Knox Press, 1957); *The Struggle of the Soul* (New York: The Macmillan Co., 1951); *The Gift of Power* (The Macmillan Company, 1955).

[25] (New York: Holt, Rinehart & Winston, 1953).

teaching and what are their wants and needs?" Reviving and releasing the spontaneous will-to-learn (stifled by years of uncreative echoing back what teachers wanted to hear) must be a major objective in teaching older children, youth, and adults. Cantor says emphatically:

> The central problem of education is self-discipline, self-motivation. . . . Significant learning stems from the self-directed motivation of the learner who wants something positive and creative for . . . unfilled need of his. No one can learn for another any more than a mother can help her child grow physically by eating the child's meal.[26]

For there to be genuine learning there must be tension and desire arising from unfilled need. The teacher's job is to discover and awaken the sense of need.

THE CLIMATE OF THE CLASSROOM

Ten of the nation's leading educators were asked, "If you could address all the teachers of the nation for five minutes, what would you say?" Two of the major themes in their responses were an emphasis on the crucial importance of the emotional climate of the classroom and the key role of the teacher in producing this climate.[27]

Experiments involving the measurement of blood sugar levels of elementary students in a public school revealed that the levels were characteristically high or low in certain classrooms. The researchers concluded that the emotional atmosphere of a given classroom affected the pupil's endocrine systems—a hostile, threatening, or highly competitive atmosphere tending to cause the release of sugar in the blood. In a classic experiment, pioneer social psychologist Kurt Lewin found that different group climates could be created by varying the leadership from autocratic, to *laissez faire,* to democratic. Thirty times more hostility and eight times more aggression were found in the autocratic than in the democratic groups. Overt aggression was usually directed, not toward the autocratic leader, but toward scapegoats (weaker children). In four of the five autocratic groups aggression was converted into apathy.

A negative emotional climate is created when the teacher's be-

[26] *The Dynamics of Learning*, pp. xiv-xv.
[27] "Portfolio of Teaching Techniques, No. 1" (New London, Conn.; A. C. Croft Publications, 1951). This is a brief, imaginative resource for teachers.

havior threatens the students' sense of personal worth. Many students bring angry, hurt feelings toward adults to the classroom. They respond to the teacher in negative ways, which sometimes causes the teacher to respond in a threatened and therefore threatening fashion. Thus a self-feeding, vicious cycle of interaction produces increasing deterioration of the classroom climate.

Here are some of the factors which threaten self-esteem in the classroom: (a) *Persistent criticism and shaming*—Severe criticism makes the child feel rejected as a person; the need for recognition is so intense that a child will seek it in unconstructive ways if he cannot get it by achievement. Criticism and even punishment seem better than being ignored. This is the root of many discipline problems. On the other hand, well-distributed approval, particularly of the whole group, germinates a positive classroom climate. Appreciation is the language of acceptance. (b) *Expecting too much from an individual or group*—Demanding much more than a child can produce creates fears, hostility, and failure-feelings. The continual presentation of concepts that are far beyond the life experience and ability to comprehend creates confusion and resentments. (c) *Repeated experiences of failure*—Each student needs to experience success in some areas. Instead, many classroom situations allow some to excel and others to fail continually. Nothing fails like failure! Each failure makes it easier to fail again. Only active intervention by the teacher can rescue a child from a spiral of chronic failure. (d) *Authoritarian methods*—Heavy-handed authority stifles a student's need for growing autonomy and self-directedness. The learning process is paralyzed by passivity, submissiveness, and lack of personal involvement, on the one hand, or chronic rebellion, on the other. (e) *Over-permissiveness*—In the Lewin experiments, it was discovered that *laissez faire* leaders who set no limits produced considerably more hostility and scapegoatism than did the democratic leaders. Anna Freud and others have pointed to the dangers of classroom overpermissiveness.[28] Children and adolescents need a dependable adult-defined structure within which they can discover their identities. The church school

[28] See Anna Freud, *The Psychoanalytic Treatment of Children* (New York: Schoken Books, 1946), and Barbara Biber, "Schooling as an Influence in Developing Healthy Personality," in *Community Programs for Mental Health,* Ruth Kotinsky and Helen L. Witmer (eds.) (Cambridge, Mass.: Harvard University Press, 1955).

should strive to balance structure and content, on the one hand, with freedom of expression (within the structure), on the other. Allin-smith and Goethals state: "If a teacher demands too much docility, the pupils may some day have trouble in thinking independently and imaginatively; if too much time is spent in 'free expression,' mastering basic skills may suffer." [29]

(f) *Lack of challenge and stimulation*—Dullness is the besetting sin of many church school classes. Slovenly preparation, lack of imagination, and poor teaching facilities all contribute to this. A teacher's enthusiasm or lack of it will be caught by his class. Plato's conception of the ideal school was that it would be an intellectual playground. The church school should be an intellectual-spiritual playground. In an article called "Thanks to Books," Stefan Zweig lyricized: "Tiny fragments of eternity, mutely ranged along an un-adorned wall, you stand there unpretentiously in our home. Yet when a hand frees you, when a heart touches you, you imperceptibly break through the workaday surroundings, and as in a fiery chariot your words lead us upward from narrowness into eternity." [30] Sparks of interest will fly in a church school class when this spirit is present in the teacher's attitudes toward the Bible and the magnificent ideas of our religious heritage.

(g) *Lack of participation*—In her excellent pamphlet on behavior problems in the classroom, Nina Ridenour says: "Good schools to-day are shot through with the 'let's find out' approach to teaching. Lucky the youngster whose teacher has a gift for stimulating in him genuine pleasure in finding out for himself." [31] Learning-by-doing is a fundamental principle of effective education. The children in a primary class were finding out about God's world, in particular, the world of air and weather. Making and flying kites was an un-forgettable learning experience for them. Participation and the emotional involvement which results from it produce a climate of contagious enthusiasm.

(h) *Neurotic problems of the teacher*—The prime determinant of classroom climate is the personality of the teacher. If he is cold and

[29] *The Role of Schools in Mental Health*, p. 5.
[30] *The Saturday Review* (February 8, 1959), p. 24.
[31] *The Children We Teach* (New York: Mental Health Materials Center, Inc., 1956), p. 4.

conflicted, no amount of skill in "educational techniques" will suffice. If he is warm, giving, and alive, reasonably healthy children will tend to respond in kind. Personality needs (students' and teacher's) will be satisfied and a healthy emotional climate will be obtained.

TRANSMITTING THE GOSPEL VIA MEANINGFUL EXPERIENCES

Contemporary approaches to religious education aim at providing meaningful experiences through which the Christian message and experience can be communicated. Attitudes are formed and reformed through experiences of interaction in relationships. To illustrate the application of this principle, a youth group followed their discussion of techniques for diminishing prejudice by role playing the experiences of minority group members. By this means they were able to experience to a degree, how it feels to be discriminated against and treated with contempt.[32] Even this limited empathy with minority group feelings led the young people to join in a project aimed at reducing discrimination in housing in their community.

The church school should give persons of all ages those experiences which will awaken their sense of need to search for an adequate and satisfying faith. It should also provide experiences which will give guidelines and resources in their search and provide the opportunity to know firsthand the living truths which they can then make their own. For example, a small group in which persons experience something of the *koinonia* quality of relationships will awaken Christian discipleship more effectively than many lecture sessions on the topic.

One facet of teaching with particular relevance to preventing mental ill-health is that which encourages children to feel their emotions, and to work them through in creating imaginative stories, finger-painting or clay-modeling. In a chapter of *New Ways in Discipline* entitled "New Ways of Discipline in the Schools," Dorothy W. Baruch describes a wide variety of techniques which are useful in helping children work through their "bad" feelings. The church

[32] For a discussion of the effectiveness of role playing in changing attitudes see Gordon Allport "Is Intergroup Education Possible?" *Harvard Education Review*, XV (1945), 83.

school should include approaches such as this so that potentially harmful feelings can be expressed in nondestructive ways and thus diminished or redirected. Unless this happens somewhere within the child's experience he will tend to take his negative feelings out on himself in the form of personality, religious, or psychosomatic problems, or on society in the form of delinquency.

Clark Moustakas holds that "listening to children as they express themselves without trying to press our thinking and feelings upon them is perhaps one of the most fundamental ways of promoting mental health in the classroom." [33] He believes that a teacher should provide an accepting climate in which feelings about the teacher and the school can be expressed.

Developments in teaching materials in recent years have been felicitous from a mental health standpoint. The "Christian Faith and Life Series" (United Presbyterian) and the Seabury (Episcopal) The Wesley Series (Methodist) and the United Church of Christ Series are examples of curricular materials which reflect contemporary psychological insights without sacrificing solid biblical-historical content. Katherine Wensberg's and Mary Northrop's *The Tuckers*[34] (Unitarian), a volume of stories for children, aims at stimulating greater self-understanding.

Nathaniel Cantor summarizes the factors upon which genuine growth through education depends:

(1) The student's discovering for himself *in the process of learning* what he *really* wants out of that course and (2) the skill with which the instructor utilizes and meets the *real* needs of the student . . . What takes place between instructor and student provides the dynamic conditions which will be used by the student in his own way. Whatever genuine learning takes place occurs when the help offered by the teacher . . . is accepted willingly by the student as an aid toward making the meanings his own.[35]

TEACHER-PARENT RELATIONSHIPS

If the church school is to make its maximum contribution to mental health, teacher-parent cooperation must be vigorous. Most of

[33] *The Teacher and the Child* (New York: McGraw-Hill, Inc., 1956), p. 42.
[34] (Boston: Beacon Press, 1952).
[35] *The Dynamics of Learning*, p. 90.

the child's fundamental life-attitudes are caught in the family matrix. In terms of deep attitudes about oneself, others, and God, parents are the most important teachers of religion. At best, the church school complements and undergirds the constructive side of what the family does in this area. When a child has acquired severe distortions of the Christian message from his parents, a teacher may gently but firmly introduce a more constructive way of understanding the message, exercising care not to damage the child's respect for his parents as persons. Hopefully, adult education experiences in the church school will help rectify the distorted views held by parents.

The family-oriented approaches to church-school curriculum, used by several denominations are sound from a mental health viewpoint. Direct involvement of parents in religious education occurs through home assignments, teacher-parent and teacher-parent-child workshops, and through the use of parents as rotating "helpers" in classes. These methods help foster good teacher-parent communication.

Church school teachers' morale (and their mental health influence) is sometimes damaged by parents who criticize in ways reflecting the poverty of their knowledge concerning current Christian education methods and goals. A common instance is the volunteer teacher who, while trying to use creative methods, comes under fire from misguided parents because their child isn't "learning enough Bible verses." A parent owes both his child and the teacher a serious effort to understand the aims and methods of his church school. The teacher's morale can be undergirded by parents offering to help in the program and by expressions of honest appreciation.

The morale of church school teachers is also enhanced by the existence of a warm *esprit de corps* among them. The "teacher's fellowship" should be among the most vital groups in a church, both in terms of interpersonal relationships and opportunities for growth. Other factors in morale are the teachers' relationships with the superintendent and the minister. A supportive, competent superintendent and an interested minister can boost teacher morale as much as the opposite types can hurt it. Trained substitutes and/or a team teaching approach allowing every teacher regular "breathing spaces" away from this demanding task, enhance morale and improve teaching. Fundamentally, high morale is the result of teaching being rewarding as well as demanding. It is when religious education helps to meet the interpersonal, intellectual, and spiritual needs of both students and teachers that they become co-learners and co-growers toward greater wholeness as persons.

HELPING UNHAPPY AND DISTURBED CHILDREN

A child who is temporarily upset by disappointment or a family crisis can be helped by an understanding teacher. The same is true of the mildly but chronically disturbed child who is shy, over-aggressive, or unpopular with other children. The severely disturbed child, however, is another matter. In such a situation, the important thing for the church school teacher is to recognize the severity of the disturbance and to do everything possible to encourage the parents to obtain professional help for themselves and the child. A teacher should have a therapeutic influence on his class, but he should not attempt to be a "therapist" with children who need a child guidance clinic and the complex skills of one trained in play therapy.

Identification of serious emotional disturbances is ordinarily made by parents, family physicians, or public school psychologists. Although the church school teacher usually plays a minor role, if any, in the process, it is well for him to be able to recognize the warning signs of serious disturbance. Occasionally he may have an opportunity to encourage early treatment. To illustrate the importance of early treatment, research has shown that in cases of phobias concerning school, "treatment is far more efficient and likely to result in complete remission when a child is referred soon after developing the phobia." [36]

Here are some of the signs which may indicate serious emotional disturbance in children: (a) *Exaggerated aggressiveness*—chronic defiance of authority, destruction of property, bullying weaker children. (b) *Excessive daydreaming*—finding a large proportion of one's satisfactions in the world of fantasy; withdrawal from reality. (c) *Gross inadequacies in peer relationships often linked with clinging dependency on adults.* (d) *Grossly regressed or retarded behavior inappropriate to one's age group.* (e) *Intense irrational fears, guilt feelings, obsessive thoughts, or compulsive actions.* Obsessive-com-

[36] *The Role of Schools in Mental Health*, p. 43.

pulsive problems are repetitive patterns which cannot be changed by reasoning. (f) *Chronic lying or stealing*—A child may lie because he feels trapped between his need for approval and the excessive demands of adults. Stealing by an emotionally-starved child may be both a symbolic way of grasping for love and an attack on his parents. (g) *Psychotic symptoms*—Warning signs include abrupt and radical personality changes, hallucinations, extreme suspiciousness, depression, and extreme mood swings.[37]

A church school teacher who suspects the existence of a serious disturbance should discuss the matter with his minister. In a suburban church, a fourth grade teacher approached the minister of counseling following his talk on discipline problems. The teacher described a moody, withdrawn student about whom she was concerned. The minister of counseling sensed that the child was in need of psychiatric help. In spite of her uneasiness, the teacher agreed to visit in the home and talk with the mother. She found the mother not only appreciative of her concern but already aware, from public school reports, of the child's problems. At the appropriate moment the teacher mentioned the availability of the local child guidance clinic and suggested that the parents talk with the minister if they desired further suggestions concerning therapeutic resources. Subsequently, the parents contacted the clinic directly and the child received help.

An ounce of preventive therapy in childhood can avoid tons of unhappiness in adult life. It should be stated emphatically that many emotional difficulties which may not foreshadow major psychiatric problems justify psychotherapeutic treatment. Some church schools have mental health professionals who are on call to advise with teachers concerning problem children. For example, one church school has a social worker who, at the invitation of a teacher, visits that class to observe and work with a troubled child.

Here are some suggestions for handling garden-variety problems of children. (Nina Ridenour's *The Children We Teach* contains a more comprehensive discussion of these.) To the casual observer, some children (and adults) *have* problems, others *are* problems. Actually both the troubled and the troublesome are disturbed per-

[37] For a more detailed description see *The Children We Teach*, pp. 44-48.

sons. The troubled person internalizes his disturbances so that they produce shyness, worry, guilt, and depression. The troublesome one externalizes his disturbances, acting them out in his interpersonal relationships. Some disturbed persons do both.

Shyness in children has several causes. Preschoolers may be shy when they begin Sunday school simply because of their inexperience in handling new relationships. Children may be insecure when they are away from home because they do not feel certain that their home is a secure place to which they can return. Frightened babies and small children should never be traumatized by being allowed to cry for long periods. Church schools should follow a firm policy that parents of such a child should be called and asked to remain in the room until the child feels safe in his new environment.

Adolescents are often shy because of self-consciousness about their bodies, their powerful, guilt-laden sexual feelings (and fantasies), and their struggle for a clear sense of who they are as individuals. A teacher should avoid doing anything which increases an adolescent's painful self-consciousness. The teacher should encourage participation without being coercive.

When a child or adolescent has chronic agonies of shyness, these feelings should not be taken as "just a phase." Often such a person is sending out silent distress signals saying, "I need help! My feelings are too big for me to handle unassisted." A shy child who does not respond to the individual attention of a teacher may need professional help. The internalizing child may be overlooked because he is not a discipline problem. He may even be regarded as a "model child," in spite of the fact that he may be more disturbed than an aggressive child.

Some children are naturally less aggressive and more given to inwardness than the blossoming extrovert type regarded as "normal" in our culture. To try to fit all children into an extrovert mold would stifle healthy inwardness which may produce some of the finest flowering of creativity. It is our culture which needs changing rather than such a child.

Chronic destructive behavior is usually a disguised "cry for help." The key question for the teacher to ask is "Why?" Is the child acting "bad" to protest against unrelenting pressure from his parents to be "bright" or "successful"? Is he trying desperately to define his identity by taking a stand against society? Perhaps he is saying, by his negative behavior, "I'm starved for someone to pay some attention to me!" or "My parents are on the verge of a divorce and my world is crumbling about me!" or "I desperately need the security of some dependable limits set and enforced by adults," or "To hell with the severe, rigid discipline which I experience without the love which would motivate me to become self-disciplined!"

If a teacher knows or suspects the causes of a child's behavior problems, specific remedies can be devised. For example, a discipline problem caused by the recent birth of a sibling rival can be diminished, to some extent, by generous helpings of attention from the teacher and the opportunity to ventilate feelings of jealousy. Unfortunately, the causes of behavior problems are often hidden from any except a highly trained therapist, who may require months of careful work to discover them in the nuances of the family's interaction.

In general, there are three approaches to discipline problems which frequently are helpful: (a) *Provide opportunities to get "bad" feelings put into the open,* as described earlier. Storytelling and opportunities to work out feelings through muscular activities are useful methods of draining off the child's head of emotional steam. Most important, the church school teacher should avoid saying those things which might cause the child to feel guilty about his feelings. (b) *Give extra attention to the troubled child.* This is important. It is difficult to do this without neglecting the other children. One of the many advantages of team teaching is that it makes it possible for one of the teachers to give special attention to a disturbed child. Allowing the child to lead, excel in some project, or otherwise gain approval from his peers often helps. (c) *Make certain that the limits are clearly defined and fairly enforced.* This is necessary to protect the class as a whole and avoid disrupting the educational process. It is also precisely what some problem children need. The limits should be firm and, if possible, friendly. Children who persist in not conforming to reasonable, necessary limits should be punished by the temporary removal of privileges. (If the child is misbehaving because he is emotionally malnourished, punishment may make his behavior worse.) If all three of these approaches are to no avail, removal of the disturbing child until he has had psychotherapeutic help may be necessary to save the class from chaos.

THE EXCEPTIONAL AND THE HANDICAPPED CHILD

Providing special religious education resources for the physically handicapped, the retarded, and the brilliant child is a responsibility which a growing number of churches are undertaking to meet. Team teaching is one answer to this need. It permits one or more teachers within a team to be free to concentrate on the special needs of a blind child or a small group of high-I.Q. children who require a more demanding curriculum. Special classes for moderately retarded children are available to some churches.

The First Methodist Church of Wausau, Wisconsin, has developed a Tuesday afternoon "opportunity group" for physically and mentally handicapped children. Nine patient, loving women compose the teaching staff. About fourteen children attend. The purpose of the program is to develop social skills through stories, games, music, art, and field trips, and to bring the children kindness and love. University Park Methodist Church, Dallas, Texas has an "Opportunity Class for Exceptional Children" which meets on Sundays. For most of the children the class is the high point in the week. The existence of the class has fostered understanding and concern within the congregation as a whole.[38] Programs such as these can give moral support and guidance to the parents of a handicapped child.

There are between five and six million mentally retarded children and adults in our country—approximately three percent of the population. Each year produces some 126,000 new cases. In some slum areas ten to thirty percent of the school-age children are mentally or culturally retarded.[39] There is new hope in this entire area. The special medical panel appointed by the late President Kennedy to study mental retardation reported that "with present knowledge, at least half and hopefully more than half, of all mental retardation cases can be prevented." [40] The rate of mental growth can be accelerated among the children who are mentally retarded

[38] *Together* (November, 1963), p. 30.
[39] "Message from the President of the United States Relative to Mental Illness and Mental Retardation" (February 5, 1963), reprinted in *Pastoral Psychology* (May, 1964).
[40] *Ibid.*, p. 16.

because of cultural deprivation. The social functioning of many other retarded children can be improved greatly by guidance, training, and modern rehabilitative procedures. Our churches should have a dynamic role in devising imaginative new approaches to this long-neglected problem.

THE STRATEGIC FOCUS ON PRESCHOOL CHILDREN

Every age group, from the nursery to the senior citizens, offers rich, undeveloped opportunities for developing positive mental health programs. However, two groups offer particularly strategic opportunities—preschool children and their parents. These should be given top priority in a church's mental health approach. Periodically the commission on education should ask itself: *Is our program of education seriously taking into account the findings of the social scientists which demonstrate that the foundations of mental, emotional, and spiritual health are laid during the preschool years?* Is our church doing everything possible to provide a positive, security-giving experience in the church school classes for these children? Are we doing everything we can to help prospective parents and parents of young children be what they most want to be—adequate parents—during these crucial years? The programs of many church schools would receive radical revision if these questions were asked and answered with action. More than any other institution in our society, the church has an opportunity to strengthen lives at their very foundations.

MENTAL HEALTH EDUCATION IN THE CHURCH SCHOOL

On the youth and adult levels, church school curricula ought to include serious study of mental illness, its causes, treatment, and the church's role in prevention. On all levels, the things that make for positive mental and spiritual health should be a prominent concern in the church school. For instance, the church school should supplement whatever the public schools do in the area of sex education and preparation for family life by relating these areas to the Christian understanding of the good life.

Mental health flourishes in churches, marriages, vocational life, parent-child and other relationships, to the extent that the basic hungers of personality are satisfied in these relationships. The church school has an exciting opportunity to help persons understand the

146

nature of these fundamental human needs and the ways in which they are satisfied in interpersonal relationships. Here is one way of describing these basic "foods of the spirit":

To have good mental health, every person needs—

S—*security*   The inner feeling of safety and stability that comes to a person in a relationship in which he feels wanted and accepted.

  service   The investment of oneself in others that brings the awareness that one can make one's life count. Giving love to others is a fundamental human need.

E—*esteem*   The awareness that one is recognized, respected, and appreciated by others.

  enjoyment   Experiences of the pleasures of the mind and the senses, including physical, intellectual, aesthetic, interpersonal, and spiritual satisfactions, as well as the adventure of new experiences.

L—*love*   The experience of knowing that another cares, warmly, intensely, and acceptingly. This is the most basic and indispensable need of any human being.

  limits   The sense of living within a dependable structure —the laws of nature, the principles of the psychological and spiritual life, the requirements of life in society.

F—*freedom*   Experiencing a growing sense of autonomy and self-directedness appropriate to one's capacity for responsibility. The discipline of external limits gradually becomes the self-discipline of responsible freedom in the course of normal development.

  faith   A satisfying philosophy of life and a hierarchy of personal values giving meaning to living, along with a sense of trust and of mystical relatedness to the universe and to God.

147

These are the vitamins, the minerals, the essential food elements of human personality. Persons become and remain healthy children, parents, spouses, employees, ministers, church members, friends, and so forth, to the degree that these basic needs are satisfied in their interpersonal relationships. As in the case of physical malnutrition, severe shortages of psychological food have their most damaging effects during the early years when growth is the most rapid and personality the most plastic. A person who had abundant satisfaction of his personality needs in the preschool years is like the house built on a rock in Jesus' parable. Conversely, the person who experienced severe psychological malnutrition during those years is like a house built on sand—highly vulnerable to the storms and stresses which occur in later life.

WISDOM—THE FAR GOAL OF CHRISTIAN EDUCATION

In a moving discussion of "The Glory and Agony of Teaching" Loren Eiseley recalls this poignant experience:

In Bimini, on the old Spanish Main, a daughter of the island once said to me: "Those as hunts treasure must go alone, at night, and when they find it, they must leave a little of their blood behind them."

I have never heard a finer, cleaner estimate of the price of wisdom. I wrote it down at once under a sea lamp, like the belated pirate I was, for the girl had given me unknowingly the latitude and longitude of a treasure." [41]

The hope and dream of every church school leader should be that his learners will push on beyond knowledge about religious truth to the pulsating reality of religious experience, and that many, as the years pass, will catch a vision of the depth dimension of the inner life—spiritual wisdom. As Eiseley says so well, the quest for wisdom often is a lonely quest in which one must pay a very personal price. But it is as individuals discover this treasure that the spiritual legacy of mankind is enriched.

[41] "The Glory and the Agony of Teaching," *Think*, October, 1962, p. 25.

CHAPTER 7

Mental Health and the Group Life of the Church

> *For where two or three are gathered in my name,
> there am I in the midst of them—Matt. 18:20*
>
> *That their hearts may be encouraged as they are
> knit together in love, to have all the riches of assured
> understanding and the knowledge of God's mystery
> —Col. 2:2*
>
> *There are many things which a person can do
> alone, but being a Christian is not one of them*[1]
> *—William T. Ham*

Groups, large and small, are the fabric from which a church's program is shaped. Many church groups provide rich opportunities for developing interpersonal skills, leadership abilities, spiritual depth and intellectual discipline. The existence of a variety of sizes and types of groups in a local church is an invaluable asset in fulfilling its ministry of growth, healing, service, and reconciliation. The spiritual vitality of a local church is directly correlated with the health of its groups—particularly its small groups where heart-hungers are most apt to be satisfied. Here a sense of Christian community can flourish.

Unfortunately, many church groups do not discover their untapped potentialities for growth and healing. They fail to find the secret of group creativity. Rather than providing growth-stimulating experiences, they become drags on the mental health of their members. Instead of sharpening the creative edge of living, such groups have a dulling effect, encouraging the investment of precious human life in

---

[1] From John L. Casteel (ed.), *Spiritual Renewal Through Personal Groups* (New York: Association Press, 1957), p. 169.

trivial activities. Out of a sense of duty, guilt, or habit, persons continue in such groups, cluttering their schedules with a plethora of meetings. A perceptive student of church groups states a fact that stands as a judgment on our churches: "We affirm that our churches are Christian fellowships, households of faith, beloved communities. But many churchmen find deeper fellowship in a union, a trade association, or a lodge." [2]

Church groups, once established, tend to become self-perpetuating. Even if they become sick, they grind on like cogs in a machine, year after year. To measure a group's viability, the minister and lay leaders need to ask these crucial questions: Is this group useful in achieving the kingdom goals for which the church exists? What are its effects on personality? Is it contributing significantly to the service of humanity, the growth of persons, or the deepening of relationships?

How can a church's groups make their maximum contribution to mental and spiritual health? As the central issue of this chapter, this question will be treated with a dual focus: How can the health of the existing groups be enhanced and how can such new groups be created as are necessary to meet the needs of a church's members and its community?

THE MYSTICAL IDENTITY OF A CHURCH

What is "Christian community"? A church as a psychological reality is not just a collection of groups any more than a family is only a collection of individuals. There is a unifying identity which is more than the sum of its members and groups. This makes the church-fellowship-as-a-whole a psychological entity. The over-all identity of a given congregation is a mystical unity which transcends the collective identities of the subgroups within its structure. The identity of the local church is, in turn, strengthened by an awareness of sharing in larger circles of identity—the denomination, other branches of the mystical Body of Christ, and in the largest circle—the family of God. The theological and historical dimensions of a church's corporate identity account for its uniqueness as a social organism. Unlike other groups, a church fellowship participates in a century-

[2] M. E. Kuhn, *You Can't Be Human Alone* (New York: National Council of Churches, 1956), p. 1.

spanning heritage which finds the ultimate meaning of existence in man's relationship with God.

Coming into a particular congregation opens the door for the individual to participate psychologically in this many-faceted corporate identity. The depth of an individual's participation depends on the degree to which he is able to enter into the fellowship and its heritage. The corporate identity of a congregation is most apt to come alive for the individual as he builds strong relationships in the church's groups. Persons who find the richest satisfactions in church membership are almost invariably immersed in the fellowship of one or more of its smaller groups. Conversely, the "fringe member" is one who has not gotten into one of the centers of group life.

Participation in the psychological identity of a church fellowship undergirds one's sense of individual and family identity, thus strengthening personality health. As Arnold B. Come has stated, "Participation in the life of the church has a formative power below the level of consciousness." [3] This vital contribution to the mental health of millions of church members is so ubiquitous that it is easily taken for granted.

THE SMALL GROUP AND THE CHURCH'S PURPOSES

Robert C. Leslie, a leader in the field of group pastoral counseling, has observed: "One of the healthiest signs of renewal in the life of the church is the increasing number of small, intimate, sharing groups which are springing up on all sides." [4] The flowering of small groups in the churches is one of the most significant religious developments of our times. The labels are varied—"sharing group," "growth group," "discovery group," "personal group," "encounter group," "quest group," "healing group," "therapy group," "Yoke-fellow group," and so forth. All emphasize personal sharing, depth communication, and growth in the spiritual life. Collectively these emerging groups represent a tremendous wellspring of mental health influences.

Church historians have noted that the training of small groups has been a part of every major surge of spiritual vitality in the

[3] *Drinking: A Christian Position* (Philadelphia: Westminster Press, 1964), p. 78.
[4] "The Uniqueness of Small Groups in the Church," *Pastoral Psychology*, XV (June, 1964), 33.

church. In *The Human Group,* George Homans points out that early Christianity grew through the spread of its "network of new and tough groups." [5] In his dissertation, "Group Therapy as a Method for Church Work," [6] Robert C. Leslie identifies these salient points at which small groups played a vital role in church history: Christ and his disciples, the Apostolic church, Montanism, monasticism, the Waldenses, the Franciscans, the Friends of God, the Brethren of the Common Life, German pietism, the Anabaptists, the Society of Friends, the Wesleyan revival, the Great Awakening, the Iona Community, the Emmanuel Movement, and the Oxford Group Movement (from which came Alcoholics Anonymous). The contemporary renaissance of small groups in the churches follows an ancient, time-tested path.

If a church is to be "a creative cell in our mass society," [7] it must offer people abundant opportunities to experience Christian community. Large groups have a vital function in achieving the instructional and inspirational objectives of a church. Think, for example, of the spiritual lift which comes from being a part of a congregation singing the mighty Easter hymns of renewal. But a church's smaller groups are the settings in which lonely people can best experience the reality of religion as creative relationships—with self, others, and God. In the lay academies of the continent, the "house churches" of Britain, the ecumenical retreat centers in the U. S. and elsewhere, in denominational and local church camps, youth assemblies, parent education and Bible study groups, hundreds of persons are discovering the excitement of life-to-life communication in small groups. Many are finding a fresh baptism of the biblical experience as a small, honest group becomes a channel of God's grace for them. There is no doubt that the small group renaissance is a powerful factor in the recovery of Christian community and of the healing mission of the church.

SMALL GROUPS AND PERSONALITY NEEDS

Human beings have a spontaneous tendency toward grouping resulting from the fact that man is essentially a social being whose

[5] (New York: Harcourt, Brace and Company, 1956), p. 658.
[6] Unpublished Ph.D. dissertation, Boston University, 1948.
[7] Alan Walker, address at Garrett Theological Seminary, August, 1957.

deepest personality needs can be satisfied only in relationships. In early childhood his personality is created through interaction with his family. Throughout his life span the maintenance of personality health depends on the adequate satisfaction of his personality needs through positive relationships.

The basic "heart-hungers" or personality needs were described in the last chapter. Each of these hungers is satisfied to some degree in an effective church group. Feelings of *security* are derived from belonging to an accepting group. Opportunities for meaningful *service* should be present in every church group. (In a personal sharing group this may be the service of helping others discover themselves.) *Self-esteem* is enhanced as one feels esteemed by one's fellows. Group activities allow for the *enjoyment* of a variety of shared experiences. An effective group helps bridge the separateness of individual life by empathy, affection, and concern. The sum of these is *love,* the absolutely indispensable personality food. A group elicits loyalty because it satisfies personality needs. This loyalty to the group gives the group power to influence the values and set *limits* on individual behavior. A health-enhancing group respects the need for encouraging individual *freedom* within necessary limits.

The religiously oriented group is the instrument par excellence for nurturing that experience of trust which is called faith. Trust is contagious and the place where it is most likely to be caught is in a group committed to the religious quest. In a small, accepting group many persons discover that the kingdom is already among us!

Small groups are particularly important in our period of history. It is psychologically true, as in John Donne's familiar line, that "No man is an Island, entire of itself." But the fact is that millions of persons experience themselves as islands, cut off from the continent of humanity. Many are not aware of the depth of their loneliness. They live in what Tennessee Williams describes as "a lonely condition so terrifying to think about that we usually don't." [8] Cut off from real communication with others, they feel like grains of sand, washed back and forth by the waves of impersonal forces, having friction with others but no organic relatedness. In this kind of society, small, lively groups in a church offer sorely needed opportunities

[8] Tennessee Williams, *Cat on a Hot Tin Roof,* introduction.

for persons to drink deeply from the fresh springs of relationship, discovering the reality of the New Testament experience of being "members one of another."

CREATING A TRUE GROUP

In the psychological sense, a group is not just a collection of individuals in geographical proximity. Fifty people packed like sardines in a subway train do not constitute a true group. A group comes into existence when, through interaction, there is a partial merging of the "psychological field" or "life space" of two or more individuals. The significant world of each is to some extent involved in the other. There are definite, predictable stages through which an aggregation of people go in the process of becoming a true group. When this process is well advanced, there is a strong sense of group identity, of group boundaries and of cohesiveness, interdependency, and belonging.

Although the process of becoming a group is a natural one, certain factors in our society tend to block it—for example, competitiveness, fear of intimacy, and general reluctance to relax our defensive masks. Consequently, many so-called groups meet for years without achieving more than superficial interaction. Unfortunately, glib talk about "Christian fellowship" will not produce it. Only as a group satisfies the conditions under which vital interpersonal relationships can grow will genuine fellowship be experienced.

A group tends to develop a distinctive "personality"—a persistent emotional climate and style of relating which distinguishes it from other groups. Many groups have personality problems. Since groups can be robust or sickly, energetic or anemic, it behooves church leaders who work constantly with groups to be able to diagnose and treat the factors which limit group creativity.

For any group to come into existence there must be "physical, social, and interactional proximity." [9] Physical proximity must be combined with continuity of meeting. It takes time together to develop a sense of group identity. Social proximity refers to the common goals or interests which bring certain individuals together. The sense of group identity grows as mutual need-satisfaction develops

[9] Quoted from Eugene Jennings of Michigan State University in *You Can't Be Human Alone*, p. 6.

and psychological fields overlap through interaction. Emotional involvement in the group flowers as its members communicate and share meaningful experiences. The more intense the experience in which they participate, the more powerful the bond—witness the rapport among men who have been through a battle together.

In the growth of a healthy group, openness and honesty of communication are essential. Speaking of small groups in the churches, John Casteel declares: "The vitality of the group's life together depends upon the freedom, honesty, and depth with which members come to share their questions, problems, insights, and faith with one another." [10] The kind of participation which produces emotional involvement is based on the awareness that one's feelings and opinions are recognized, valued, and taken into account in group decisions.

A unique aspect of a church group which contributes to its health is its vertical as well as horizontal reference. The growth of individual group members is seen in relationship to God and the needs of the world. This tends to balance the necessary introspective aspects of a sharing group. In her description of the spiritual pioneering of the Church of Our Savior in Washington, D. C., Elizabeth O'Connor put the issue squarely: "The group does meet for the nurture of its own members, but it also meets in order that God may have an instrument through which His power may come and through which His life may break in new ways for the world." [11]

GROUP-CENTERED LEADERSHIP

The most crucial single factor in group health is the quality of its leadership. In an authority-centered group, honesty of communication tends not to occur. Members hide their real feelings and withhold themselves from wholehearted participation. The more a leader assumes responsibility for what happens in the group, the more the group forces him to carry the ball. In a leader-centered group, members give only enough of themselves to "get by." Uncreative conformity and its Siamese twin, "foot-dragging," flourish. Coercive devices such as penalties and rewards become increasingly necessary to keep the wheels turning.

Various studies have shown that authority-centered patterns of

[10] *Spiritual Renewal Through Personal Groups,* p. 201.
[11] *Call to Commitment* (New York: Harper & Row, 1956), p. 37.

leadership produce negative effects on personality health. The morale of workers and the emotional stability of children have been found to be enhanced by job situations and homes, respectively, in which they participated in some of the decisions affecting them.[12] The distribution of leadership in the "therapeutic community" approach in mental hospitals (including patient self-government and even participation in decisions regarding the discharge of fellow patients) has produced remarkable therapeutic results.

The leadership model which maximizes the growth-stimulating effects of groups is described by Thomas Gordon in *Group-Centered Leadership, A Way of Releasing the Creative Power of Groups.* Here are some of the functions of a group-centered leader:

(1) He seeks the maximum distribution of leadership among the group members. (2) He sees that all members of the group have an opportunity to participate in group decisions. (3) He encourages freedom of communication. (4) He seeks to increase opportunities for participation. (5) He attempts to create a non-threatening group climate in which feelings and ideas are accepted. (6) He conveys feelings of warmth and empathy, thus encouraging others to do likewise. (7) He sets the tone by paying attention to the contributions of others, perhaps of reflecting what they are saying with, "Let's see if I understand what you mean . . ." (8) He helps build group-centered (as contrasted with self-centered) contributions by his linking function in which he points to the relationships among various individuals' contributions to the discussion.[13]

Such a leader is a catalyst and midwife—a facilitator of the group process. As group-centeredness grows, dependence on the leader decreases and the functions of the leader are gradually taken over by the group. It is important to emphasize that the degree to which members give of their abilities to the group's thought and work is determined by the extent to which emotional involvement is elicited through the distribution of leadership and meaningful participation.

Democratic (or group-centered) leadership is not the same as

[12] From Thomas Gordon, *Group-Centered Leadership* (Boston: Houghton Mifflin Company, 1955), pp. 8-9.
[13] Paraphrased from Thomas Gordon, "Group-Centered Leadership and Administration," in *Client-Centered Therapy* by Carl R. Rogers (Boston: Houghton Mifflin Company, 1959), Chap. 8.

laissez faire leadership or leader passivity. The democratic leader actively helps the group to release its own potentialities. He knows that the only way this can happen is by not doing the things for the group that they can learn to do for themselves. His respect for persons and for the group process assures him that he can depend on the group's discovering its identity and power. As midwife, he helps in a "natural childbirth" process by which a creative group is born. His job is to help the group achieve an emotional climate and a level of communication which will facilitate natural group-birth.

The spirit rather than the mechanics of leadership is at the heart of this matter. To illustrate, an authority-centered person can misuse a knowledge of group dynamics (or even the methods of group-centered leadership) to manipulate a group in subtle ways. On the other hand, the person-centered leader, believing deeply that the group-centered approach releases human potentialities, will carry this spirit into those situations requiring more directive approaches. Church groups require a variety of leadership skills, including the constructive use of authority. Like counseling, leadership calls for different facets of a leader's personality in different situations. On the same day, a minister may function with a family temporarily paralyzed by a tragic loss, a ministerial association meeting involving numerous routine administrative matters, and a planning retreat for his church leaders. The use of any one leadership style in all of these situations would miss the needs of at least two. The first calls for a firm, parental, supportive approach. The second needs efficiency in leadership in order to save the group's time for important matters. But in the third situation—the planning retreat—genuine group-centered methods are essential in order to reduce leader-dependency and allow each person the freedom and incentive to contribute his creativity to the planning process.

TYPES OF SMALL GROUPS IN A LOCAL CHURCH

There are at least four types of group functions which have useful roles in a church program— (a) *work and service,* (b) *study,* (c) *supportive-inspirational, and* (d) *modified therapy.*[14] Many church groups combine two or more of these functions. Each of the four

[14] I am indebted to Robert C. Leslie for his elucidation of this term in "Group Therapy: A New Approach for the Church," *Pastoral Psychology,* VI (April, 1955).

types can play an essential role in contributing to the health and growth of persons.

Work and service groups (called "task-oriented" in group literature) accomplish the essential administrative, fund-raising, social action, and community service functions of a church. They can contribute to mental health by providing the therapy of worthwhile work and satisfying the need for self-investment. Take, for example, the group in a west-coast church which produces an excellent church paper. The mental health values to these persons include participation with congenial friends in achieving worthy goals (producing a channel of information and inspiration) and the reward of well-deserved appreciation from church members and minister. The editor's leadership is the key to understanding the *esprit de corps* of the staff. He delegates responsibility in ways that reveal his respect for persons and calls regular staff-meetings at which important decisions are made regarding layout and policy.

The methods frequently employed in work groups to "get things done," ride roughshod over feelings and stifle individual initiative. In an article on "Group Dynamics in a Local Church," Philip H. Anderson asks rhetorically: "Are we so sure that the committee which ignores the feelings of individual members in order to get a job done is the most efficient and productive in the long run?" [15] Even if it could be proved that a steamroller approach is the most efficient way of getting certain work done (as it may well be in the short run), the fundamental issue is the negative impact of this methodology on personality.

Study groups, like work groups, have varied effects on the mental health of their members. As indicated in the preceding chapter, sound educational methods encourage involvement, enhance self-esteem, and stimulate growth. To maximize its mental health impact, a church should have a wide variety of study groups for all ages. Most churches have hardly scratched the surface of their opportunities to offer adults horizon-widening encounters with new dimensions of truth. Having a face-to-face contact with many more adults than any other agency in our society gives the churches a tremendous natural opportunity in adult education. Through lively study-

[15] *Pastoral Psychology*, III (January, 1953), p. 21.

discussion groups, persons from young adulthood through senior citizenship can discover the zest of loving God with their minds.

One church in the South has a "Christian great books club." Twenty-five couples each contribute the price of one book per year. A committee from the club recommends twenty-five choice books, drawing both from contemporary theological writings and the religious classics. The books are circulated. Each month a panel of members leads a discussion on two of the books. At the end of the year, the books are added to the church library. This approach provides a group incentive to read solid religious books and to wrestle collectively with ideas from many facets of religious literature. The group bond is strong because they are sharing a highly significant experience. Invariably the group discussions focus on the relevance of the books to a broad range of practical problems in living. A study group thus becomes a kind of modified therapy group, encouraging growth in the adequacy of one's total life.

Many churches are forming *koinonia* groups. Their primary focus is disciplined study with an emphasis on personal commitment. Robert Raines describes the operation of *koinonia* groups in his church.[16] He holds that they are an effective way of training a hard core of dedicated, growing disciples who can leaven a local church. Bible study is the core of the groups' activity, for three reasons: (a) Rediscovery of the biblical message is the shortest path to the God of the Bible. (b) The Bible gives the authoritative content of the faith which provides substance for the small group experience, helping members avoid the "self-centeredness and sentimentality" of many prayer groups. (c) An invitation to work out an intellectually respectable faith through grappling with questions and doubts about the Bible is the most efficient way of getting large numbers of adults into small groups.

Koinonia groups usually meet two evenings a month for two hours. After fifteen minutes of devotions, one and a half hours are spent discussing the material for that session. Study is based on a two-year cycle of books, beginning with a survey of the Bible followed by the Gospel of Mark. New groups are led by carefully trained laymen with previous *koinonia* group experience. In describing group ses-

[16] *New Life in the Church* (New York: Harper & Row, 1961).

159

sions, Raines comments: "No matter how academically I would start the discussion, the people would invariably bring it down to their daily lives where they needed help." [17] The goal of these groups is to reach and change people quickly in the direction of Christian discipleship. There is no doubt that these groups have therapeutic (healing) effects. In fact, they may be more therapeutic than many "therapy groups" simply because they have a center outside themselves and a goal which is more inclusive than simply the growth of their members. Raines reports that these groups have transformed lives and revitalized his church from within.

Some church groups are primarily supportive-inspirational in their function—that is, fellowship groups give emotional support to their members. Typical prayer groups are supportive-inspirational. Their goal is the deepening of the members' spiritual lives through experiencing a vital relationship with God. Canon Ernest W. Southcott, founder of the "home church" movement in England, writes in *The Parish Comes Alive:* "We need fellowship—the fellowship of the Holy Spirit—in 'upper rooms' where two or three are gathered together in His name, so that He can be in the midst of us." [18] His movement aims at taking the church into the homes of people primarily through the celebration of home communion.

The usual assumption in group therapy thinking is that a group cannot be both insight-oriented and "repressive-inspirational." One of the significant things that small group experiences in church settings have demonstrated is that a group can be inspirational without being repressive. Put another way, a group can have an inspirational dimension without putting the lid on the emergence of insight. In fact, experiments like the *koinonia* groups suggest that an inspirational aspect may facilitate the process of self-discovery in certain people by providing a sense of support and safety. This reduces their anxiety level sufficiently to allow them to examine previously avoided areas of their inner lives.

The leadership of a group makes a decisive difference in determining whether inspiration is used repressively or to facilitate self-awareness. Leaders with group-therapy training can encourage a

[17] *Ibid.,* p. 84.
[18] (New York: Morehouse-Barlow Co., 1956), p. 121.

Bible study group to use the great biblical insights as stimuli and guides to deeper explorations of their intrapersonal conflicts and interpersonal relationships. Because of its refreshing candor regarding big feelings—for example guilt, fear, anger, sibling rivalry (Cain and Abel)—the biblical record, when skillfully employed, is an ideal instrument for depth explorations.

THERAPEUTIC GROUPS VERSUS GROUP THERAPY

Should the typical church group be thought of as a form of group therapy? Definitely not! Group therapy is one form of psychotherapy. It is an effective instrument only in the hands of a well-trained group therapist. Any general attempt to convert church groups into therapy would produce widespread (and justified) resentment and would miss the broader educational, prophetic, and service goals of a church. Church groups in general cannot and should not be "therapy" groups, but they should be increasingly therapeutic in their effects. Every class, committee, society, circle, board, commission, and fellowship group should strive to become more and more healing and growth-stimulating. That this happen in the life of a church is vastly more important than that the church sponsor "group therapy," per se. However, the church leaders' (lay and professional) understanding of the principles of group dynamics and therapy can be immensely useful in helping groups realize their creative possibilities.

This comparison of two adult classes in the same midwestern church illustrates the distinction between therapeutic and non-therapeutic groups:

Class X: The interpersonal climate is warm, accepting, enthusiastic. There is a strong sense of belonging among its members. Newcomers are attracted by the positive spirit of the class. It is unnecessary to promote attendance. People come regularly because attendance is a need-satisfying experience. Most of the members participate in the programs and the decisions of the class. Top leadership rotates regularly every six months. A variety of speakers is used in its programs which are planned by the members.

Class Y: The group climate is decidedly cool and there is little sense of cohesion. Except for a small clique at the center who make the decisions and plan the programs, there is little sense of member-involvement. In spite of strained efforts to promote "friendliness," the social distance separating individuals within the group is large. There is a constant and coercive effort on the part of the three officers to increase attendance and arouse enthusiasm. The programs are executed (in more ways than one) by the officers who complain that "people won't take responsibility." Most of the members of class Y are essentially spectators, attending sporadically and investing little of themselves in the experience.

Class Y mirrors the problems of our culture—aloneness, manipulation, noninvolvement, and "spectatoritis." Class X effectively challenges these pathogenic patterns by providing experiences of warm, interpersonal relationships, participation, and belonging.

REJUVENATING A CHURCH'S GROUP LIFE

If a church's groups are to make their maximum contribution to the health of persons, the health of the groups needs to be checked periodically. One church did a self-study of its entire membership and program to ascertain the extent to which the program was meeting the basic needs of the congregation. It used as participation criteria four categories in which information was readily available— church attendance, financial support, group membership, and leadership in the church's program. It found that an alarmingly high percentage of members was not involved in any group and that the leadership function was not broadly distributed. This self-study included a careful analysis of the church's group structure against the background of the obvious needs of the congregation. A study of the age distribution revealed that a higher percentage of the members was in the over-sixty category than had been generally recognized. In the light of this, several new groups for retired persons were launched, as well as a short-term group (repeated periodically) to help prepare persons for the stresses of retirement.

Each group within that church was encouraged to do a self-study of its own effectiveness. A "Group Vitality Check List" was distributed to the leaders to assist them in this process. It contained items such as group growth, major problems, degree of participation, attention to newcomers and absentees, rotation and distribution of leadership. One of the results of these group self-studies was a request from several group leaders for a leadership training course. This was set up on a small group, modified-therapy basis, recognizing that the most efficient way of acquiring depth understanding of group interaction is to experience such interaction under supervision. The church's minister of counseling led the group using a laboratory method. After discussing the influence on group morale of various types of leadership, the training group experimented by role-playing authoritarian, over-permissive, and group-centered leaders. The group was used as a lab to experiment with various group techniques including buzz groups, post-session evaluation techniques, opinionaires, brainstorming, and dialogue-stimulating methods. Leadership training is the key to rejuvenating a church's existing groups and preparing for the development of future groups.

Faltering groups frequently find new vitality in "renewal retreats" in which the officers or the entire group spend a weekend together at a remote spot. These retreats aim at rethinking the purposes of the group and searching for new resources for achieving them. During such a retreat interpersonal barriers are lowered and bridges strengthened. This may have more to do with the success of such experiences than the plans they produce.

There are in many churches one or more groups which suffer from severe personality problems and are meeting only the neurotic needs of a few persons. If vested interests and emotional involvement in such groups are high on the part of a few, it may be necessary for those responsible for the overall adequacy of the church program simply to bypass the sick groups and create other groups to meet the needs of the congregation. This is usually more constructive than attempting to do away with the infected groups.

CREATING NEW GROUPS TO FILL GAPS

To meet the challenge of our society, a church should experiment with new patterns of group life. This is precisely what vital churches in many places are doing. In evaluating its group structure, a church's leaders should ask themselves these questions: *Is it possible for persons of every age, with a wide range of interests, to find meaningful group experiences in our church? What are the unique needs of people in this community in the second half of the twentieth century? What are the gaps in our group structure? What new group ap-*

proaches can help to meet the needs of our members and the needs of our community, beyond our congregation?

Every human being, whatever his age or social position, needs a small group to nurture his personal growth. Increasing numbers of persons are finding their nurture groups within a church. The goal toward which a church should strive is to encourage each of its members to participate in a significant small group relationship in which depth communication can occur. If this is to happen, churches must be imaginative and daring in their creation of new groups. The classic example of a church that has done this through the years is the First Community Church of Columbus, Ohio. Under the leadership of the late Roy Burkhart, that church took as its aim the guidance and spiritual enrichment of life "from birth through all the years of life in the tabernacle of the body." Long before the current surge of small groups, that church developed a wide and varied group structure to meet the growth needs of its members.

In a significant paper, "Theological Dimensions of Renewal through Small Groups," [19] James B. Ashbrook holds that the vitality of church life depends on the presence of a number of "cellular units" which are discovering new life in the Spirit. He describes the way in which his church developed ten small groups paralleling the regular organizational structure but not formally a part of it. Their purpose was to seek the authentic life of the Spirit. Each group had its own life history. When a group had outlived its usefulness, it was allowed to die so that new life might come into being. The idea of creating vital parallel groups, as at the same time one works to energize existing "institutionalized" groups, has much to commend it.

THERAPY AND MODIFIED THERAPY GROUPS

Among the new groups which a church should create there ought to be one or more with explicit counseling goals such as growth in self-understanding, opportunity to deal openly with feelings and problems, and opportunity to grow in the health of one's interpersonal relationships. These could be group psychotherapy and/or modified therapy groups. Pure (unmodified) group psychotherapy has the following characteristics:

[19] *Pastoral Psychology*, XV (June, 1964), 23-32.

(1) It has an avowed therapeutic purpose which the members know in advance. (2) Its activities are limited to those which are directly psychotherapeutic. There are no projects, agendas or instruction in the formal sense. (3) The basic concern of the group is the growth of its members in self-awareness, self-acceptance and in their relationships. (4) Free and honest expression of feelings is encouraged, including negative feelings about other members and the leader. (5) There is a continual focus on interaction within the group, on the assumption that this reflects the member's general interpersonal patterns. (6) Such groups are usually limited in size, six to eight being a common number. Many such groups continue to meet over considerable periods of time.[20]

The leader of such a group must be highly skilled in order to help the group per se become a therapeutic agent and to minimize the following dangers: (a) Transference distortions. Archaic feelings of intense love and hate inevitably come to the surface in such groups, attaching themselves to the leader and to group members. These feelings may disrupt relationships. Given sufficient time, they can be worked through in therapy groups providing the leader is well trained. If not well-handled, these transference feelings can produce difficult interpersonal problems. (b) *Acting out.* Because of the intimate communication over a long period of time, therapy group members tend to develop strong bonds which sometimes leads to sexual pairing. The acting out can also be of a hostile variety. Here again, skilled leadership is very important.

It is obvious from the above that a minister (or anyone else) with only limited training in counseling should avoid attempting anything resembling group psychotherapy. Even if he has the necessary training, the pastor of a church who attempts to do group therapy is probably investing more time in a few people than he can afford. Fortunately, whatever training a minister has in the principles of group therapy need not be wasted since these principles can be applied in modified therapy groups designed to help "normal" people raise their levels of effectiveness in living. Psychiatrist Jerome D. Frank points out that "intimate sharing of feelings, ideas and experiences in an atmosphere of mutual respect and understanding enhances self-respect, deepens self-understanding, and helps a person

[20] Adapted from G. R. Bach, *Intensive Group Psychotherapy* (New York: Ronald Press, 1954).

live with others. Such an experience *can be* helpful to persons at any level of illness or health." [21]

Unless a church has a minister of counseling with advanced training in group therapy (or a member of one of the mental health professions with such training), it should concentrate on modified therapy groups for relatively healthy (or mildly disturbed) persons. Such persons can often profit greatly from growth groups. If a church has a well-trained person on its staff there is no reason why it should not consider sponsoring group therapy for more disturbed persons as an expression of its ministry of healing.

The pure group therapy approach can be modified in several ways to make it applicable to church groups with less highly trained leadership and designed to help relatively normal people. The therapeutic process will ordinarily be less intense (and therefore more easily used constructively) if one or more of the following changes are made: (a) The size of the group is increased. (b) The purposes are broadened to include educational or inspirational goals. (c) The frequency of meetings is reduced (therapy groups usually meet weekly for 1½ hours). (d) The length of the group's existence is limited in advance. (e) The leader functions as a teacher. (f) The leader focuses away from expressions of feelings concerning other group members.

Robert C. Leslie suggests these simple ground rules which he believes make it possible for church groups to focus on relationships without excesses such as emotional explosions and unwholesome confessions:

1. The situation of the moment, the here and now in this room and around this table, is never lost sight of. . . . investigation into past behavior is inappropriate. . . . 2. Attention is centered on the first person, on *my* feelings, *my* reactions, *my* associations. . . . 3. There is no place for personal criticism. That is, instead of saying: "You have a very annoying way of interrupting me," the feeling of annoyance is expressed as *my* problem rather than as *yours:* "I find myself getting very annoyed when I am interrupted." . . . 4. Investigation of motives has no place in the group, but reactions to behavior are always relevant. . . . 5. The cre-

[21] "Group Methods in Therapy" (Public Affairs Pamphlet #284), pp. 3-4. (Italics added).

ation of an atmosphere in which personal feelings can be discussed at the moment that they are aroused by characteristic behavior patterns is a major concern, so that the group gains increasing freedom in dealing with its own habitual operations.[22]

These ground rules represent a practical way of modifying orthodox group psychotherapy rendering it less hazardous without losing the therapeutic values of honest discussion of personal feelings.

Within the church setting, modified therapy approaches can be applied to meet many types of needs. For example, Edgar N. Jackson has experimented with short-term parent groups involving four to six couples. In his pastoral work, he frequently encountered a strong sense of need among parents of sixth grade preadolescents. So, he invited several couples to meet for eight to ten sessions to explore their mutual concerns related to their roles as parents of soon-to-be adolescents. Each session was opened with a brief statement by Jackson on such matters as the psychology of sixth graders and of parent-child relationships. This statement, a seed-planting operation, produced a lively discussion which quickly moved to the level of the parents' feelings, problems, and self-images. This approach has applicability to a wide range of problems which normal church members encounter during the "common ventures of life."

A modified therapy approach was employed by a west-coast church in its teacher-training program. The minister discovered that several of his children's division teachers felt grossly inadequate as teachers, were baffled by problems of doubt, and felt shaken by parents' criticism. Fortunately, he had had training in group counseling. His suggestion that they have a series of informal meetings to deal with some of these problems was eagerly accepted. The minister met weekly with a dozen or so of the teachers for a period of two months. They felt this experience to be of substantial help in clarifying and working through the feelings which were inhibiting their effectiveness.

A Long Island church of which I was pastor used a modified therapy group approach in its continuing program of child-study for mothers of preschoolers. After preliminary discussion of the need for such a group, the nursery superintendent and the minister invited

[22] "The Uniqueness of Small Groups in the Church," pp. 35-36.

all the mothers of preschool children to an exploratory meeting. Those who responded decided to start a "Child-study Nursery Group" which would meet one morning a week throughout the school year. They elected a steering committee with a rotating chairmanship. This committee planned the child-study program in consultation with the minister and the superintendent after circulating an "Interest Finder" questionnaire among the entire group. Here is a sampling of their programs: systematic study of Dorothy Baruch's *New Ways in Discipline*,[23] a mental health film entitled "Angry Boy," a talk by a pediatrician, a trip with their children to a zoo, a talk by the minister on "Handling a Child's Fear of Death," and a panel of members on "Sex Education of Young Children."

While the mothers met in the church parlor their children attended nursery school in the basement under the supervision of trained volunteers. Each mother contributed fifty cents a week to cover costs of nursery school equipment as well as coffee and juice. Occasional evening meetings were scheduled so that the fathers could share in choice programs. In the evaluation session at the close of the first year, comments such as these were voiced: "This group has given me self-confidence as a mother. I don't feel so pushed around by what others on my street think." "Our family is spending more time together and *liking* it! We went on our first picnic in the country last week."

This group continued for a number of years. Some dropped out as their children reached school age. Other mothers joined, keeping the group at about twenty-five. This group was effective because it met real needs of mothers and children. It allowed the mothers an opportunity to deal with their feelings and attitudes as well as acquire useful information. It was self-directed so that it stayed close to the needs and interests of the participants. The group association helped to overcome the loneliness often felt by mothers whose activities are confined by small children.

Modified therapy groups have been used extensively with adolescents (who respond especially well to such approaches). After a satisfying yearlong confirmation class with the minister of a Michigan church, several highschool youth expressed a desire to continue

[23] (New York: McGraw-Hill Book Company, 1949).

the group. The minister inquired if they would like a group on "Solving Personal Problems" which would meet weekly for twelve weeks. Six of the young people responded and they continued on a group counseling basis.

The minister of counseling in a downtown church in Southern California takes the initiative in inviting teen-agers whom he feels could benefit to join small (seven or eight members at the maximum) "self-discovery" groups which meet with him weekly throughout the school year. The aims of these groups are to help the youth learn to relate more meaningfully, to bring their hidden fears and feelings out into the light, to handle their problems more adequately, and to grow toward a mature faith.

Group counseling (another label for modified therapy [24] groups) has also been used productively in premarital couple counseling. It is noteworthy that couples often move more rapidly to a significant level of discussion in groups of three to five couples than when they meet separately with the minister. The less inhibited couples tend to open up delicate areas of discussion and encourage the more restrained to participate. What is more, the couples have an opportunity to learn from the experiences of one another as well as from the minister.[25]

In summary, the possibilities of using modified therapy groups constructively in the church program are almost unlimited. Such groups are particularly helpful for those facing a common crisis or period of stress. They are ideally suited as instruments of depth education. A modified therapy group retains certain features of group psychotherapy—the goal of growth in self-awareness, the encouragement of honest discussion of those feelings which are "off limits" in most social groups, and the focus on the personal concerns of the members. These features of group psychotherapy are combined with educational and/or inspirational elements within the framework of limited duration and specific goals such as increasing the in-

[24] Words like "therapy" and "counseling" have negative overtones for many people. In setting up such groups it is usually best to employ a less threatening label such as "sharing group," "personal group," or simply, "group."

[25] See "Group Premarital Counseling," by Lena Levine and Jeanne Brodsky. Available from Planned Parenthood Federation of America, 501 Madison Ave., New York 22, New York.

dividuals' adequacy in handling a particular relationship or problem. Modified therapy groups do not aim at radical personality changes and avoid dealing with transference feelings or other products of the unconscious.

A recovered alcoholic who is also a devoted churchman declared, "Tragically many people find so much more acceptance in A.A. than in the church that they make A.A. their church." This need not be true if we are willing not just to belong to the church but to *be* the church—a community of forgiven sinners striving to become transmitters of that unearned love which brought us to life spiritually. A.A. is a refreshing example of the power of dynamic, spiritual groups. Fortunately many churches are discovering within their own life that small groups of many kinds can become channels of the healing, empowering, reconciling Spirit of God.

CHAPTER 8
Creative Church Administration and Mental Health

It all started some years ago when Mr. Wahlstrom bought an old bombsight and took it apart just for the fun of it. When he began to put it together he found in his workshop some parts of an old alarm clock. He became fascinated to see how he could add these to the bombsight. Thus it began, and in the years since he has been adding wheels, belts, bells, and cogs until today there are some ten thousand parts in Wahlstrom's wonder. When he throws the switch three thousand of them move while the whole apparatus revolves on a turntable. Bells ring, lights flash, and hundreds of wheels go round. It is an awesome sight! The only thing about it is Mr. Wahlstrom's wonder doesn't do anything. It just runs! Wheels within wheels, cogs within cogs.[1]—Gene E. Bartlett

And when the living creatures went, the wheels went beside them . . . for the spirit of the living creatures was in the wheels—Ezek. 1:19-20

FRIEND OR FOE OF MENTAL HEALTH?

For better or for worse, organizational work and administration are involved, to some degree, in everything a church does. Many ministers see such activities as burdensome necessary evils which must be tolerated. Frequently, the recent seminary graduate collides

---

[1] "The Minister: Pastor or Promoter," *Pastoral Psychology* (September, 1957), p. 13.

head-on with an unpleasant fact—that he *is* the executive and administrator of a complex organization. This role greedily gobbles huge chunks of his time and energy. Having entered the ministry to "help people" and/or "serve God" through preaching, teaching, counseling, and pastoral work, he finds to his dismay that he is expected to "keep the machine running." He spends hour after hour each week in administrative chores—attending meetings, raising the budget, recruiting youth leaders, pushing the latest "emphasis" from headquarters, pouring oil on a leader's ruffled feelings, arranging to get the church roof fixed, and helping to plan for the community 4th of July celebration.

"How," the harassed young minister asks himself, "can I do all these things and still find time to prepare inspiring sermons, minister to a host of sick and disturbed persons, keep 'spiritually ready' through reading and prayer, and still be a reasonably adequate husband and father?" Emotionally, spiritually, and physically exhausted at the end of a typical week, he sees the ministry as a reflection of Ezekiel's vision—wheels within wheels. In response to the administrative rat race, some men leave the ministry. Others grit their teeth, get a larger appointment book, and endure the whirl. Fortunately, others find ways of decreasing the frustrations of administration by streamlining their efficiency as executives and utilizing the pastoral opportunities which inhere in every situation involving people.

In his study of Protestant clergymen [2] sociologist Samuel Blizzard found that the average minister spends nearly two-fifths of his time in administration and another tenth on organization (working with organizations, recruiting leaders, and so forth.) The study indicated that these were the functions which the ministers enjoyed least and felt most inadequately prepared to handle. Think of it—spending half one's time doing things which are unsatisfying, if not distasteful! Given these feelings, adminstrative work is done without enthusiasm and often with mediocre results which serve to confirm the negative evaluation attached to this work at the outset.

Considering how much time ministers and lay leaders invest in administrative activities it is important that whatever creative potential they hold be realized in practice. The way a church is organ-

[2] "The Minister's Dilemma," *The Christian Century* (April 25, 1956), pp. 508-9.

ized and administered actually has a great deal to do with its impact on mental health. Contrast the experiences which members of a failing, fragmented church have with those in a vigorous, united congregation. The minister's leadership in guiding, inspiring, and stimulating the growth of vibrant organizational life geared to meeting the needs of the maximum number of people is one of his major contributions to mental health. By providing effective leadership, he can help increase the overall vitality of the church organism which, in turn, gives each member a lift. Through counseling, a minister can help a maximum of several score individuals in a given year. Through creative leadership of the total church, he can help enrich the lives of several hundreds or more in the same period. A minister who neglects his role as leader of a religious community is sacrificing an opportunity to help create a redemptive fellowship which, as an organism, can become the instrument of healing and growth. If, on the other hand, he makes the concept of the church as " a vital outpost of the Kingdom" [3] operational in his ministry, he discovers that the most effective way of meeting the personality needs of the majority of his flock is through vital activities and program. In leading the church program, he finds abundant opportunities to utilize his pastoral skills. The same is true of the laymen who lead church groups.

The focal concern of this chapter is this—*How can the organizational structure and administrative methods of a local church have the maximum positive influence on the growth and health of persons?* This is an extension of the concern of the preceding chapter. Organization and administration have to do with the group life of the church, particularly work and service groups.

THE HEART AND GOAL OF CHURCH ADMINISTRATION

Unfortunately the terms "administrator" and "executive" have a metallic, manipulative ring, suggesting for most people the image of the organization man in a grey flannel suit. Even the term "pastoral director," in contrast to the intent of its originators, has a manipulative, managerial flavor. Because of the ubiquity of the big business image in our culture, administrative words in general carry a freight of negative overtones. Somehow, in the church, we must

[3] I am indebted to James Ashbrook for this phrase.

transcend the verbal symbols to capture a rich appreciation of the office of leader, builder, and shepherd of a redemptive community.

The heart and essence of church administration are interpersonal relationships! Church "machinery" is simply the organizational vehicle through which people relate with a certain continuity. The jaundiced look which some people cast at the church institution is appropriate only if the institution's fundamental purpose—to provide channels for serving individuals—has been forgotten and the institution has become an end in itself. Since the church "majors" in people, it needs to be keenly alert to the influence on personality of the way its machinery operates. Methods, programs, goals, and structures should be continually reevaluated in the light of the ultimate purpose of a church's organizational-administrative activities: *The development of a redemptive fellowship in which the maximum number of persons can grow in their love of God and neighbor!* "Organization exists to help the church in its work of developing Christian persons and a Christian society." [4]

In all social movements, organizational values tend to replace original goals. This hardening of institutional arteries has occurred repeatedly in the history of the church. As Robert Lee puts it, after *doxology* (the initial religious experience) comes *theology* (systematic teachings about the experience) and then *sociology* (the attempt to preserve the experience through organization). As he sees it, the organizational dilemma of the church is that the very institutional forms necessary for the church to carry on its work continually threaten to distort and obscure the fundamental purpose for which the institution was founded. [5]

In evaluating church machinery, it is useful to distinguish means and ends. Organizations, programs, and committees are means which should be evaluated in terms of the degree to which they contribute to or detract from the ends of fulfillment of persons and redemption of society. Certain administrative approaches actually contradict these basic purposes of the church. For example, a Madison-Avenue type professional fund-raiser used high-pressure, coercive techniques

[4] Lee J. Gable (ed.), *Encyclopedia for Church Group Leaders* (New York: Association Press, 1959), p. 541.

[5] "The Organizational Dilemma in American Protestantism," *Union Seminary Quarterly Review* (November, 1960), pp. 9-10.

in a certain church's building-fund drive. These methods were in direct conflict with the respect-for-persons orientation of a Christian church's philosophy. Another example is the contradiction between a church's goal of enhancing family life and its organizational tendency to fragment families through the many family-separating activities in its program.

THE NEED FOR PERSON-RESPECTING EFFICIENCY

If the kingdom were going to come by way of committee meetings, it would have arrived long ago. The weekly schedule of many churches mirrors the frantic activism of American life in general. Thoreau's sage advice to his readers regarding the overall patterns of their lives—"simplify, simplify!"—could be applied to church organizational structures with salutary effects. One reason church administration is frustrating is that many churches are organizational monstrosities—ecclesiastical Wahlstrom's wonders. Streamlining the church's program and machinery is the job of a planning conference composed of top-level laymen and the minister. Their guiding principle should be to have the least amount of machinery necessary to achieve their church's goal. They should apply this test with incisiveness: *Does this administrative procedure or this part of our organizational structure contribute to our church's effectiveness in increasing love of God and neighbor and in redeeming society?*

Just as there is no justification for administrative top-heaviness, there is no excuse for slovenly methods. Efficient administration requires less energy and leaves more time for other pastoral duties than inefficient administration. To illustrate, a minister who keeps haphazard pastoral records, triples his headaches and paper work when report time arrives. As churches increase in size, administrative efficiency becomes more and more imperative. Christian laymen who are also efficiency-oriented business executives can render invaluable help in improving their church's fund-raising, record-keeping, and business procedures which often consume an inordinate amount of time. Ministers can well afford to learn from laymen in this area, and to delegate much of the responsibility to those who find satisfaction in making this their lay witness.

In the church, efficiency should never become an end in itself at the expense of persons. The "efficient" methods of the professional

175

fund-raising mentioned above were not really efficient from the church's standpoint, since they conflicted with the very values for which a church exists.

Good administration includes seven functions.[6] Ineffectiveness is usually the result of faulty work in one or more of these areas:

(a) *Planning.* This includes choosing goals and developing the means by which the goals can be achieved. Many church groups short-circuit this process. Broad sharing in planning is important. (b) *Organizing.* It is wise to use existing organization in implementing plans whenever feasible. (c) *Executing.* Someone must see that the plans, as formulated, are carried out through the appropriate organizational structure. (d) *Supervising.* This includes training workers, boosting morale, coaching, and revising plans which prove to be faulty. (e) *Coordinating.* Communication is essential in coordinating the many facets of church activity. Morale will suffer if groups work at cross purposes. In larger churches it is especially crucial to keep communication lines open and coordination procedures operative. (f) *Publicizing.* The goal should be that of interpreting the church's program so that the maximum number will know about it, understand it, and be attracted to support it. Many churches hide their lights under the bushel of poor publicity. Skilled laymen in the communication arts can help here. (g) *Evaluating.* Opportunity for grass-roots participation in the evaluation and replanning process can do wonders for the spirit of a church group. Taking an active part in such a process is good for the mental health of members. The use of post-meeting evaluation sheets following a Lenten study series, for example, permits broad participation and helps keep program planning relevant to the needs and interests of the members.

Gene E. Bartlett tells of a conversation years ago with his father who, at that time, had completed twenty-five years in the ministry. His father said: " 'In these years I have discovered that the number of people who will be changed by an idea inculcated through my preaching is comparatively small. But the number of people who will grow when they are put to work in the church is comparatively

---

[6] Adapted from Lee J. Gable, *Encyclopedia for Church Group Leaders,* pp. 546-48.

large.' " [7] Committee meetings may be, as James Ashbrook points out, "oases of fellowship in deserts of loneliness" for some people. Sharing with others in significant projects often develops as a by-product a deeper sense of Christian community than do direct efforts to create "fellowship." A person-centered committee or organization has an esteem-enhancing effect on its members. For persons caught in routine occupations with little or no opportunity to take initiative or express their personalities the opportunity to "speak their piece" and participate in "running the show," is deeply satisfying.[8] This helps immeasurably to overcome the depersonalized feelings of our mass culture. Growth, like learning, occurs through participation.

CHURCH ADMINISTRATION AS PASTORAL CARE

At a meeting of professors of pastoral care in Berkeley, California, in 1960, Paul Morentz, a psychiatrist, Lutheran minister, and seminary teacher suggested that the future of pastoral care is in creative church administration. I find a good deal of validity in this assertion. A minister (or lay group leader) should utilize a pastoral (shepherding) approach to every phase of his work. If he does this, administration becomes an important form of pastoral care affording him frequent opportunities to touch the lives of persons in helping, healing ways. Bartlett puts his finger on the key issue:

The question is whether the minister becomes an executive who occasionally functions as a pastor, or remains a pastor who also functions as an executive. . . . As long as a man remains a pastor in all his relationships, whether preaching, or calling or sitting on a committee, he will find that all of these things can become means of ministry.[9]

A pastoral administrator (or lay leader) can employ profitably whatever sensitivity he has derived from counseling training. His awareness of interpersonal dynamics is a distinct asset in selecting leaders and in the constructive handling of situations involving conflict. His knowledge of group dynamics can be used in leadership training and in assisting groups which are stalemated be-

[7] Bartlett, "The Minister: Pastor or Promoter," p. 12.
[8] James B. Ashbrook, "Creative Church Administration," *Pastoral Psychology* (October, 1957), pp. 12-13.
[9] Bartlett, "The Minister: Pastor or Promoter," p. 15.

cause of personality factors. The wise pastoral administrator gives moral support and is available as a resource person, but he avoids "carrying the ball" for a group.

Implied in the previous discussion is the idea that there should be a mutually beneficial reciprocity between pastoral counseling and pastoral administration.[10] Counseling skills contribute immensely to creative administration. On the other hand, administration opens doors to counseling opportunities, both formal and informal. Precounseling often occurs in administrative contacts and organizational relationships. Working beside the minister on a committee allows a burdened person to size him up and decide whether to approach him for help. The minister whose interpersonal radar is sensitive can often spot subtle distress signals sent up unwittingly in the course of such meetings. If he suspects that a certain individual is hurting, he can make himself more psychologically accessible to that person by means of a series of pastoral calls.

A minister is the leader of a segment of the total Christian community. The question is not whether he will be an executive, but what kind—weak or strong, rigid or flexible, inhibiting or releasing. The now familiar term "pastoral director" (in spite of the semantic limitations of "director"), is a fruitful one, as it relates to church administration as pastoral care. The minister is a leader of leaders just as he is a teacher of teachers and a counselor of counselors. The term "director" has the advantage of emphasizing the need for active leadership in the mode of a coach or orchestra conductor. (Perhaps "pastoral coach" or "pastoral conductor" would be happy alternatives to pastoral director.) Democratic leadership does not mean indecisive leadership. Studies in industrial psychology have shown that weak executive leadership has a deleterious influence on company morale, as does authoritarian leadership.

The concept "pastoral director" also implies the distribution of leadership. By developing a team of well-trained, dedicated lay leaders, a minister lightens what would otherwise be an unbearable load on himself. He also enhances the growth rate of his people and allows his church to do a better job through utilizing their "diversity of gifts."

[10] This point is discussed illuminatingly in the Bartlett article cited above.

The model of the orchestra conductor is a pregnant one for the pastoral director's self-image. By instructing, coordinating, and inspiring, a skilled conductor helps his musicians produce the best music of which they are collectively capable. He must be sensitive to feedback from the players and must provide them with opportunities to express their own unique talents at appropriate times in a production. In addition, he must restrain the prima donnas and help integrate their contributions in ways that enhance the total performance.

The ways in which a minister utilizes his laymen will have an impact on their mental health and his. If they are treated as pawns to serve ends which he alone or his ecclesiastical superiors have chosen, the minister will soon encounter a psychological barrier of diminishing leadership returns. On the other hand, if laymen are regarded as full partners in the kingdom enterprise, their growing leadership potential will be released. They will sense whether or not their minister really believes in the mutual ministry of all Christians.

The process of distributing the leadership function to help a congregation mature is not easy. As James Ashbook puts it, "The central difficulty is to effect the transition from a dependent relationship to one of mutual interaction and responsibility." [11] Many congregations are conditioned by generations of minister-dominated administration to run to the current minister for "the word" on all manner of major and minor issues. This dependence is antithetical to responsible adult behavior. The follow-the-leader pattern tends to be a self-perpetuating, vicious cycle. The more a person succumbs to it, the less adequate he is to function as an adult. To be successful, the transition from dependence to interdependence must occur gradually. The attempt by a minister who is new in a church to introduce the distribution of leadership principle quickly is usually abortive. His efforts encounter a wall of hostility derived from having threatened a long-standing parent-child style of relating.

The personality costs of minister-dominated administration are exorbitant, indeed! By encouraging dependency on himself, a minister decreases his people's ability to function as adult decision-

[11] "Creative Church Administration," p. 15.

makers and initiators of action. As Ashbrook points out, covert, if not overt hostility will build up under such an approach:

One of the things which depth psychology has taught us is that dependent people resent their dependence. The hostility may be deeply repressed but it is present. As human beings we cannot give up our capacity for self-direction, under coercion or voluntarily, without feeling angry and frustrated. The parishioner may consciously desire the minister to dictate policy and program, but on a deeper level he resents such suppression of the image of God in him.[12]

Covert hostility is usually expressed in "passive-aggressive" forms. Members quietly sabotage the minister's well-laid plans by dragging their heels, coming late to meetings, "forgetting" essential items, or simply leaving the success of the entire enterprise in the minister's crowded (with dependent parishioners) lap.

The minister's authority role is the key issue in this matter. A committee member's response to the minister is inevitably colored by the member's previous relationships with authority figures. "Transference feelings" may make him submissive, ingratiating, rebellious, or cooperative. As ministers, we tend to encourage the acquiescent and resent the rebellious. But it is as destructive to foster childish dependence as to reject the persistent resister. The members' responses to the minister's authority role constitute one of the minister's opportunities to help them and himself to mature.

METHODS OF DISTRIBUTING LEADERSHIP

Like most other people, the typical minister's feelings toward relinquishing a controlling position are ambivalent. Most of us have a little thirst for power somewhere within us. Techniques designed to broaden a church's leadership base will be effective only if the minister's pro-democracy side outweighs his power motives. If he is deriving major (neurotic) satisfactions from "running the show," his use of democratic techniques will be a half-hearted farce, foredoomed to failure.

With the requisite pastoral wholeheartedness, team planning is a valuable means of distributing the leadership function. A planning conference or retreat to which all the leaders of a church are invited

[12] *Ibid.*, p. 14.

is a good way to accomplish this.[13] Planning for a planning conference should itself be done on a group basis by key leaders. It is desirable to hold the planning conference at a spot away from the local church to encourage continuity of attendance and the growth of fellowship. The uniqueness of a planning retreat is its perspective —allowing participants to obtain a wide-angle overview and to gain enough distance from the mundane details of operating a church program to consider fresh ideas and new directions. It should be a "creative conference" in which there is a minimum of agenda items and a maximum opportunity for thinking creatively about the long-range functions and goals of that church. Questions of short-range tactics should be left for monthly meetings. Instead, consideration should be given to long-range aims and strategies.

The motto of a planning retreat might be "Come, let us reason together." Communication is the heart of effective administration and of "creative conferences." If a conference is large, the frequent use of small groups is indicated to encourage maximum participation in the planning process. Techniques such as role-playing can help to bring parish problems to life in the awareness of the participants. By facilitating the maximum participation in the first stage of administration—planning—such a conference encourages involvement in the other six. Unless people have an opportunity to take part in policy decisions and planning, they cannot be expected to join enthusiastically in implementation.

The "leadership by default" principle used in group therapy is helpful to a minister desiring to escape from the trap of having committees and meetings ubiquitously minister-centered. The principle is that a group of persons ordinarily will not give up a comfortable dependent posture nor use their own potential until they have to, that is, until the leader stops behaving in a leader-centered manner. When asked in a committee meeting to make a decision which should be a corporate one, a minister can say, "I'm interested in what the group feels should be done about this." He can then facilitate the group process by encouraging them to explore the live options and

---

[13] Helpful discussion of procedures for developing democratic leaders is found in L. Howard Grimes, *The Church Redemptive* (Nashville: Abingdon Press, 1958), pp. 163ff, and Gable, *Encyclopedia for Church Group Leaders*, pp. 549ff.

by fulfilling the "group-centered leader" functions described in the last chapter.

Only by getting out of the center of things and helping laymen learn leadership skills can a minister enable his church to avoid the tragic waste of human capabilities so common in churches. By training and distributing leadership, a pastor can help make the "lay renaissance" a reality in his own parish.

Leadership distributing principles should also be applied in denominational circles. Denominational meetings should be experiences of creative planning and inspiration rather than pipelines which attempt (with mixed success) to transmit prefabricated programs to the local churches. Passive-aggressive techniques are used characteristically by parish ministers to block what they perceive as high-handed approaches "from the top." However, if local churches were more imaginative in creating their own programs, denominational agencies would find it less necessary to initiate so many "emphases." Real value does inhere in cooperative planning on both a denominational and ecumenical basis.

THE TROUBLED CHURCH LEADER

C. W. Morris, psychiatrist and active churchman, points out that a ministry of reconciliation is inherent in the constructive handling of church fights.[14] The minister or lay leader needs to understand something of the neurotic conflicts within the individuals who cause them. Thus he may be able to resolve such altercations with a minimum of damage to the church and with constructive effects on the persons involved.

The "obsessive-compulsive" type person often gravitates to positions of church leadership simply because he is "willing" (actually driven) to work incessantly. Such persons are hypercritical of the "laziness" of normal individuals who are not driven by the perfectionistic need to earn the acceptance of others. It takes an unusual measure of compassionate understanding on the minister's part to handle the interpersonal conflicts which result. Many ministers fall into the trap of exploiting the obsessive-compulsives' terror-driven need to work. This allows them to gain strategic positions of leadership in which their anger and fear can wreck havoc in interpersonal

---

[14] "The Terror of Good Works," *Pastoral Psychology* (September, 1957), p. 29.

relationships. Participation in the life of a church does not "cure" the obsessive-compulsive person. However, if he is given a job in which he can channel his problem (keeping precise, detailed records, for instance) , with a minimum of interpersonal contacts, it may help both him and the church.

An obsessive-compulsive Bible student began attending a certain church and immediately made himself unpopular by dominating every discussion with an ostentatious display of knowledge.[15] He could not understand why others did not accept him. Fortunately, the minister was both insightful and redemptive in his approach. First, he got to know this "problem child" well. Behind the man's contentious use of biblical knowledge the minister sensed a cry for acceptance and help. Then he discussed the case confidentially with several of his strongest laymen, asking their help in integrating the man into the life of that church. He suggested that they give the man ample opportunity to air his views in "private hearings." The minister counseled with the laymen during the process helping them see the necessity, however difficult, of patience and kindness. Gradually the man's neurotic defenses were relaxed and, consequently, his objectionable behavior diminished. He eventually became able to lead productive discussions of the Bible in church groups.

In this case laymen and the pastor cooperated in a redemptive ministry which saved a man from rejection (which his anxiety made him invite) for useful service. That such a ministry of reconciliation is very difficult is obvious. That it is what a church should be doing is equally obvious. What often happens in such cases is that the person's neurotic behavior is increased by the anxiety which rejection arouses. He becomes more domineering and resorts to more pontificating which increases the rejection and isolation. The minister's neurotic defenses become involved in the power struggle and the vicious cycle whirls on. In administration, as in counseling, the people who test one's maturity the most severely are the very ones who need it the most desperately.

THE CHURCH STAFF: BATTLEGROUND OR BROTHERHOOD

Church relationships in general demonstrate that the treasure of the gospel is carried in some very earthy vessels. At no point is this

[15] *Ibid.*, pp. 29-31.

more painfully obvious than among church staff members. Intra-staff squabbles are unconducive to either the staff's mental health or that of the congregation.

Understanding the dynamics of these conflicts is the place to start. Nonministerial staff members (secretaries, custodians, and so forth) tend to suffer from low morale because they are underpaid, over-worked, taken for granted, and manipulated by both the minister and aggressive church members. Elementary principles of good em-ployee relationships such as clear-cut job definitions, adequate pay and vacations, hospitalization insurance, retirement benefits, and ap-preciation when deserved, constitute the needed treatment. A church's social witness powder is very damp if it exploits its own workers.

Many factors produce friction among the ministerial staff. In those cases in which the head minister is a prima donna who is in-capable of relating to peers, being aware of their emotional needs, or sharing the limelight, a parade of "assistant ministers" will come and go in rapid succession. What is needed is to replace the narcissist with a minister who has the maturity to build a sense of community in the church, beginning with the staff. But since narcissistic min-isters often appear to be skilled pulpiteers (as judged by some lay-men) and homiletical finesse is usually given top priority by pastoral relations committees, staff effectiveness is frequently sacrificed in-stead.

If the head minister is reasonably mature several things can be done to build good ministerial staff relations. One is to allow every minister on a staff to preach at least occasionally. This will strengthen his status as a "minister" in the congregation's eyes. It will also distribute more equitably the ego food which comes from preach-ing. If the personality-hungers of an assistant minister are unmet, he will tend to become very jealous (consciously or unconsciously) of the preaching minister's weekly feast. Satisfying pastoral func-tions such as weddings and baptisms should also be shared among the ministerial staff, as should the frustrating chores which must be done in any church.

Each minister should have clearly defined areas of responsibility, with recognition on the congregation's part that he is ministerial leader in those areas. A "minister of education," for example, should be the head minister in that area, directly responsible to the church board. Titles such as "assistant minister" and "associate minister" are incompatible with the development of genuine community within a staff, since they connote an inferior status. Titles which describe the area of primary responsibility are much better.

Frequent staff meetings and occasional staff retreats help build a sense of teamwork and iron out frictions before they grow into full-scale fracases. Communication—open and honest—is the pathway to a sense of community. The achievement of this within a staff pays rich dividends. As one experienced minister observed: "The church staff that achieves spiritual maturity infects the congregation with its spirit. Christian insight and practice in a staff lift the life of the church.[16]

THE CHURCH'S OUTREACH

Church administration is simply a means of providing channels for the growth of *koinonia*. A vital aspect of this is the development of ways of reaching and attracting those who need what a church can give. Unfortunately, the word "evangelism" is so loaded with negative connotations for many thoughtful Christians as to limit its usefulness. For them, its overtones are imperialistic (invading the lives of others), revivalistic (connoting intellectual shallowness and emotionalism), and manipulative (pushing people by arousing guilt and fear). For them, the word "evangelist" has lost its root meaning —"bearer of good news."

But somehow the healthy center of the evangelical thrust must be rescued from the mass manipulator and made a vital part of a church's program. If a church is satisfying heart-hungers and contributing to the growth of persons, it should try to offer its ministry to as many as possible of the spiritually hungry people in its community. Unless a church has the spirit of active outreach and sharing, its springs of creativity will dry up in the drought of ingrownness. A church's circle of active concern should include the whole family of

[16] J. E. Carothers, "Disciplines for a Church Staff," *New Christian Advocate*, June, 1959, p. 33.

God. As William T. Ham writes, "The Christian church has a secret at her heart and she wants to share it." [17]

To reach out in service to persons whether or not they join one's church is a vital aspect of this outward thrust. To make the "good news" good to particular persons in need—this is the challenge. Paul M. Miller has produced a resource for helping apply mental health principles to a church's outreach activities.[18] He emphasizes the factors which make a Christian group unique and describes methods of preparing a congregation for "fellowship evangelism."

To contribute to mental health a church's outreach emphasis should have these characteristics: (a) *It should be motivated by the desire to share what each member has found deeply meaningful and to learn from what others have found significant in their lives.* Its spirit should be: "These insights and experiences have brought new life to me and I therefore offer them to you. What have you found that speaks to your condition and from which I can learn?" (b) *Its method should be that of establishing depth relationships with others through which mutual growth can occur.* It should involve bringing people into meaningful relationship with the church fellowship. (c) *It should use attraction rather than coercion, trusting the magnetic power of a need-satisfying fellowship rather than employing guilt-fear motivators.* (d) *The program to attract new members should be only the beginning of a continuing program of education for personal maturity.* By using a modified therapy approach in membership-training groups, new members can become emotionally involved in a meaningful group relationship from the beginning.

CHURCH ADMINISTRATION AND THE BODY OF CHRIST

Anton Boisen, father of the clinical pastoral training movement, points to a "wise observer" who has said in effect that a weakness of psycho-analysis inheres in the fact that it lacks a church—a fellowship of the faithful to help him carry on. However one views this familiar statement it is unquestionably true that from the standpoint of mental health the existence of the ongoing fellowship of a local church is one

---

[17] Casteel, *Spiritual Renewal Through Personal Groups* (New York: Association Press, 1957), p. 187.

[18] *Group Dynamics in Evangelism* (Scottsdale, Pa.: Herald Press, 1958); see also *Pastoral Evangelism* by Samuel Southard (Nashville: Broadman Press, 1962).

of the most significant facts about it. If this fellowship even begins to approximate a quality of relationships which can be described as "Christian," that fellowship becomes an open channel for the living Spirit. The renewal and growth which occurs within its fabric of relationships is clear evidence that that church is, in fact, a part of the Body of Christ, ministering to lonely, troubled persons at their point of greatest need. Creative church administration by ministers and laymen can help to provide such an organism through which the Spirit can be expressed in the world.

CHAPTER 9
Fostering Mental Health by Strengthening Family Life

The family is the basic unit of growth and experience, fulfillment or failure. It is also the basic unit of illness and health.[1]—Nathan W. Ackerman.

And the rain fell, and the floods came, and the winds blew and beat upon that house, but it did not fall, because it had been founded on the rock—Matt. 7:25

THE FOUNDATIONS OF MENTAL HEALTH

A church's basic contribution to fostering positive mental health and preventing mental illness is what it does to strengthen family life. Personality is homegrown. The family is the garden in which every new personality is created and grows. Here the roots of mental health are established in some and the roots of mental illness in others. Whatever a church can do to increase the adequacy of parents and the richness of family life will have a direct, positive effect on the mental health of its people. The minister's continuing face-to-face relationship with the families who compose his parish gives him a strategic role in the matter.

From birth to age ten, the average child is under direct home influence nearly ninety-five percent of the time, at school only five percent and at Sunday school or church less than one half of one percent. For every hour a school-age child spends in church, he spends thirty at school and 137 at home. It is obvious that the de-

---

[1] *The Psychodynamics of Family Life* (New York: Basic Books, Inc., 1958), p. 15.

cisive factor in laying the foundations for future personality health is the health of today's homes. A church's most potent impact on the mental health of children is its positive influence on parents. Parents hold the key to the doorway leading to a bright, mentally healthy future for their children.

This chapter will center on the question, *How can a church's family life program make the maximum contribution to the growth and health of persons?* The goal of such a program is to help create in all the homes of a parish that quality of relationship through which persons of all ages can grow toward their God-intended fulfillment by having their basic personality needs satisfied. Through positive family life the basic "foods of the spirit" (described in Chap. 6) are made available to infants, children, youth, and adults. The adequacy of this spiritual nutrition determines the emotional growth rate and the degree of personality health produced in that family.

THE FAMILY AS AN ORGANISM

To understand the absolute importance of the family in influencing personality health it is helpful to see the family as an interpersonal organism. A family consists of an organic network of complex social, economic, and psychological interdependencies. Psychiatrist Nathan W. Ackerman has shown that a family possesses these qualities of an organism—it has functional unity; it is a living developing process; and it has a natural life history.[2]

As in the case of an individual organism, a family has definite growth stages and critical transition periods. One student of family life delineates seven periods: (a) Beginning families; (b) families with preschool children, (c) families with school children, (d) families with adolescents; (e) launching families; (f) middle-aged families; (g) aging families.[3] What appears to be the same family is actually a different family at each stage of its life history. Different interaction, pressures, roles, satisfactions, and self-images are found among its members. The continuing health of a family organism depends, to a considerable degree, on whether it can make the

[2] My discussion in this section draws heavily on Nathan W. Ackerman's approach in *The Psychodynamics of Family Life*, pp. 15-25.

[3] Evelyn M. Duvall, *Family Development* (New York: J. P. Lippincott Co., 1957).

necessary adaptive changes as it moves from stage to stage. A church's family-life program should develop a strategy for helping families in each of the seven stages meet the special challenges of that stage creatively.

The humanness and identity of a child are developed within the family matrix. Each family has a unique emotional climate which, though constantly in flux, provides the psychological environment within which personality develops. At birth, a child has no self, no personality, only the hereditary potentialities for developing a personality. In the give and take of day-to-day family interaction, the personhood of the child emerges and is molded by the family organism. His personal identity and his ways of relating to others are derived from and will always be linked to the identity and relationship patterns of his family-of-origin. If the fundamental relational pattern satisfies the heart-hungers of family members to an adequate degree, their personality-health will be robust. The mental health of children flourishes when the need-satisfying adults around them are mentally healthy.

It is impossible to exaggerate the profundity of the impact of the family's dominant relationship pattern on the personality development of all its members. It influences everything about their personalities—their anxiety levels, choice of defenses against anxiety, perceptions of reality, models of success and failure, their roles, self-images, conflict patterns, values and life goals. The identity and behavior of each is influenced by all the others in a kind of positive or negative complementarity. Negative complementarity is evident in the sick family organism in which one member is unconsciously "chosen" by the family to be the "black sheep" or mentally ill member. If the black sheep reforms or the ill member recovers, another family member often takes his place. The deviant or mentally disturbed member satisfies some hidden need in the inner dynamics of the family organism. A striking illustration of this is the manner in which some "respectable" parents of delinquents unconsciously use their children to obtain vicarious gratification of their own forbidden destructive or sexual impulses. In short, most personality illness becomes intelligible when understood as a manifestation of a disturbed family organism. Conversely, to a considerable degree an

190

individual's personality strength and health is an expression of the vitality of his original family organism.

ENRICHING HUSBAND-WIFE RELATIONSHIPS

The emotional health of today's families was profoundly influenced by the experiences which these parents had as children and youth in yesterday's families. Emotional illness and health tends to be transmitted from one generation to the next over bridges of parent-child relationships. The health of the families of the next generation is already being deeply influenced by the experiences of children in present-day homes.

Though difficult, it is possible to interrupt the transgenerational process by which emotional problems are transmitted. Based on his extensive experience with troubled families, Ackerman declares: "Under optimal conditions it is possible to achieve a level of positive emotional health beyond that which characterized the families-of-origin. The younger generations of parents may raise healthier children than the older one, even while overreacting against their parents' 'mistakes.' " [4]

Many experiences beyond the parental home have influenced parents since their childhood. Hopefully these enriched their lives and enhanced their resources for raising healthier children. The church with a dynamic family life emphasis becomes this kind of broadening-strengthening influence in the lives of scores of parents and potential parents.

The personal identities which two people bring to a marriage are never fully formed. Each is attracted to the other by deep yearnings, including the yearning to complete himself through psychological union. Maleness is completed by femaleness and vice versa. A new identity emerges from the complementing interaction between the psychological worlds which the partners bring to the marriage. This new marital-pair identity is not simply the sum of their two personalities, although it incorporates many aspects of each. It is a new creation resulting from the ways each unique personality interacts with the other. A good marriage relationship has dimensions of health and strength which neither could possess alone. The marriage-pair identity provides a new base from which personal growth

[4] *The Psychodynamics of Family Life,* p. 22.

can occur. As children arrive, the marriage identity provides the core for the emerging, expanding family identity. The marriage identity is modified by interaction with the children. Fundamentally, the personal identity of the child (his answers to "Who am I and what am I worth?") are shaped by the marriage identity and its derivative, the family identity. If his parents have clear, positive answers (on a feeling level) to the question, "Who are we as individuals and as a couple?," the child will grow a sturdy sense of self-esteem and a solid identity. His self-image will eventually include aspects of the self-images of each of his parents, of their marriage identity, and of the family identity, all combined in his own unique way.

Since the child's personality growth is inextricably bound up with his parents' relationship with each other, it is imperative that that relationship be as strong and well-nourished as possible. If the parents' relationship is impoverished so that their sexual and ego needs are frustrated over long periods of time, they will become unable to satisfy the child's heart-hungers. What is worse, they will tend, through loneliness, to try to satisfy their adult emotional needs in their relationship with the child. This makes the child feel exploited and caught in the cross fire between two people, both of whom are essential in his psychic economy. The woman who uses motherhood as a compensation for failure in wifehood is a case in point. The old saying to the effect that the most important thing a father can do for his child is to love the child's mother (and vice versa) contains an inescapable truth.

One of the ways in which a church program can enrich husband-wife relationships is by providing sound education for marriage beginning with high school youth. Ideally, such long-range preparation should occur in small groups using a modified therapy approach with self-understanding as the major goal. Since personality problems and emotional immaturity rather than lack of information are at the heart of most marriage failures, effective preparation for marriage should place heavy emphasis on feelings, attitudes, and relationships. If young people knew themselves better, they would be less pushed by neurotic needs in their choices of "roommates for life."

Premarital counseling (or better, premarital guidance) should be

192

the culmination of a long preparation-for-marriage process. Pre-marital guidance sessions should have these goals: (a) *Strengthening the bridge of relationship with the minister and the church.* What-ever else happens during the sessions, the minister should do every-thing he can to establish strong rapport with the couple. This will make it easier for them to return to him in the future should they need help. It will also strengthen their link with the church fellow-ship, which can undergird their marriage. (b) *Helping the couple understand the difference between "holy matrimony" and just "get-ting married."* The former is a religious service symbolizing the ways in which both God and the religious community are deeply involved in the marriage relationship. The ceremony, understood as the establishment of a sacred covenant, is a significant way of helping a couple enter into the vertical dimension of family life. The emerging identity of a growing family is supported by the larger identity of the religious community. (c) *Reducing the couple's anxieties about the mechanics of the ceremony by providing this information.* This in-struction can free their minds for more vital considerations. (d) *Supplying the couple with whatever information they may desire related to achieving a strong, satisfying marriage relationship,* in-cluding information about sex, finances, in-laws, children, planned parenthood, religion, and so forth. This is basically a seed-planting operation (as in Jesus' parable of the sower). Only a small part of the information will fall on the receptive soil of the couple's sense of need. (e) *Giving them at least a taste of the experience of increas-ing their awareness of their relationship.* Acquaintance with what Reuel Howe calls the "language of relationship" can point them in the direction of growth. By encouraging the couple to reflect on the new spiritual entity which they are beginning by establishing the core of a family, the growth of their sense of couple-identity is stimulated. (f) *Helping acquaint them with the importance of recog-nizing and satisfying emotional needs*—each other's and their chil-dren's. This should encourage them to see marriage as a relationship which must be worked at if it is to grow. (g) *Offering the couple the opportunity for more extended counseling,* before or after the ceremony if they desire it or if serious emotional problems are evident. A minimum of three premarital sessions should be held with every couple.

Following the wedding, the minister should help the couple become involved *as a couple* in meaningful church activities. Worshiping together, sharing in a *koinonia* group, or enjoying the fellowship of a young couples club—these and other activities can provide food for a growing husband-wife church relationship.

A California church invited couples who had been married within the past two years to a series of four informal meetings to discuss their relationships. The minister led the group of five couples who responded. Their problems proved to be mainly the "grinding of the gears" type, typical of the adjustment period of new marriages. In the second session, the minister suggested that they role-play a potential conflict situation—forgetting a spouse's birthday—and then discuss how they would handle it. As the couples shared their feelings about their marriages, rapport developed among them, permitting deeper communication. After the series, several of the participants reported that greater openness of communication within their marriages had resulted from the group experience.

A family-centered church program should include a variety of couple activities, without children. Parents need to recharge their batteries by enjoying each other and relating to other adults. Children can be appreciated most if family togetherness is judiciously balanced with apartness.

EDUCATION FOR POSITIVE PARENTHOOD

Effective on-the-job training for parents can make a valuable contribution to family mental health. Here are some of the goals of parent education:

(1) To help parents enjoy and believe in their children.

(2) To strengthen their feeling of adequacy as parents.

(3) To help them enjoy their marriage more.

(4) To increase their self-understanding, including understanding of themselves in their roles as parents and marriage partners.

(5) To increase their understanding of the "ages and stages" of themselves and their children.

(6) To enhance their ability to recognize and satisfy the emotional hungers of their children and each other.

Psychiatrist Harry Stack Sullivan once called for "the teaching of every parent the fact that children do not grow like green plants on chemicals activated by solar energy, or in any other way that may be taken for granted, but rather by assimilating ideas and examples given them by significant elders. Parents must be made to see that children are . . . held in trust as future members of the community." [5]

To achieve these goals, parent education needs to have parents' hearts as well as their heads as targets. Discussions of handling a child's anger constructively should be accompanied by small-group opportunities for the parents to work through their own feelings in this area (which is so vital to mental health). This, of course, takes time and skilled leadership. Open discussion of the parents' feelings about sex should also be encouraged in good parent education. If a parent is stiff and anxious in discussing sex with his child, no supply of enlightened ideas will make it a constructive experience. Attitudes toward sex and anger are usually too deeply rooted to be altered radically by modified therapy approaches. However, it is possible and valuable for parents to achieve heightened awareness of these deeper feelings. This awareness can help them minimize the negative effects of the feelings, by discussing them openly with the child. The fact that a parent is able to talk with candor about his uneasiness in discussing sex helps to protect the child from the subtle contagion of such anxiety-loaded attitudes.

Much parent education focuses too much on content and children, and too little on parents and their feelings. Of course, it is more comfortable to talk about the former than the latter. Unfortunately, the frequent result is to heighten the parents' unproductive self-consciousness, making them awkward with their children because they are afraid of "breaking the rules" of child-rearing. To lessen this response, the resource person in a child-study group should emphasize the importance of the general tone of relationships in a family and point out that there is no one "right way" of rearing children. A cartoon depicted a pair of preteen boys reading a book entitled "Your Child." One is saying to the other, "Boy! This *next* phase we go through is a *dilly!*" Something of this light touch in

[5] Discussion of "The Psychiatry of Enduring Peace and Social Progress," by G. B. Chisholm, *Psychiatry* (February, 1946), p. 44.

handling the often-somber data of "child psychology" is needed in parent education to reduce the threat resulting from overevaluation of such writings.

Most couples acquire the sense of need which will allow them to learn from parent education only after the first child is on the way. Groups for expectant parents have been used effectively in some churches. If a low birth rate in a particular church makes it unfeasible to hold such a series periodically, and if no community agency sponsors classes for expectant parents, it is wise for the pastor to meet with the couples separately to help prepare them for their demanding new roles. Whether it is done in small groups or couple-by-couple, pastoral preparation of expectant parents should emphasize the emotional needs of infants, a subject which physicians often do not emphasize adequately. A book like Margaretha Ribble's *The Rights of Infants* [6] or Dorothy Baruch's chapter on "Better Beginnings" in *New Ways in Discipline*,[7] are valuable resources in this area. The husband and wife should both be encouraged to discuss their feelings about themselves and each other as expectant parents. These feelings often conflict and are disturbing to the marriage. Representing the concern of the religious community for them and their soon-to-be-born child is a part of the minister's responsibility. This helps to undergird their lives during this period of stress.

The next natural opportunity for continuing parent education arises during the pastoral call which should occur soon after the child is born. Like all pastoral calls, this should be for more than a social visit. The couple should be given ample opportunity to articulate their feelings about themselves and their baby. Arrangements can be made for infant baptism (or dedication, as the case may be), and the couple may be urged to participate in a group for new parents, and/or in the broader parent-education program. Carefully selected pamphlets or books on the psychological needs of infants can be presented to the couple. A pastoral prayer of thanksgiving is a natural and essential part of such a call in most cases.

It is well for the minister to be alert to the marital problems which sometimes result from pregnancy and childbirth. Marriages based on adolescent romance are often severely shaken by these events. Emo-

[6] *The Rights of Infants* (New York: Columbia University Press, 1943).
[7] *New Ways in Discipline*, pp. 85 ff.

tional immaturities come to the surface of the marriage. Occasionally husbands have affairs around this time because they cannot tolerate the anxiety of being married to a mother, because they are jealous (unconsciously) of their wife's biological creativity, or because they cannot tolerate sharing their wife's attention with an infant competitor (which revives old sibling rivalries). If the minister senses serious problems such as these, or if the baby is handicapped, he should help the couple work through their difficulties or find other professional counseling.

Prebaptismal counseling offers a splendid opportunity for continuing the parent-education process. It is unfortunate that relatively few churches utilize this natural opportunity to the full. In one survey of clergymen, only half reported holding any regular interviews with parents of children about to be baptized.[8] It is my experience that prebaptismal sessions tend to be more fruitful, from both educational and counseling perspectives, than most premarital sessions. The reason for this is simply that most new parents have a stronger sense of need for help than do typical couples hovered on the brink of matrimony. If the minister and his family life committee plan the prebaptismal sessions with care, they can provide both a major learning experience and an impetus to continuing involvement in the church's parent education program.

Ideally, prebaptismal counseling should take place in groups of from three to seven couples, utilizing a minimum of three sessions of two hours' duration. Here is the way one west-coast church conducted their sessions. The minister led the series of three Sunday afternoon meetings during the month preceding a date set for infant baptisms. Six couples participated. The first session began at the point of the parents' immediate anxiety—the mechanics of their part in the baptismal service. This led into a consideration of the Protestant views of infant baptism and a detailed discussion of the meaning of each step in the ritual. Particular emphasis was given to the vows which the parents would be asked to take. A lively discussion ensued on the question of how parents could implement these vows. In concrete terms, how does a parent lead a child, by

[8] Roy W. Fairchild and John C. Wynn, *Families in the Church: A Protestant Survey* (New York: Association Press, 1961), p. 231.

precept and example, "into the love of God and the service of our Lord Jesus Christ"?

At the close of session one, sections from Reuel Howe's *Man's Need and God's Action* [9] were assigned as "homework." His conception of baptism as "the gift of new relationship" provided an ideal transition to the second session. This dealt with how parents can help young children experience the meaning of the gospel through the "language of relationships" in the family. The leader pointed out that it is impossible to separate the physical, psychological, and spiritual needs of infants. He then presented Erik Erikson's illuminating concept, "basic trust" [10]—the fundamental feeling that grows in a healthy mother-child relationship during the first year of life. The leader declared, "Your child's most important lessons in religion are the ones he experiences before he learns to talk." This precipitated vigorous group discussion concerning how one communicates love and trust to a baby so that he will have a foundation for later relationships of trust. Several had read *The Rights of Infants* which emphasizes the crucial importance of abundant cuddling, body contact, and sucking. One mother quoted, in effect, Margaretha Ribble's statement that "the parents who shrink in horror from the 'animal' side of life make it impossible for the child to develop the very qualities of intelligence and spirituality that they think they stand for." [11] Several of the parents challenged this view. One of the feelings behind their response eventually came out. It was the feeling of having failed older children who had been treated in ways the parents now recognized as inadequate. The minister indicated that his wife and he had these feelings about their oldest child, but that children are remarkably resilient and that becoming aware of errors in the past often creates the opportunity to make up for them in the present. [12]

The third meeting was used by the parents to discuss problems in child rearing and to compare experiences. Among the points which were raised was an emphasis on the importance of the father's being

[9] *Man's Need and God's Action* (New York: The Seabury Press, 1953).

[10] Erik H. Erikson, *Childhood and Society* (New York: W. W. Norton & Co., 1950), pp. 219-22.

[11] *The Rights of Infants*, p. 110.

[12] Dorothy W. Baruch makes this helpful point in *New Ways in Sex Education* (New York: McGraw-Hill Book Company, 1959), p. xv.

involved in caring for the baby and on the necessity of keeping the marriage relationship growing during this period of pressure. The entire group was urged by the Family Life Committee chairman to join in the church's ongoing child study and family life program. The minister indicated that these three sessions were only an introduction and that the church had a continuing interest in helping the parents implement their baptismal vows and in enriching the lives of all of its families. This final session was closed with a period of devotions in which the key ideas discussed during the series were brought together in the spirit of gratitude for the high privilege of being cocreators with God.

The period between birth and starting public school is the time when the basic structure of a child's personality is established. As indicated in Chap. 6, these years constitute the period during which effective parent education can have its most decisive impact. A community's churches have an open pathway to more families in this crucial period than all the other community agencies combined. What a tragic waste of a superb opportunity when, as often happens, a church loses contact with a family for several years following a child's baptism! Reaching and influencing parents in this age group should have highest priority among the goals of a church's family life committee!

The "Child-Study Nursery Group" described in Chap. 7 is an illustration of how a modified therapy approach can be used in a continuing group for parents of preschoolers. In a larger church it is possible and desirable to have at least two groups of this kind divided on the basis of the children's ages. Children change rapidly during the preschool years, as do the interests and problems of their parents. Continuing long-term groups are valuable because they build strong, supportive relationships among their members. But there is also value in short-term (three to ten meetings) parent-education groups focused on particular age groups or problems.

Each stage of life has its own particular "developmental task," the accomplishment of which is essential to the maintenance of vigorous mental health. An overview of the changing needs and growth challenges of each period of life provides a useful format for structuring a comprehensive family life program. Erikson's widely used "Eight

199

Stages of Man" [13] can be helpful to sophisticated parent groups in understanding their own as well as their children's evolving needs. Translating some of Erikson's psychoanalytic language facilitates communication.

Stage	Approxi-mate age	Radius of significant relations	Person needs to achieve	Negative alternative
I	Birth to 15 mo.	Maternal person	Basic trust	Basic mistrust
II	15 mo. to 2½ yrs.	Parents	Autonomy	Shame and doubt
III	2½ (or 3) to 6 (or 7)	Basic family	Initiative	Guilt
IV	6 (or 7) to puberty	Neighbor-hood, school	Industry	Inferiority
V	Puberty to 20	Peer group, leader models	Identity	Identity diffusion
VI	Young adult-hood	Partners in friendship, sex, cooper-ation	Intimacy	Isolation
VII	Middle Adulthood	Divided labor and shared household	Generativity	Stagnation
VIII	Later years	Mankind	Ego integrity	Despair

A closer look at the developmental goal of each stage is now in order. Basic trust is the deep feeling that existence is trustworthy and worthwhile. It results from the warmth and dependability of the mother-infant psychological bond (see Chap. 3). Autonomy, the life task of stage 2, is the child's realization that he is a separate en-

[13] *Childhood and Society*, pp. 219-33ff; see also "Identity and the Life Cycle," *Psychological Issues*, Vol. I, No. 1, 1959.

tity from the mother and that this is basically good. During the third stage (called the "oedipal phase" by Freud), a child normally develops a sensuous attachment to the parent of the opposite sex. This is a crucial preparation for eventual happiness in marriage. To illustrate, a little girl in a healthy family discovers in the warmth and strength of her father that it is a good, safe thing to relate to males. The same applies to boys in their relationships with their mothers during this stage. The term "initiative" refers to the feeling that it is good to be oneself in a thrusting, possessing way.

Experiencing a warm oedipal attachment between three and six years is essential to normal development. But since it consists of wanting the parent of the opposite sex entirely to oneself, it both raises fears of the same-sex parent and comes into conflict with the child's love for that parent. This dilemma is normally resolved around six or seven when the child relinquishes his oedipal wishes and identifies with the same-sex parent. During the next state (called "latency") a boy learns to feel and behave in male ways as he perceives them in his father. His identity as a male person is shaped decisively as he joins all-male groups and experiments with male roles. During this period, he normally learns to work and produce, mastering the use of certain tools and savoring the satisfactions of diligence and of the successful completion of a project. The developmental goal of this stage is a sense of industry, the solid awareness that he can accomplish things.

Stage five, adolescence, is the period of the identity crisis when a youth struggles to gain a firm sense of who he is as a person, separate from his parents. The dependence-independence ambivalence is often acute during this period. During adolescence, oedipal feelings toward the parent of the opposite sex are reactivated. Normally these are resolved by being transferred to others of that sex and eventually to a marital partner.

The goal of young adulthood (stage six) is the establishment of intimacy—psychological and sexual closeness to others. During this period, persons marry, establishing what Gibson Winter calls a "covenant of intimacy." They produce children and the cycle begins again, while the growth stages continue in the parents. Having developed the capacity for intimacy, young adults enter the mature years with the ability to bear responsibility and achieve their maximum productivity. The developmental task of this stage (seven) is to realize their creative potential and to achieve what Erikson calls "generativity," the investment of themselves in the coming generation, and in the currents of education, art, and science. If this is not achieved, they turn in upon themselves in personal stagnation. Between forty-five and fifty-five most couples face the challenge of establishing a new kind of family identity minus children in the home. This tests the inner vitality of the marriage relationship. The "crisis of middle-age" is often acute for women because of the near-simultaneous occurrence of menopause, death of parents, children leaving the home, and the confrontation with inescapable signs of aging. The crisis for men centers on fear of aging (and death) coupled with feelings of not having realized the dreams of youth in vocational achievement.

Successful resolution of the growth crisis of each stage is dependent on adequately handling the previous stages. Ego integrity, the goal of the eighth stage, is the fruit of psychological success in the previous seven stages. It is the means by which one handles constructively the awareness of aging and inevitable death. The essence of ego integrity is experiencing oneself as a center of meaning and value. In the presence of this experience, death loses its sting. During the second half of life the Jungian emphasis on the necessity of discovering inner meanings, values, and creativity is another way of approaching the same truth. Certainly a church has a vital role in helping middle-aged and older persons achieve the essential reorientation of their lives from centering mainly in the outer world to finding rich satisfaction in the world of the spirit.

The lifelong process through which individuals and families pass can be understood as the evolution and fulfillment of the capacity to love. Evelyn M. Duvall [14] describes the development of love as a ladder on which the first rung is the narcissistic, self-love of the infant. Successive rungs upward include parent-child love (the primary focus shifting from one to the other), sibling love (and rivalry), affection for playmates, acquisition of "best friend," attraction to the opposite sex, selection of a marriage partner, devotion to

[14] Evelyn Millis Duvall, *Facts of Life and Love for Teen-Agers* (New York: Popular Library ed., 1953), pp. 138ff.

one's children, and altruistic love for mankind. The flowering of the capacity to love occurs most readily in the social womb of the family. Wholeness in the capacity to love is identical with the flowering of mental health. Tillich describes the theological dimension of this process: "Man can love himself in terms of self-acceptance only if he is certain that he is accepted. . . . Only in the light and in the power of the 'love from above' can he love himself." [15] It is this vertical reinforcing of the horizontal love relationships in a family that is religion's unique contribution to family life.

There is something precious about the empathic understanding of their children (and each other) which parents often acquire through family life groups. Before moving across the country with the family one mother was concerned about the effects of the move on her six-year-old. Fortunately, she had learned, in a parents' group, to listen to her child. One day she overheard him carrying on an animated conversation with a caterpillar on a tree branch outside his window. He began, "Mr. Caterpillar, would you like to move to a new house?" She felt an inner glow as she realized that he was playing out his unhappy feelings, as all healthy children do. She sat silently, sharing in the God-given healing process by which a child copes with life.

DEVELOPING POSITIVE ATTITUDES TOWARD SEX

Sex, as Freud made crystal clear, is a powerful, ubiquitous phenomenon in human life with profound effects on mental health. One of the church's major contributions to mental health is to help youth and adults appreciate sex as one of God's best gifts, to be used appropriately, like all his gifts. Reuel Howe speaks from both a psychological and Christian perspective when he says: "The power of the sex drive springs from the longing of the incomplete being for completion. . . . a divided creation groans and suffers, longing for union and fulfillment. The union longed for, however, is more than sexual. It is a longing for personal union of which the sexual is but a part and not the whole." [16] William Genné gives this definition of Christian love: "The overwhelming desire and

[15] Paul Tillich, *Love, Power, and Justice* (New York: Oxford University Press, 1954), p. 121.
[16] Reuel Howe, *The Creative Years* (Greenwich, Conn.: The Seabury Press, 1959), p. 95.

persistent effort of two persons to create for each other the conditions under which each can become the person God meant him to be." Sex finds its delicious fulfillment and life-enhancing beauty only within such a context of mutual love, respect and responsibility. Sex in marriage has at least three vital purposes: (a) *Procreation*—continuing the race and fulfilling ourselves in our children. (b) *Pleasure* —a satisfying sexual relationship adds a dimension of ecstasy and wonder to marriage. (c) *Unification*—a way of overcoming our separateness, of both expressing and strengthening the communion of two spirits. It helps to bring into being what one of T. S. Eliot's characters describes as "The new person—us!"

Basic attitudes and feelings about sex (and the physical side of human life in general) are caught by children in the home. Parents' responses to their child's normal exploratory and pleasure-producing sex play color the child's feelings about sex. The parents' warm appreciation of their own sexual complementarity helps children to realize that sex, when linked with love, is very good. In subtle ways, the parents' positive or negative attitudes toward their own sexual relationships will be communicated to their children. An excellent volume which can enrich the sexual side of a couple's relationship is *Sex in Marriage, New Understandings*.[17] If a couple has serious problems in this area, they should seek professional counseling. In her valuable sex-education guide for parents and teachers, *New Ways in Sex Education*, Dorothy W. Baruch writes: "This is the aim of sex education: to find full-hearted and full-bodied satisfactions in mature and warm mutuality, securely entered into and happily complete. The END and AIM of sex education is developing one's FULLEST CAPACITY for LOVE." [18]

FAMILY CENTERED CHURCH PROGRAMS

Here is an announcement from a church bulletin:

Premiering the New Family Group: To meet monthly in the gym, from 6:30 to 8:00 p.m., featuring devotions, volleyball, games, films, and occasional potlucks. Bring the whole family.

[17] Dorothy W. Baruch and Hyman Miller (New York: Harper & Row, 1962).
[18] *New Ways in Sex Education*, p. 7.

This is one of many patterns for encouraging family church activities. Such all-family events have the greatest value if they are planned in moderation to avoid burdening the busy schedules of the kinds of families who most often attend such functions.

Family participation in meaningful, enjoyable church activities develops their awareness of the church fellowship as a part of their extended family. Studies have shown that a valid way of measuring the vitality of a given family is to evaluate the strength of its relationships with the circle of friends immediately outside the family. Many students of our culture have pointed to the rootlessness and aloneness of contemporary families. Ackerman observes: "Individual identity requires support from family identity, and family identity in turn requires support from the wider community." [19] The support of the small county-seat town and the clan of nearby relatives is no longer available to most families. This loss contributes to upsetting the equilibrium of family relations, reinforcing internal conflict, and increasing the traumatic impact of family crises. Uprooted and mobile, the contemporary family needs a group where it can find friendship and support quickly. A family-centered church is the best way of meeting this need.

THOSE WITHOUT FAMILIES

The emphasis on couple and family activities raises awkward problems for those without family ties—for example, the nine million Americans who live alone. A strong family-oriented emphasis unwittingly creates an excluding climate which tends to increase the heavy loneliness load of such persons. Meeting the needs of non-family persons is a challenge to any church. In a sense, this is the acid test of a church's person-centeredness. Can its group program be so varied, inclusive, and need-satisfying that it will provide a substitute family for the family-less?

Single people need groups where they can satisfy social needs with other single persons, but they should be included in every other group in which they have an interest. One of the most lively church groups of my acquaintance is composed of single persons from forty to sixty. Most of them are widows, widowers, or single persons who have accepted their singleness. This allows them to relax and enjoy

[19] *The Psychodynamics of Family Life,* p. 21.

social, educational, and service activities together. The group includes enough men to give it an interesting coeducational atmosphere.

WHAT IS A "HAPPY HOME"?

What sort of home tends to grow happy, well-adjusted, emotionally healthy children? A study was made at a state teachers college in Wisconsin of 261 children who seemed to fit this description.[20] They came from all economic and occupational levels and a wide variety of religious, racial, and national backgrounds. The economic advantages which most parents struggle to give their children seemed to be of little importance to the emotional health of the children studied. Fifty-six of the children were only children. Others came from large families. The homes had their share of misbehavior, jealousy, and bickering, but the stormy periods didn't seem to last long or cut deeply into the underlying foundation of family unity.

The families studied were found to share a large number of activities as families. They liked doing things together. The typical pattern of religious activities was expressed by one parent: "We participate in religion as a family just as we do in everything else." The parents agreed in general on the importance of respecting the feelings and opinions of their children. They differed on methods of discipline, but most of the parents showed reasonable firmness without being heavy-handed. Orderly living was far more the result of positive planning and working as a family than of negative restraints and punishment. There was almost universal agreement that a child needs responsibilities commensurate with his age. Whether or not there were formal religious practices in the home, the parents put effort into encouraging basic values such as fair play, honesty, helpfulness, and respect for all sorts of people. In the variety of family life patterns represented in the study there were certain common threads of respect for privacy and the willingness to talk out grievances. The parents thought of themselves as "just everyday parents," but it was obvious that parenthood was something they enjoyed.

[20] R. M. Goldenson, "Why Boys and Girls Go Wrong or Right," *Parents Magazine* (May, 1951). These criteria were employed in choosing the well-adjusted children: Plays well with other children, appears to be a happy child, has reasonable control over his emotions, can be depended on, is achieving somewhere near his capacity, is able to think for himself, is kind and helpful to teachers and classmates, is liked and respected by his peers.

One of the fathers interviewed in this study expressed what may be the master clue to why the children were happy and emotionally robust: "Most important of all is loving your children and letting them know it, thinking of them as people and treating them so, appreciating what they do and trusting them and telling them so— and above all, *letting them know they are wanted.*" [21]

A FAMILY LIVES ITS RELIGION

When relationships like those just described exist in a family, that family is living religiously. This is more important to the personality health of its members than for them to engage in formal religious practices in the home. Such practices can have value only if they are consistent with the relationship climate of the family. If a family's interaction is leavened by respect for persons, wise love, creativity-stimulating freedom, mutual trust, and concern for the wider community, then family prayers and rituals can be a meaningful way of drawing together and enriching the family's experiences.

The way a family handles its non-loving feelings often reveals its religious quality most clearly. Peter, age four, has his "nose out of joint" because of the arrival of a baby sister. If his parents make him feel that his natural jealousy is bad, he will be forced to hide his intense, painful feelings from them, in order to retain their love. Fortunately Peter's parents respond in ways that protect his personhood. They know that all children feel jealous under these circumstances and that it is important that his feelings be kept in the open, so that he can learn to deal with them constructively. By giving him extra attention and warmth, they help to quiet his fears that his baby sister will take over completely. By expressing their love for him, rather than punishing him for his jealousy, they lessen its intensity. Further, they provide him with substitute ways of expressing his feelings—a board to pound and clay from which to model squashable little figures. They reflect and accept his feelings but they make it very clear that he must not express his feelings in ways that will hurt his sister. Learning this distinction between having destructive feelings and acting on them is very important to Peter's mental health and his ability to live with others.

Let us suppose that Peter's parents handled his jealousy in a moral-

[21] *Ibid.*, p. 81.

istic, repressive way and had subsequently, during the saying of grace before a meal, thanked God for the "gift" of a baby sister. Their intention would be to help Peter love his sister and share in what for them is a "blessed event." Undoubtedly they would be baffled by his temper tantrum and his refusal to eat his meal. Because they did not understand his inner feelings and needs, they would have done something irreligious (in its effects on personality) in the name of religion. Unwittingly they would have made Peter angry at God and guiltier about his jealousy.

Since Peter's jealousy is being handled constructively, the day will come when he will be glad for the new life that has joined his family, though as in all human relationships, he will continue to have mixed feelings about his sister. Eventually—perhaps when he becomes a father—a wider world of wonder will open in Peter's mind as he senses the miracle of new life in which a whole family participates. The awareness that a family, in all its creative experiences, is organically related to the creative forces of the universe is a moving religious experience. There is a security which comes to a person with this awareness of the way in which the person-regarding values in the family are supported by values in the universe, giving ultimate meaning to family life. This security is particularly important at times when the family organism is threatened by inner crises or outer pressures.

Regina W. Wieman summarizes: "The family that lives for the sake of great things itself becomes great. . . . Complete commitment to the Creativity of God is the great source of security, of freedom, of richness, and of meaning for the family." [22] The commitment of any person or any family is a process with successes and failures, ups and downs. When a family is living its religion the prevailing direction of its guiding concerns is toward those relationships which cause persons to grow.

Martin Buber has a choice passage which illuminates the importance of creative family life:

Man wishes to be confirmed in his being by man and wishes to have a presence in the being of the other. The human person needs confirma-

[22] *The Family Lives Its Religion* (New York: Harper & Brothers, 1941), pp. 216-17.

tion because man as man needs it. . . . Sent forth from the natural do-maine of species into the hazard of the solitary category, surrounded by the air of chaos which came into being with him, secretly and bashfully, he watches for a Yes which allows him to be and which can come to him only from one human person to another. It is from one man to another that the heavenly bread of self-being is passed.[23]

The healthy family is the womb of healthy personality, a haven of relatedness, the place above every other place where "the heavenly bread of self-being is passed."

[23] Martin Buber, "Distance and Relation," trans. Ronald G. Smith, *The Hibbert Journal*, XLIX (January, 1951), 113.

CHAPTER 10
Pastoral Counseling and Mental Health

In itself psycho-analysis is neither religious nor non-religious, but an impartial tool which both priest and layman can use in the service of the sufferer. I am very much struck by the fact that it never occurred to me how extraordinarily helpful the psycho-analytic method might be in pastoral work.[1]—*Sigmund Freud*

The most significant direct contribution of clergymen to mental health is their counseling and shepherding of troubled persons.[2] In his report on the activities of the churches in the mental health field, Richard V. McCann declares: "The minister as counselor is perhaps the one role in which the relations between religion and mental health are most sharply illuminated."[3]

No one really knows how much time the typical clergyman spends in counseling. The ministers in McCann's study averaged only 2.2 hours per week in formal counseling relationships. In contrast, a survey of the activities of thirty-four clergymen in suburban Pittsburgh showed that they spend thirty percent of their time in counseling—at least thirteen hours each week.[4] In any case, the total investment of pastoral energies in counseling is impressive. If the

[1] Sigmund Freud and Osker Pfister, *Psychoanalysis and Faith,* trans. Eric Mosbacher (New York: Basic Books, 1963), p. 17.
[2] *Action for Mental Health,* p. 134.
[3] *The Churches and Mental Health,* p. 46.
[4] J. W. Eaton, *et al.,* "Pastoral Counseling in a Metropolitan Suburb," *Journal of Pastoral Care* (Summer, 1963), pp. 93ff.

246,600 clergymen serving churches in this country average only 2.2 hours per week, a remarkable total of over half a million (542,520) hours of pastoral counseling occurs weekly. The fact that these hours are frequently spent with persons whose mental health is in jeopardy gives counseling a qualitative significance for mental health which far outweighs the quantitative investment of pastoral time.

Troubled people are more apt to seek help from a clergyman than from a member of any other professional group. This puts the minister in a strategic and demanding position. An oft-quoted study of a cross-section of the American adult population revealed that one out of every seven Americans has sought professional help with a personal problem. Of these, forty-two percent went to clergymen, twenty-nine percent went to family doctors, eighteen percent to psychiatrists and psychologists, and ten percent to a special agency or clinic.[5] Ministers are on the front lines in the efforts to help the burdened and the troubled.

In most small communities the only professional people available for counseling are ministers, physicians, and lawyers. Although the minister's counseling training may be less than adequate, he ordinarily has considerably more such training than persons in law and medicine. In the study just cited, sixty-five percent of those who had consulted clergymen reported being "helped" or "helped a lot"; another thirteen percent indicated that they were helped to a lesser degree.[6] Clergymen led the helping professions in the proportion of counselees who expressed satisfaction with the results of counseling. In spite of the limited training in counseling of many ministers, the majority apparently function with impressive effectiveness. As more and more clergymen receive clinical and academic training in counseling, the quality of ministerial work with the heavy-laden will continue to rise. The mental health potentialities which can be realized by increasing the availability of skilled pastoral counseling are immense!

In addition to formal counseling, the general work of pastoral care involves rich opportunities for informal counseling. Pastoral care is the multifaceted ministry of caring for the spiritual welfare

[5] *Americans View Their Mental Health*, p. 307.
[6] *Ibid.*, p. 319.

and growth of persons of all ages. This function is invaluable as a sustaining, nurturing influence in the lives of millions of people. The minister's caring symbolizes the caring of the religious community and of God and is expressed in many ways—for example, a friendly word as people leave the worship service, a congratulatory note when a member is honored by his company, a visit to welcome a new family to the community, and the vital pastoral ministries in the pivot points and crises of life—marriage, birth, death, confirmation, sickness, accidents, and so forth. For countless persons, this supportive ministry is indispensable to the maintenance of robust mental health. Over the years many times as many people are helped through a minister's general pastoring as are helped through formal counseling.

THE HERITAGE OF PASTORAL CARE AND COUNSELING

The clergyman as counselor has a heritage which is many centuries older than those of the mental health disciplines. As Robert Leslie indicates, "For centuries the church was the only agency concerned with the maladjusted." [7] Counseling is one aspect of a concern for healing which has been integral to the Hebrew-Christian tradition through the centuries. In recent years there has been an astonishing flowering of this ancient pastoral concern; it has been watered by streams of new insight concerning man which flow from the behavioral sciences and from the new methods of the psychotherapeutic disciplines. These new resources enable clergymen to fulfill their traditional helping functions with new vigor and effectiveness.

The counseling pastor walks in the footsteps of the great pastors of the past. He seeks to follow the example of one who was called the "Great Physician" whose healing influence brought release of the captives of inner conflict, recovery of sight to the spiritually blind, and let the broken victims of mental illness go free. To some, it must have seemed that he devoted a disproportionate amount of time to the sick. But he knew that it is the sick who need a physician, that those in crises are both more in need of and more open to help. The counseling pastor works beside the modern Jericho roads with people robbed of happiness and beaten by their fears, their guilts,

[7] Unpublished Ph.D. dissertation, Boston University, 1948, p. 10.

and by the savage cruelty with which disease, pain, and death often strike. It is in response to the raw stuff of human suffering that a person-centered minister functions as counselor.

THE NATURE AND UNIQUENESS OF PASTORAL COUNSELING

Counseling is the utilization of a one-to-one or small group relationship to help persons handle their problems in living more adequately. In contrast to psychotherapy, it is usually short-term (ten sessions or less) and does not aim at radical changes in personality. It deals mainly with contemporary relationships and problems rather than exploring childhood relationships. Its aim is to help a person mobilize his inner resources for handling a crisis; for making a difficult decision; for adjusting constructively to an unalterable problem; or for improving his interpersonal relationships, including his relationship with God.

The heart of counseling is the establishing of a warm, accepting, honest relationship between pastor and parishioner. As Carroll Wise has pointed out, the counseling relationship is simply an intensification of the same quality of relatedness which should exist throughout the life of a church. Experiments conducted under Carl R. Roger's direction demonstrated that growth tends to occur in a counselee when three qualities are present in the counselor: *congruence* (authenticity, inner openness, self-honesty), *unconditional positive regard* (warm caring and respect for persons), and *empathic understanding* (entering into another's inner world of feelings and meanings).[8] Carl G. Jung also emphasized the importance of the counselor's personality: "Learn your theories as well as you can, but put them aside when you touch the miracle of the living soul. Not theories but your own creative individuality alone must decide." [9]

A psychiatrist (who is an active churchman) writes: "My hope is that we may develop a more intensive *in*-reaching mission, a ministry to those lost within themselves in our own congregations." [10] This is the goal of pastoral care and counseling. It is an instrument

---

[8] Carl R. Rogers, *On Becoming a Person* (Boston: Houghton Mifflin Company, 1961), pp. 263ff.

[9] Carl G. Jung, *Psychological Religious Reflections* (New York: Pantheon Books, 1953), p. 73.

[10] "The Terror of Good Works," p. 25.

for implementing the basic purpose of the church—increase of love of God and neighbor—by helping to release the ability to love in those in whom this ability has been blocked or crippled.

The mental health potentialities of counseling by a minister can best be realized when he is cognizant and appreciative of the uniqueness of his counseling role. What are the clergyman's particular contributions within the general field of counseling and psychotherapy?

(1) To some extent the minister is unique among the counseling professions in his *training*. Unlike most other counselors, he is trained in philosophy, theology, comparative religions, and psychology of religious experience. This training should equip him to be of special help to those whose problems root in an unsuccessful search for a philosophy of life which would give meaning to their existence. The minister's training should help him develop expertness in facilitating growth in the relationships of persons with God. Paul Tillich describes pastoral counseling as a "helping encounter in the ultimate dimension." [11]

(2) The clergyman is unique among counselors in his *explicit goal of spiritual growth*. Any counseling which enhances a person's ability to relate to another makes for greater vitality in his relationship with God. Most religiously oriented counselors, however, regard the development of a more mature relationship with God as essential for personality wholeness. The fact that a minister has a continuing concern for the quality of his counselee's relationship with God, whether or not this is ever discussed in theological terms, inevitably influences the nature of the relationship and the direction of counseling. For many people, God is dead. He can come alive for them only as they are able to remove the blocks to awareness of his living presence. These blocks usually stem from distortions in early relationships which can be reduced through experiencing grace— unearned acceptance and love—in a counseling relationship (or elsewhere).

A minister should be aware of the theological realities with which he deals constantly in counseling—guilt, grace, sin, alienation (from God, oneself and others), the terror of meaninglessness and death, the dark, "demonic" destructiveness of inner conflicts, the struggle

[11] Address at the National Conference on Clinical Pastoral Education, Atlantic City, November, 1956.

for rebirth to wider dimensions of relationships, and the powerful, God-given drive toward wholeness. It may be helpful for the counselor to point out to persons from religious backgrounds that they are dealing with profound theological (as well as psychological) realities in the counseling experience. With others, the use of "religious" language may actually block religious growth. A theological student, reflecting on his clinical training experience, described it as "theology on an experiential level." This is precisely what effective pastoral counseling is. The ultimate goal of such counseling is spiritual rebirth through loving reconciliation with oneself, others, and God.

(3) The minister is unique among counselors in his professional *role*. Because he is a religious authority figure, people spontaneously project on him a rich variety of associations from their early life, including powerful feelings about such matters as God, heaven, hell, sex, parents, Sunday school, death, sin, and guilt. This provides a sensitive clergyman with a superb opportunity to help people mature in these emotionally charged attitudes. Through their relationship with him, he can help them grow in their relationships with all authority figures, including the supreme authority, God. This will occur most readily if his professional self-identity is clearly that of a minister.

Unique dimensions in pastoral counseling are derived from the minister's role as leader of a local congregation and his function of shepherding persons from birth to death. His continuing contacts with families (often stretching over many years) give him advantages in counseling which those in no other counseling profession possess. Many people seek his help because a bridge of relationship already exists with him. Often they have trusted ministers since early childhood.

Another advantage derived from his role is the expectation that he will go to his people in their homes and places of work without a special invitation. He can often detect problems in their early stages and bring help before they have reached the final, destructive stages. As a pastor, he is normally with his people during periods of stress when major problems often develop. Unlike most counselors, he can be consulted informally, without calling the helping process "counseling" or necessarily going through the often difficult matter of appointment-making. The setting of a religious fellowship within which the minister functions as counselor offers a rich variety of group resources which can undergird, broaden, and complete many of his counseling efforts. As a counselor, the clergyman has many things in his favor.

(4) There is uniqueness in the *religious instruments* which the minister naturally employs when appropriate in his counseling. When used carefully, prayer, scripture, sacraments, and devotional literature can be of distinct value, particularly in supportive and crisis counseling. When used indiscriminately, these instruments can block rather than facilitate the emotional and spiritual growth of persons. Whether or not the minister uses religious tools in a particular relationship, the counselee knows that he represents the religious community and the vertical dimension of existence upon which both can draw in counseling.

Pastoral counseling should always be done in the spirit of prayer —that is, openness to and dependence on the growth forces of the universe which constitute the source of all healing. Growth in counseling is the result of the release of these God-given resources which have been blocked within the person. The effective counselor is only a catalyst in the person-to-person interaction through which these growth-healing resources become available to the individual.

In order to avoid using religious instruments in irreligious ways (which block growth), they should be employed in counseling only after one is aware of their meaning to that person. It is wise to explore their impact on the person by inquiring after a prayer, for example, "What was going through your mind as I prayed?" The use of instruments and symbols of religion tend to strengthen the dependency aspect of a counseling relationship by stirring up childhood feelings. In some cases, this may arouse guilt feelings which block the catharsis of anger, jealousy, and sexual or destructive fantasies. The content of some prayers tends to arouse expectations of magical solutions not involving struggle on the counselee's part. In general, religious instruments should be used sparingly in insight counseling, more frequently in supportive counseling, and generously in the wider ministry of pastoral care. A prayer of thanksgiving at the close of a counseling relationship can be a beautiful way of articulating the gratitude which both pastor and parishioner feel for the mystery and miracle of healing.

TYPES OF PARISH COUNSELING

The client-centered approach has dominated pastoral counseling literature too long. This approach constitutes one valuable aspect of a minister's training, helping him master the art of disciplined listening and lessening the occupational tendency toward facile verbalizing. However, a minister must modify the client-centered approach in a variety of ways if he is to serve those who seek his help. A minister with only a client-centered string on his counseling fiddle often feels guilty or blocked in counseling situations requiring the constructive exercise of authority, functioning as a teacher-counselor, or serving a parishioner emotionally in a feeding role.

The father of client-centered counseling states clearly that many troubled people cannot benefit from an insight-oriented, client-centered approach because of excessive instability, aging, or unfavorable environment.[12] In my experience, a majority of those who seek a pastor's help cannot respond to a pure Rogerian approach. This approach is sometimes effective with reasonably intelligent, highly verbal, young or middle-aged neurotics who are strongly motivated to obtain help. Attempting to use it with troubled persons who lack these characteristics usually results in what a social worker, Gordon Hamilton, describes as an adventure in passivity[13]—a rambling relationship which becomes an exercise in mutual frustration. Many people's capacity for insight and self-directedness is so limited, crippled, or ossified that they cannot respond to an insight-oriented approach. But, they can be helped to greater adequacy in living by varied counseling approaches involving the selective use of guidance, authority, instruction, along with a focus on improving interpersonal relationships (rather than effecting major intrapsychic changes) and seeing one's situation from a more constructive perspective.

The full person-helping potentialities of a minister's counseling can be released only if he develops skills in several basic types of

[12] Carl R. Rogers, *Counseling and Psychotherapy* (Boston: Houghton Mifflin Company, 1942), pp. 61-80.
[13] Howard J. Parad (ed.), *Ego Psychology and Dynamic Casework* (New York: Family Service Association of America, 1958), p. 26.

counseling. To some degree, these types utilize different facets of his personality. Here are the basis types of counseling which the minister is normally called on to do: (a) *Marriage and family counseling,* (b) *supportive (including crisis) counseling,* (c) *counseling for referral,* (d) *short-term educative and decision-making counseling,* (e) *superego counseling,* (f) *informal counseling,* (g) *group counseling,* (h) *religious-existential problem counseling.* Several of these types usually are employed in the same counseling situation.

Before looking more closely at these types, the ingredients which all effective counseling approaches have in common should be mentioned:

(a) Establishing a growing therapeutic relationship through warm nonjudgmental concern. (b) Disciplined listening to and reflecting the parishioner's feelings. (This encourages the pouring out or catharsis of bottled-up feelings which is like draining the poison off a wound.) (c) Seeking a growing understanding of the person's "internal frame of reference." (d) Gaining a diagnostic impression concerning the nature of his problems, his weaknesses, and inner resources. (e) On the basis of this tentative diagnosis, suggesting an approach to help. These general procedures have been discussed in standard books on pastoral counseling.[14] The mastery of skill in establishing and utilizing a therapeutic relationship in these ways is the foundation upon which the minister can build a differential approach to the major types of pastoral counseling.

Marriage and Family Counseling

A minister needs to be reasonably proficient in all eight varieties of counseling, but he should acquire a high degree of expertness in three types—marriage counseling, crisis counseling (especially bereavement), and counseling on religious-existential problems. In these types he should be among the most skilled persons in his community. Because of his socially defined role, he occupies a strategic position of opportunity to help persons in these areas.

In the nationwide mental health survey mentioned earlier in this

---

[14] See, for example, Seward Hiltner, *Pastoral Counseling* (Nashville: Abingdon Press, 1949), Rogers, *Counseling and Psychotherapy,* pp. 83-173, and Carroll A. Wise, *Pastoral Counseling: Its Theory and Practice* (New York: Harper & Row, 1951), pp. 39-114.

chapter, nearly sixty percent of clergy counseling opportunities were family problems (forty-two percent marriage, twelve percent parent-child and five percent other family relationship problems) .[15] The clergyman's natural entrée to families gives him a major advantage in this type of counseling. There can be no doubt that skill in marriage and family counseling is essential for an effective ministry!

There are two basically different approaches to marriage counseling. One method consists of individual counseling with one or preferably both parties. The goal is to help both achieve sufficient personal growth so that they can relate more maturely in marriage. The assumptions of this approach are that problems between people always reflect problems within them (which is true) and that the problems within must be dealt with to improve their relationship (which is not always the case). For the pastor, this method has serious drawbacks. It requires extensive training and ordinarily is highly time-consuming. Distorted feedback between the partners sometimes damages the counseling relationships. "The minister said . . ." is misused in moments of anger between the partners. The counselor has the arduous task of keeping strict track of who said what, so that he does not unwittingly violate confidences. Considerable insight and growth may be achieved by the better-motivated party without substantial improvement in the sick marriage.

The newer approach is called "role-relationship" counseling or "couple counseling." [16] This approach tends to be more efficient time-wise and also more effective in healing a sick marriage by improving the quality of marital interaction. It usually does not have long-range effectiveness with grossly disturbed persons whose weak egos and need to act out their inner problems vitiate the effects of counseling. But I regard it as the method to try first in most marriage counseling. If it does not prove helpful, individual counseling in more depth or referral to a psychotherapist or a family service association is in order.

Role-relationship counseling aims neither at basic personality changes nor at depth insight. Its goal is more modest—to help the couple make their relationship more mutually need-satisfying. The

---

[15] *Americans View Their Mental Health*, p. 305.

[16] A useful book on this method is Charles W. Stewart's *The Minister as Marriage Counselor*. Rev. ed. (Nashville: Abingdon Press, [1961] 1970).

marriage relationship itself is sick. It is the patient. The focus of counseling is on the interaction which occurs in and shapes their relationship. The "between" of a marriage is seen as far more than the sum of the problems within the two persons. The "couple identity" (see Chap. 9) is a psychological entity which has been created by their interaction. Frequently, significant improvement in the quality of interaction can occur without basic changes in the underlying personality patterns. Marital interaction occurs on many levels and can be improved on many levels. For adults, counseling procedures which aim at improvement on the relationship level are usually the most helpful.

The Greens are having serious trouble with their marriage. They seek their minister's help. Using a role-relationship approach, his goals with them will be: (a) *To help them reestablish meaningful communication (that is, on the level of feelings, hopes, and personality hungers) so that they will have the instrument for working at their problems.* (b) *To interrupt their negative, self-perpetuating interaction pattern of mutual attack and retaliation.* Because both have been hurt so severely they probably cannot extricate themselves from this vicious cycle unassisted. The cycle's momentum can carry a couple into the divorce court. (c) *To help them become aware of the nature of their interaction and the conflicts in the role expectations which each has had for himself and the other.* Most interaction in sick marriage is blind, automatic, and maladaptive. (d) *To assist them in discovering ways to modify their attitudes, role-expectations, and marital behavior so as to decrease friction and increase mutual need-satisfaction.* This includes helping them decide on some mutual goals (which both desire) and then beginning to work toward them. (e) *To help them learn how to relate with their more mature rather than their more childish sides.* (f) *To help them accept the things about their partner which cannot be changed.* This means giving up their futile campaigns to reform each other. When this pressure is removed, many couples actually begin to change in significant ways.

In counseling with the Greens, the minister is a combination referee, who sees that each gets an opportunity to voice his views on each issue, and coach, who helps them learn how to play the marriage game more constructively. After an initial joint interview in which the minister senses the nature of their interaction, he decides to see each person separately for a few sessions. This drains off some of the extreme pressure of hurt and anger, which otherwise would block couple counseling. It establishes rapport with each person and gives each the opportunity to divulge information or feelings which would not come out in a joint session. After three or four separate sessions, counseling proceeds mainly by triangular interviews, the couple meeting together with the minister. He helps them communicate and encourages them to explore specific incidents of conflict in depth. "How did you feel when that happened?" is directed first to one and then to the other. Occasionally the minister summarizes how each perceives or feels about a given incident or aspect of their relationship. The focus is, "What can we learn from this fight (or satisfying experience)?" Through practice during the counseling sessions the Greens gradually acquire the ability to be aware between sessions of what is occurring in their relationship. Awareness of their patterns of interaction is the first step toward changing these patterns. Couples with a reasonable degree of ego strength can often acquire the ability to help themselves within as few as six to ten sessions.

For the minister with strong training in counseling, a method called *family group counseling* offers a useful tool for helping families with a disturbed member or with parent-child problems. As Jerome D. Frank says so well: " 'No man is an island' and the degree and permanence of change in any individual will depend in part on corresponding changes in those close to him and on support of his wider milieu." [17] The family group counseling approach is useful in cases of troubled adolescents where intrafamilial communication has broken down. After an initial conference with the parents to explain the need for family sessions and gain their cooperation, subsequent sessions include the entire family. The assumptions and goals are similar to couple counseling. Since the family is an interpersonal organism, the most efficient way to help a disturbed member is to increase the health of family interaction. The goals are to help them

[17] Jerome D. Frank, *Persuasion and Healing* (New York: Schocken Books, 1963), p. 234.

reestablish meaningful communication, develop awareness of the roles and interaction patterns of various family members, experiment with modifications in roles and behavior, and, most important, to allow the family to experience its essential unity and interdependence. The counselor's presence as referee and coach allows the family to experiment with new patterns of relationships.

To do family group counseling well, a minister needs considerable skill and sensitivity to interpersonal relations. Clinical training and participation as a member of a therapy group are valuable as background training experiences. A minister who wishes to use this approach should study John E. Bell's monograph, "Family Group Therapy" [18] and then arrange to have his work supervised by a well-trained psychotherapist, preferably one who has done family group therapy. The minister who masters this approach has an invaluable instrument for rendering relatively short-term help at the source of personality problems.

Supportive and Crisis Counseling

There are at least four varieties of supportive counseling: *crisis, stopgap, sustaining,* and *supportive growth-action* counseling. All four make significant contributions to mental health through providing supportive relationships.

1. *Crisis counseling.* Gerald Caplan [19] shows how a person's mental health is enhanced or depleted by the way he handles crises. No matter how psychologically healthy a person is there are times when his inner resources are severely strained by crises such as accidents, illness, bereavement, natural disasters, unemployment, handicaps, and family traumas such as alcoholism. At such stress-points, many individuals are helped by a supportive counseling relationship.

In a sizable church, a minister's counseling is often primarily crisis counseling. During a given week, he may be called to the home where a child has died, asked to appear in court to help a teen-ager in trouble with the law, consulted by a woman suffering from menopausal emotional problems, called on by a man who has just learned he has cancer, and another whose self-esteem is shaken

[18] Public Health Monograph #64, U.S. Government Printing Office, Washington 25, D.C.; see also Virginia Satir, *Conjoint Family Therapy* (Palo Alto, Calif.: Science and Behavior Books, 1964).

[19] *Principles of Preventive Psychiatry* (New York: Basic Books, 1964).

by mandatory retirement. The crisis ministry to such persons may prevent the development of major personality illnesses. Such a ministry ordinarily combines three things—walking with the person through his dark valley by maintaining a supportive relationship, giving emotional first-aid by means of informal counseling and guidance, and watching for possible signs that the individual's built-in recovery resources may not be adequate. If a person is not pulling out of the emotional tailspin caused by the crisis, intensive pastoral counseling (if the minister has the time and training) or a psychiatric referral are in order.

Fortunately most people have latent resources which allow them to handle even staggering blows. By standing with a person in crisis the minister helps him to mobilize these inner resources and also to draw on the resources of the religious tradition and community. During stormy crisis periods, a person's sense of worth and meaning are temporarily depleted, his world shattered. The support of his pastor can help keep the floundering ship of his life from sinking. Ordinarily, when the storm's fury diminishes, the ship will right itself.

Bereavement, the universal crisis, strikes an average of two American families per minute. Active bereavement involves at least a million Americans at any one time. Nearly every feeling known to man can be involved in this crisis. Sigmund Freud commented on the death of his father: "He had passed his time when he died, but inside me the occasion of his death has reawakened all my early feelings. Now I feel quite uprooted." [20]

The loss of a loved one is a psychological amputation. A part of one's world of meaning and identity has been cut off. One's response depends on the nature of the relationship. The psychological mechanisms employed are the same which one uses in coping with other frustrations. In normal recovery the psyche has an orderly process which it follows in working through the loss over a period of months or years. Experiences during this process include feelings of unreality and shock, physical distress, preoccupation with the image and memory of the lost one, pouring out of grief, idealization of the deceased, guilt feelings, anger, loss of interest in usual activities, the

[20] Ernest Jones, *Life and Work of Sigmund Freud* (New York: Basic Books, 1953), I, 324.

unlearning of thousands of automatic responses involving the deceased, relearning of other responses, resumption of normal patterns of living, and the establishment of substitute relationships.

The minister's role in normal grief is essentially to support, to encourage catharsis of feeling, and to make religious resources readily available. Proximity to death arouses deep death-fear in the survivors (including the minister). This existential anxiety can be handled constructively only by the experience of religious trust. Through his priestly role the minister brings familiar rituals and theological beliefs to serve as vehicles of trust. He should avoid blocking the natural flow of grief by implying that it is somehow unchristian to experience or express deep sorrow. Mourning—experiencing the awful pain of loss—is an essential part of the healing-recovery process.

Abnormal or pathological grief reactions are like infected wounds which cannot heal. As Edgar N. Jackson puts it, if working through the grief does not occur at the time of loss, "it will be done later at a much greater cost to the total personality." [21] Here are some warning signs which may indicate abnormal grief: an absence of mourning, increasing withdrawal from normal life, undiminished grieving, psychosomatic illnesses, severe depression which does not lift, personality changes, severe undiminishing guilt. It is the persistence of such symptoms over a considerable period of time that shows most clearly that normal psychological healing is not occurring. Repressed feelings of guilt, anger, and dependence deprivation are usually involved.

Pastoral counseling and/or psychiatric treatment should be instituted as soon as possible, hopefully before the problem moves into a chronic, difficult-to-treat stage. The goals are to help the person in releasing the "emotional tie to the deceased, despite the attending discomfort of sorrow and subsequently to replace the type of interaction lost." [22] The method is to focus on memories of the loved one, assisting the person to become aware of and resolve his powerful, conflicted feelings about the loss. The process is painful, but

[21] Edgar N. Jackson, *Understanding Grief* (Nashville: Abingdon Press, 1957), p. 143.
[22] Henry H. Brewster, "Grief: A Disrupted Human Relationship," *Human Organization* IX (1950), 19-22.

there is no other road to healing. Medical help should be sought when psychosis, severe depression, or psychosomatic problems are obvious or suspected.

2. *Stop-gap supportive counseling.* A seriously disturbed young man contacted a minister in the town to which he had moved recently. The minister recognized immediately that he needed psychiatric treatment. Limited financial resources made the community mental health clinic the only feasible referral. After an initial screening interview, he was placed on the clinic's waiting list. During two months of waiting, the minister saw him regularly, making no attempt to engage in insight counseling. He merely allowed the man opportunity to pour out his fears and troubles in a supportive, accepting relationship. This relationship probably allowed him to remain functional until psychiatric help was available. In many similar cases, a pastor can render invaluable stopgap aid to a person in desperate need.

3. *Sustaining counseling.* For some persons who have low ego-strength or are irreversibly crippled emotionally an ongoing relationship with an authority figure allows them to continue to function. The minister's symbolic role makes him a natural supportive counselor. Dependent persons are inevitably attracted to him because he represents a parental strength upon which they need to lean. They can identify with him as he functions in various leadership roles (see Chap. 3) and their dependency needs can be distributed among other leaders in the church organizations. These factors make it possible for a minister to help sustain a network of dependent persons with an economical expenditure of counseling time. An occasional counseling contact in which they tell him "how things are" and he gives them whatever guidance is needed will have greater meaning to them than many sessions with another counselor. Their awareness that he knows them and is concerned about them, has an ongoing ego-sustaining effect. Many people are able to keep going in desperately difficult situations because of this kind of relationship in their lives.

In ascertaining whether dependency relationships are constructive two questions are relevant: Does the minister need to collect such relationships? Does he do things for people (make decisions,

225

for example) that they could do for themselves? If both can be answered in the negative, such relationships are probably not blocking growth and, on the contrary, are serving a vital need.

4. *Supportive growth-action counseling.* Supportive counseling with certain people does much more than simply sustain them. It provides the interpersonal environment in which they can grow in their ability to handle life constructively. The heart of such counseling is a steady, dependable relationship with the minister. The person acquires strength, not by achieving depth insight, but by the exercise of making decisions, taking responsibilities (often small, at the beginning), and handling the stresses of his life-situation while in a supportive relationship. Self-esteem grows as the person is helped to hold a job, experience modest success in his relationships, and reduce the disorganization of his life. In short, the supportive relationship permits the person to function constructively. From this he gains strength which gradually allows him to function with less support.[23]

Alcoholics Anonymous provides a vivid example of a supportive-growth group. By successfully interrupting the "runaway symptom" of drinking to overcome the effects of previous drinking, A.A. enables the alcoholic's personality resources to become available to him for handling his problems in living. It provides a supportive social environment in which the alcoholic's desocialized, semiparalyzed ego can acquire enough strength, by identifying with an accepting group, to renew its functioning. This functioning in interpersonal relationships eventually restores ego strength. Through A.A.'s supportive-growth approach nearly 300,000 "hopeless" alcoholics have recovered, most of them with no attempt or need to explore the deep personality conflicts which probably caused the addiction.

In supportive-growth-action counseling, the pastor focuses on present reality, current relationships, and the practical problems of handling one's life situation more adequately. He is as interested in what a person does about his problems as how he feels. No attempt is made to ferret out deep underlying causes. Rather than search in the irrational and immature side of a person's life the min-

---

[23] For a more comprehensive discussion of supportive-growth counseling see H. J. Clinebell, Jr., "Ego Psychology and Pastoral Counseling," *Pastoral Psychology* (February, 1963), pp. 26-36.

ister relates to his rational and mature side. The goal is to help the person's adult side (which, as Eric Berne shows,[24] even the most inadequate person possesses) gain strength by functioning, so that it will rescue control of the person's relationships from his child side. Such counseling aims at discovering and activating whatever areas of potential strength and competence a person possesses. The realization that significant enhancement of a person's general adequacy in living can occur without anything approaching depth insight opens a wide door of new effectiveness for the counseling minister.

"Insight" has been the ultimate goal, the magic word in pastoral counseling for too long. For persons who have the time, money, and emotional resources to acquire self-understanding in depth, it can be a life-transforming experience. But it is unrealistic to expect this in short-term pastoral counseling. Many people lack an appreciable capacity to acquire depth insight. Many of these, and others who have the capacity, do not require insight in order to enhance their relationships and increase their effectiveness in living.

A teen-ager who has withdrawn from his peer group because of emotional problems becomes progressively less able to relate to other adolescents because he misses important learning experiences in relating. His emotional problems are increasingly aggravated by his actual lack of social skills. A vicious failure-withdrawal cycle develops. If this is recognized early enough and the underlying emotional problems are not too severe, the most helpful "treatment" is getting him back into an accepting peer group. Often an emotionally secure teen-ager who "belongs" can be found to serve as a bridge to such a group. If this is successful, no psychotherapy may be needed.

A school dropout often gets caught in a runaway, self-perpetuating failure cycle—the more he fails, the more he expects to fail and the less his chances for success. Helping him interrupt and reverse this vicious cycle by some experience of success is often more useful to him than psychotherapy. Countless other examples of this could be cited. If taken seriously by the minister counselor the supportive growth-action approach provides him with a counseling tool which he is naturally equipped to use and which will allow him to help

[24] *Transactional Analysis in Psychotherapy* (New York: Grove Press, 1961).

scores of people who do not respond to a client-centered approach.

Some form of supportive counseling is indicated when working with persons having weak or rigid personal structures. This includes most alcoholics, drug addicts, overt and borderline psychotics, those with severe psychosomatic problems, religious fanatics, rabid "positive thinkers," and those with a protracted history of chronic failure in adult roles (marriage and job). A supportive, rather than an uncovering (insight) approach is also the most helpful one with most "senior citizens." Personality structure generally becomes less resilient with the passing years.

Referral Counseling

Since many people trust his judgment and turn to him spontaneously when trouble strikes, a minister is in a strategic position to assist them in finding competent, specialized help. A wise referral is one of the most significant services he can render a suffering parishioner. A family who, in the midst of a traumatic problem, is guided by its minister to effective help, is usually eternally grateful to him. A minister can multiply his service to the troubled manyfold by using all the helping resources of his community to the hilt. It is unfortunate that some ministers feel that referral is an admission of weakness or failure. *Action for Mental Health* reports: "The helping process seems to stop with the clergyman and physician in the majority of cases, and far more so with the clergyman than with the physician." [25]

As soon as a clergyman arrives in a new parish, he should begin to assemble a "referral file" of community resources. If his community has a welfare planning council, it may provide a directory (or a phone information service) listing health and welfare services. Professionals who have been in the area for a while are often sources of reliable information. Accurate evaluations of the relative competence of counselors and psychotherapists may be difficult to acquire except by firsthand contacts and by observing the results of referrals. It is helpful for the minister to have personal acquaintance with such persons and with key agency workers before he needs to make a referral. Having lunch with such persons, attending an open A.A.

[25] *Action for Mental Health,* p. 104.

meeting, or visiting the local mental health clinic can strengthen one's referral-making ability.

Here are some basic guidelines for referral counseling: (a) *Create this expectation*—When the minister's availability for counseling is presented in the church paper, his function of assisting persons in finding specialized help should always be mentioned. (b) *Mention the possibility early in any relationship in which one suspects a referral might be in order.* The longer one waits, the more referral will arouse feelings of rejection. If a counselee doesn't improve after four to eight sessions, he probably should be referred. (c) *Use rapport with the minister as a bridge over which the person can walk into another relationship.* This is facilitated if he knows that the minister knows and trusts the person to whom he is referred. (d) *Attempt to remove any emotional blocks which may prevent him from going to the person or agency suggested.* This may take several sessions or even several months of counseling. When a referral is recommended, the minister should routinely ask what the person has heard about that person or agency and how he feels about going there for help. It is essential to search out the fears, misinformation, and emotional resistances which otherwise will cause many referrals to be unsuccessful. It is also wise to ask the person to report back, indicating a continuing interest in his obtaining the best available help. (e) *If possible, the person should make his own appointment.* This keeps the initiative where it belongs and also begins a relationship with the new helping resource. (f) *The minister should let the person know that his pastoral concern and care will continue undiminished after the referral.* This will lessen the sense of rejection. However, it is essential that a person referred for counseling or psychotherapy not also continue to counsel with the pastor. One counselor at a time!

Short-term Educative and Decision-Making Counseling

In many counseling situations, the minister needs to combine the skills of the educator, the guide, and the counselor. Effectiveness in such short-term "pastoral guidance" depends on the minister's wise use of his special knowledge and authority. Awareness of when to use advice, instruction, and guidance to facilitate rather than

229

block growth is one aspect of the sensitivity of a well-trained counselor. Lacking this sensitivity, a counselor's advice, like that of Job's "comforters," is apt to be a burden rather than a blessing.

The pastor's authority is "strong medicine" and should be used in counseling (as elsewhere) with caution and moderation, under circumstances such as these: (a) *When a person's decision-making ability is temporarily crippled.* Encouraging a grief-crushed person to choose a coffin within his price range is an example. (b) *To block a precipitous, impulsive action with serious, irreversible consequences.* A minister is obliged to use persuasion, coercion, and even physical restraint if necessary to save a person bent on suicide. In cases where any dangerous, impulsive actions are planned, the minister's role is to interrupt the person's momentum, to encourage him to explore the probable consequences, and to consider alternatives. (c) *With those who are mature enough (in their relations with authority) to accept or reject suggestions* after weighing their merits, it is relatively safe to advise. Except in an emergency, a wise counselor will never give advice or attempt to instruct a person until he understands something of that person's inner world.

A seasoned pastor has a wealth of knowledge from his training and experience which counselees lack and some of which they need as grist for the decision-making process. The minister's legitimate fear of "playing God" in the lives of other people should not prevent him from sharing his knowledge when appropriate. He should, of course, be alert to the emotional problems which frequently lurk behind requests for information. When advice and/or instruction are used in counseling they constitute only part of the process. They should always be combined with work on the feeling level. It is usually more constructive to help a person explore alternatives than it is to suggest one course of action. The counselor should respect people's freedom to make their own mistakes and their own decisions even when they seem to him to be in error. (He should shield them, if possible, from mistakes which have disastrous or irreversible consequences.) There are many things that a person cannot be taught. He can only learn them for himself.

One thing a minister needs is faith in the effectiveness of skilled short-term counseling. Experience at family service centers has shown that many people can be helped significantly in one or two sessions at a time of crucial decision or crisis.[26] An impulsive decision to initiate divorce proceedings made during the heat of a domestic battle, often proves, when the smoke has cleared, to be unfortunate. Because of the chain-reaction of lawyers' maneuvering and mutual recriminations which follows such a decision, the action may be difficult to reverse. This is why a minister is usually justified in using pressure, if necessary, to persuade a couple in a marriage crisis to agree to a moratorium on legal action until they have had several months to explore alternative ways of resolving their conflicts.

Robert Frost's poem, "The Road Not Taken," has a certain relevance to short-term pastoral guidance. In vocational counseling, for example, a fork-in-the-road ministry may be all that is needed. A minister who encourages a bright adolescent to take the college fork rather than its alternative may in one interview have a decisive positive influence on that person's next sixty years. In many cases, of course, vocational dilemmas involve emotional conflicts which call for longer-term counseling.

If a counselor expects to be genuinely helpful in a few sessions, the odds that he will be are improved. The Court of Conciliation in Los Angeles maintains a counseling service for disturbed marriages. Sixty percent of their couples have already filed for divorce. All couples are seen from one to three times. For one third of them, this is enough to effect reconciliation. These are families in which pressures such as loss of job, ill health, in-laws moving in, and so forth, have knocked the marriage off balance. Their problems snowball. Often this runaway process can be interrupted and they can be helped to get their marriage back in balance in a short time. The other two thirds of the couples are disturbed persons who require more extended help. The remarkable thing about the conciliation service is that in spite of the advanced disintegration of many of the marriages, an average of sixty out of a hundred couples decide to try to save their marriages through a "trial reconciliation." Follow-up studies after a year show that three fourths of these are still to-

---

[26] From a discussion on April 5, 1963 with Carl Shafer, formerly director of the Pasadena Family Service Association.

gether.[27] One reason for the success of this service is its atmosphere of hope. The counselors expect to help people and they do!

The approach of this service has aspects which can be used in short-term pastoral counseling. Here is what these counselors do: (a) *Furnish disciplined listening.* (b) *Provide ego support.* The counselor helps a couple to keep their heads above water and see what is happening. (c) *Help the couple mobilize their inner resources.* They often discover these as they talk with a counselor. (d) *Help them to distinguish an impulse from a final decision.* "I want a divorce" may mean "I don't want a divorce" or "Help me" or "What do I want?" (e) *Interpret only conscious material.* The counselor may be aware of unconscious material but he does not deal with it. (f) *Use questions and confrontation.* A question, skillfully used, is to a counselor what a scalpel is to a surgeon. (g) *Focus on the marriage relationship, instead of on the inner problems of the individuals.* (h) *Use authority constructively.* At the conciliation service, seven out of ten couples actually sign a written agreement which aims at helping them reorganize their role-relationships. The ritual of working it out is often helpful.

Superego Counseling

In the period when modern psychotherapy was born, many of those seeking help were crippled by neurotic, puritanical consciences which stifled their creativity and loaded them with neurotic guilt feelings. The goal of counseling with such persons was and is to decrease the severity of their hair-shirt consciences and to help them become more self-accepting. The pastor still sees many people who need precisely this help. But he also sees persons whose inner controls or consciences are underdeveloped and weak. They have not internalized the culture's major values and therefore have not learned to control their impulses. Such "character problems" sometimes stem from homes where weak parents mistook permissiveness for love and were unable to maintain stable limits or dependable discipline. Many others come from barren, loveless homes or from homes with a physically or emotionally absent father.

A girl of seventeen came to her pastor to discuss her sexual activi-

---

[27] This report on results and methodology is from a talk on April 5, 1963 by Meyer Elkin, Director of the Court of Reconciliation counseling service.

ties. Her father was an emotionally nonresident commuter. Although she consciously felt little or no guilt about her activities, she was fearful of "getting caught." If the minister had responded to her reports of promiscuity in a passive or permissive way, she would have interpreted this as more of the weak, detached permissiveness of her father. She needed more acceptance than she was getting at home, but not more permissiveness! On the contrary, what she needed was for the minister to be both an accepting and a firm father-figure from whom she could gain strength in controlling her own behavior and in relation to whom she could establish her own constructive limits. After rapport was well developed, the minister made it clear that from his point of view, certain behavior is harmful to persons and therefore morally wrong. Using accepting confrontation he helped her face rather than avoid the probable consequences of her behavior. Most important, he helped her become aware of and work through her confused, lonely, rebellious feelings which provided fuel for the behavior. In reflecting on this experience, the minister realized that the girl was, by her behavior, pleading for some adult to set limits. In fact, this is probably why she had come to a minister.

Every minister represents the value structure of the community. This is an aspect of his socially defined role which is essential to the mental and moral health of our society. He should never be afraid, in any relationship, to stand for the things he regards as right. If his acceptance of feeling is mistaken by counselees for acceptance of their person-hurting behavior, they will be confused and letdown by him. His role as a value-symbolizer keeps some troubled persons from seeking his help. But for the many who come suffering from either weak or punitive consciences his symbolic role provides a tremendous counseling advantage. In using confrontation and firmness with those who have underdeveloped consciences, it is essential that the minister "speak the truth in love." If he has achieved reasonable awareness and self-acceptance of his own weaknesses and sin, he will be better able to stand for what he regards as right without being self-righteous, moralistic, or rejecting of other sinners.

Edmund Bergler has written that "a feeling of guilt follows every person like his shadow, whether or not he knows it." [28] As indicated

[28] *The Battle of the Conscience* (Westport, Conn.: Associated Booksellers, 1948), p. vii.

in Chap. 2, human guilt is of two intertwined varieties—normal, resulting from hurting persons; and neurotic, resulting from breaking puritanical mores. Normal guilt is healed by confession, making amends, and experiencing forgiveness. As a religious leader, the minister counselor can use the healing symbols of Christianity by which such guilt can be transformed. Neurotic guilt can be alleviated temporarily by compulsive self-punishing atonement devices. It can be removed by the maturing of the person's conscience through depth counseling.

Informal Counseling

The idea of the psychotherapist who sits in his office seeing clients for fifty-minute hours is inapplicable to much of a clergyman's counseling. Many of his best counseling opportunities occur informally, as a part of his general pastoring. One aspect of the uniqueness of the pastoral office is the opportunity to apply counseling sensitivities and insights in the ordinary encounters of parish life. It is well to recall that the counseling of Jesus apparently occurred in such informal settings as by a well with a Samaritan woman. The minister should develop the skill of turning pastoral calls and chance conversations into counseling opportunities, formal or informal. Unless he does this, he will miss many who need help but are afraid to seek it directly.

Some people who cannot overcome their resistance to admitting their need for counseling can pause for a few minutes after a meeting to tell the minister something about a situation. They may or may not move into a formal counseling relationship. Even if they do not, they can receive some supportive help and guidance from occasional informal contacts. Counseling-shy persons sometimes edge into counseling by coming to discuss other matters and then in an offhand way bring up the real problem.

In informal counseling many of the approaches of short-term formal counseling are useful—sensitive listening, reflecting feelings, seeking to understand empathetically, giving ego support, summarizing the person's perception of the problem, asking questions, examining alternatives, giving information, and, occasionally, advice. If a serious problem is evident, the minister should make every effort to continue the counseling. One Sunday morning a middle-aged parishioner paused after the other worshipers had left to mention that she was planning to seek a divorce. After listening for several minutes, the minister said, "Let's step over to my study where we can talk about this more fully." (If this had not been convenient, he could have said, "I'm going to be over your way this afternoon about two o'clock. If it's convenient, I'll stop by so that we can discuss it more fully.")

Creative pastoral calling gives rise to many opportunities for informal counseling, particularly in cases of shut-ins, the sick, the unemployed, the aged, and the rootless who move frequently in a futile effort to escape themselves. To make the most constructive use of his calling time a minister might maintain a "Special Help List" of the names of those whom he knows or suspects have special needs. In addition to those just mentioned, the bereaved, the alcoholic (hidden or open), the handicapped, and the vocationally or maritally maladjusted have a place on such a list. The minister does well to invest a greater than average amount of pastoral time in these members of his flock. His aim will be to allow a strong bridge of rapport to grow with them so that they can walk over it (psychologically) to seek his help. If they do not do so, and the relationship is strong or the need great he should not hesitate to take the initiative in offering help.

How does one keep pastoral calls from being merely pleasant social visits, dominated by the usual social "chitchat"? The minister can offer opportunities for the communication to move to a deeper level. John Sutherland Bonnell used this question to open doors of pastoral opportunity: "How are things going with you spiritually?" Subtle distress signals such as a catch in the voice, a slip of the tongue, tension in a marriage relationship, or a change in the pattern of church participation can often be picked up if the minister has his psychological antenna out to catch these cries for help. If a parishioner sounds burdened or despondent, simply saying, "You sound as though you're feeling discouraged," often opens the door to counseling.

Group Counseling

Much pastoral counseling now done on an individual basis could be done more efficiently and effectively in small groups. In his volume on group counseling in the church, Joseph W. Knowles writes:

Group counseling is integral to the ministry of the church. The doctrines of church and ministry reveal the depth nature of a counseling group, and a counseling group can become a means of grace whereby the church is enabled to *be* the church. Furthermore, the ministry of the church is the ministry of the entire people of God. Group counseling can become one means by which the pastor fulfills his essential function "to equip God's people for work in his service" (Ephesians 4:11-12, NEB), and through which laymen perform their priesthood as members of the Body of Christ.[29]

Group counseling offers the richest single field for future development within the general pastoral counseling field. (This underscores the importance of providing training in group dynamics and group counseling for theological students and ministers.) As indicated in Chap. 7, the proliferation of small groups in churches all over this country and in many other parts of the world shows that this exciting development is already well along.

Religious-Existential Problem Counseling

A relatively small percentage of those who seek pastoral help come because of overt "religious problems"—problems of belief, doubt, prayer, and so forth. When such problems are presented in counseling, they sometimes are surface-level manifestations of deeper emotional problems. A man in his early forties consulted his minister because his prayer life had lost its meaning. In the course of counseling it became clear that he was suffering from an oppressive load of guilt linked to the death by suicide of a relative for whom he had felt some responsibility. When this problem was worked through in counseling, vitality returned to his prayer life. The minister should be aware that psychological problems, including psychoses, sometimes come disguised as "religious problems."

It is equally important to be aware of the spiritual emptiness and lack of a meaningful philosophy of life which are at the root of many neurotic problems. Paul Tillich points out that those who are empty of meaning are "easy victims of neurotic anxiety"[30] and,

[29] *Group Counseling* (Englewood Cliffs, N. J.: Prentice-Hall, 1964), pp. 7-8.
[30] *The Courage to Be* (New Haven: Yale University Press, 1952), p. 151.

conversely, that a high degree of neurotic anxiety renders one hyper-sensitive to the threat of nonbeing.[31] Thus, there is a reciprocity between neurotic and existential anxiety—each reinforcing the other.

There is a religious dimension to every human problem in that existential anxiety is inherent in all human existence. When a person lacks a vital religious life he has no way of handling his existential anxiety constructively. As noted in Chap. 2, it is only as a person faces his existential anxiety and makes it a part of his self-affirmation that it becomes a creativity-stimulating rather than a deadening influence in his life. It is possible to confront existential anxiety only to the extent that one has achieved a viable personal religion, including a meaningful philosophy of life, a challenging object of devotion (and self-investment), a sense of mystery and transcendence, and a deep-level experience of basic trust in God, oneself, others, and life. When these have been achieved to a significant degree, existential anxiety becomes, in Kierkegaard's words, a "school"—a source of wisdom and growth.

The basic religious problem consists of finding these four experiences so that one can handle existential anxiety creatively. Until the middle years many people are able to ignore their unsatisfied spiritual hungers. But when a person crosses the halfway point in his life, his "value vacuum" or inner poverty becomes painfully obvious as he moves on the downward slope toward death. Frequently such persons become depressed with a sense of utter futility. Helping the person find a religious orientation and dedication is often the central task in counseling with such persons. Helping him look at his life from a religious perspective can change his basic feelings about his problems. As a specialist in spiritual growth, the minister should be able to render unique help to such individuals.

SPECIALIZED MINISTRIES OF COUNSELING

Every church of more than five hundred members should have one minister on its staff with advanced training in pastoral counseling. (His training should be such as to qualify him for membership in the

---

[31] *Ibid.*, p. 67.

American Association of Pastoral Counselors.) [32] Here is a job analysis for a "Minister of Counseling":

1. Provide a pastoral counseling service for members and constituents.

2. Develop a group counseling program for those with special needs and those who wish to raise their level of creativity in relationships.

3. Work with the leaders of church groups with the goal of increasing their groups' abilities to meet the needs of persons.

4. Develop a long-range program of premarital education and counseling.

5. Provide vocational counseling of youth and young adults.

6. Serve as a resource person for renewal and planning retreats.

7. Work with the Christian Education Committee in developing a parent and family-life education program, teacher and leadership training workshops.

8. Participate occasionally in the preaching ministry, the leadership of public worship, ministering to the hospitalized, and speaking to church groups.[33]

The emergence of pastoral counseling as a specialty within the ministry has been paralleled by the development of church counseling centers in many parts of the country. There are now 164 of these sponsored by denominations, councils of churches, individual churches, seminaries, and privately.[34] The majority of these are staffed by clergy counselors; some have interprofessional staffs. These counseling centers have opened a new, significant dimension in the churches' mental health ministry. In his study of the *Churches and Mental Health*, Richard V. McCann states that pastoral counseling centers "could be at least a partial answer to the need for substitutes for mental health facilities in small communities." [35] I share the

[32] Clinical membership requirements include: college and seminary degrees, a masters degree in pastoral counseling, ordination and good standing in a denomination, three years of parish experience, six months of clinical training and 250 hours of supervision of one's counseling, and personal therapy.

[33] This is an amended version of the goals of the ministry of counseling in which the author engaged at the First Methodist Church of Pasadena. Not all of these goals were achieved.

[34] Berkley C. Hathorne, *A Critical Analysis of Protestant Church Counseling Centers* (Washington, D. C.: Board of Christian Social Concerns, The Methodist Church, 1964).

[35] *Churches and Mental Health*, pp. 94-95.

enthusiasm of his conclusion: "The church counseling centers, in attempting to meet the mental and spiritual needs of people, seem to be the best way, organizationally, to make this aspect of the ministry available to people who need it." [36]

In the most comprehensive study of these centers now available, Berkley C. Hathorne arrived at these conclusions:

1. The church counseling centers have restored an historic tradition to the Church by meeting neglected needs. 2. . . . provide help for many who would not otherwise get assistance. 3. . . . perform a significant community service by functioning in part as a referral agency. 4. . . . may aid in the prevention of more severe disturbances. 5. . . . may provide unique opportunities for personal and spiritual growth. 6. . . . have fostered inter-professional association and cooperation. 7. . . . demonstrate another dimension of interdenominational cooperation. 8. . . . provide a clinical setting for advanced training in pastoral counseling. 9. . . . provide a clinical laboratory for research. 10. . . . confront American Protestantism with the challenge to extend and expand the ministry of counseling.[37]

The specialist in pastoral counseling, whether he works on a local church staff or in a counseling center, shares many of the counseling advantages of the parish minister and, in addition, has time and training to do depth counseling or pastoral psychotherapy. This is a salutary development, since it means that persons with theological training will now be cooperating with secular disciplines in seeking depth understanding of the human psyche.

SPIRITUAL HEALING AND PASTORAL COUNSELING

In a survey of ministers from Protestant churches one third had attempted spiritual healing in some form.[38] The current upsurge of this interest represents a revival of an ancient but long-neglected ministry. The term "spiritual healing" seems to suggest that some healing is not spiritual. Since all healing involves the release within a person of God-given growth forces, all healing is spiritual healing. Actually, what the term usually describes is approaches to healing

---

[36] *Ibid.*, p. 95.
[37] Hathorne, pp. 79-83.
[38] See Charles S. Braden, "Study of Spiritual Healing in the Churches," *Pastoral Psychology*, Vol. V, No. 44 (May, 1954), pp. 9-15.

making primary use of traditional religious forms and instrumentalities such as prayer, communion, the laying on of hands (Mark 16:18), and anointing with oil (James 5:13-16).

Both the spiritual healing and the pastoral counseling approaches are useful in a local church's program. Both have the same goal— the restoration of persons to greater wholeness. Experience has shown that some persons respond to one approach who do not respond to the other, and vice versa, while others benefit from a combination of counseling and healing services. Each approach tends to serve as a corrective of the other.

The physical danger in the spiritual-healing emphasis is that it will encourage persons to delay or neglect using the resources of medicine. A sound approach, of course, urges the use of all channels of God's healing, including the full range of medical resources. Psychologically, spiritual healing may increase unhealthy dependence on the leader and encourage the expectation of cures from the outside not involving struggle with inner problems. Theologically, this approach may cause people to feel they are manipulating divine forces to their own end, in a magical way. If a person is led to believe that enough faith will cure any condition, then failure to be healed saddles him with a load of guilt for his lack of faith. Enlightened approaches to healing strive to counteract these dangers. The emphasis is on opening the channels of one's life to the ever-available healing power of God and on healing of the personality. Physical healing may or may not be one aspect of this deeper healing of the spirit.

One danger that besets pastoral counseling is that it will lose its awareness of the spiritual element in all healing and will become infatuated, in an idolatrous way, with the human cleverness of psychology. The spiritual healing emphasis, particularly in its priestly aspects, can help a pastoral counselor retain a robust awareness of the vertical dimension in all relationships, including counseling relationships. It can remind the person enamored with counseling that the principles of the spiritual universe are much too complex to fit any machine model comfortably. There is infinitely more that we do not know than we do know about the human spirit and its relation to the Spirit of the universe.

The emphases in counseling on respect for the orderly cause-effect sequences in the world of the psyche and on the necessity of a person's growing in his responsibility for his own inner life can help to counteract any tendency in spiritual healing to function in ways which encourage magic or the temptation to shift the total responsibility to God. Training in counseling can help a minister use his authority constructively in healing rituals. Thus counseling and spiritual healing methods are complementary instruments for enhancing the wholeness of persons.

CHAPTER 11
Helping the Mentally Ill and Their Families

Madness severs the strongest bonds that hold human beings together. It separates husband from wife, mother from child. It is death without death's finality and without death's dignity.[1]—*Robert S. de Ropp*
    The socially visible characteristic of the psychotic person is that he becomes a stranger among his own people.[2]—*Action for Mental Health*

The crisis of mental illness is probably the most agonizing of all human experiences for everyone directly involved. Together with suicide, mental illness constitutes the deepest of the various forms of "deep water" through which individuals and families must sometimes go. A minister occasionally encounters persons who are on the verge or in the midst of major psychotic illnesses. More frequently he is contacted by a distraught family member who does not understand what is happening and/or does not know where to turn for help. Whether he is working with the ill person or with family members, this ministry will draw on all of a pastor's resources of empathy, interpersonal sensitivity, and compassion for those caught in the tentacles of an excruciating problem.

The clergyman has a responsibility to both the ill person and his family. In relation to the psychotic person, his role is to (a) *recognize the difficulty as mental illness;* (b) *aid the ill person in finding psychiatric help* (or guiding the family in making an involuntary com-

[1] *Drugs and the Mind* (New York: St. Martin's Press, 1957), pp. 167-68.
[2] *Action for Mental Health*, p. 59.

242

mitment, if the person is unwilling to accept help) ; (c) *maintain a supportive pastoral relationship during treatment,* whether the person is hospitalized or treated on an out-patient basis; (d) *maintain a close relationship and be available for counseling during the adjustment period following treatment.*

The minister has a major opportunity in helping the patient's family. Often they are living under a dark, miasmic cloud of fear, humiliation, and guilt. Of necessity, the mental health professionals concentrate the bulk of their attention on the mentally ill person himself. Except for a minimum of help from the social work department of a mental hospital or clinic, the family is left to handle the trauma largely on its own. The pastor's opportunity to stand with the family in their lonely, confused distress is one of the privileges of being a clergyman.

The minister's role in relationship to the family is to (a) help them *accept the painful fact that their loved one is mentally ill;* (b) *assist them in getting the person to psychiatric help;* (c) maintain a *supportive counseling relationship with them to help them understand and learn from the crisis.* This involves helping them work through their painful feelings about the "stigma" of mental illness and their feelings of guilt and rejection toward the ill person. (d) The minister must *help them relate constructively during visits to the hospital* and *help prepare them for the person's return to the family environment;* (e) *counsel with the family of the person requiring permanent custodial care;* (f) *keep in close pastoral contact with the entire family during the post-treatment adjustment,* and (g) *mobilize a caring ministry among members of the congregation.* There are few places at which a minister can invest his pastoral time more helpfully than in a supportive ministry to the mentally ill and their families.

RECOGNIZING MENTAL ILLNESS

In the early stages of some forms of mental illness, both the individual and his family may be unaware of the nature of what is occurring. The person himself often is unaware because his illness, by its very nature, causes him to lack insight about his condition. The family members may believe that the person is merely selfish, inconsiderate, or temporarily upset. If early and intensive treatment

243

are instituted, the severity and duration of mental illnesses can be reduced in many cases. Prompt recognition can lead to appropriate treatment before a serious disorder becomes set in a treatment-resistant stage.

A minister should not attempt to diagnose the specific nature of the difficulty. This is the psychiatrist's area of competence and responsibility. But the minister should know the general symptoms of mental illness. Here are some of the signs: (a) The person believes that others are attempting to harm him, assault him sexually, or influence him in strange ways. (b) He has delusions of grandeur about himself. (c) He shows abrupt changes in his typical pattern of behavior. (d) He hears voices, sees visions, or smells odors which do not exist. (e) He has rigid, bizarre ideas and fears which cannot be influenced by logic. (f) He engages in a repetitious pattern of compulsive actions or obsessive thoughts. (g) He is disoriented (unaware of time, place, or personal identity) . (h) He is depressed to the point of near-stupor or is strangely elated and/or aggressive. (i) He withdraws into his inner world, losing interest in normal activities.[3]

When a minister sees any of these signs, he should help get the person to psychiatric treatment without delay. Although the vast majority of mentally ill persons are not dangerous to others, the deeply depressed person is always a suicide risk. Occasionally the individual with hallucinations or feelings of persecution may strike out destructively at others. Whatever the symptom, the earlier psychiatric treatment is begun, the better the chances for full recovery. If the minister encounters signs of psychosis in counseling with an individual, he usually should inform the family or other responsible persons. Unless there is obvious danger of precipitating a suicidal or homicidal attempt, the minister should explain to the individual why he must bring the family into the picture—whether or not he understands or agrees with this action. Unless it is unavoidable the minister should not act behind the person's back in ways that the person may interpret as betraying him or plotting against him.

Family members sometimes deny that their loved one is really

[3] "A Clergyman's Guide to Recognizing Serious Mental Illness" by Thomas W. Klink is a useful resource. (National Association for Mental Health, Inc., 10 Columbia Circle, New York 19, New York.)

mentally ill, holding on desperately to the hope that the person will "snap out of it" or that "all he needs is a good rest." Their own feelings of distress, social stigma, fear, and guilt may be too strong for them to take appropriate steps without firm support and guidance by a trusted clergyman. The minister's logical ally in this situation is the family physician. The individual and the family should be steered in his direction for an evaluation of the problem and for assistance in arranging for psychiatric treatment. A family will often accept a physician's counsel on such matters. Also he can give sedation or other emergency medical help and arrange for hospitalization.

FINDING TREATMENT RESOURCES

Although the family physician usually should be the key person in arranging treatment of the mentally ill person, the minister occasionally has an important role in counseling with the family concerning their decision about whether or not to hospitalize the individual against his will. Many families are reluctant to utilize state mental hospitals because of the "snake pit" stereotype which is in their minds. Often they believe (in some cases rightly) that the social stigma in state mental hospitals is greater than in private psychiatric hospitals. This is unfortunate since private facilities are usually very expensive and the ill person will not necessarily receive better care there. The treatment may be inferior to up-to-date state hospitals and is likely to be less adequate than in Veterans Administration mental hospitals, which generally have higher standards than state hospitals.

In the light of the minister's and doctor's evaluation of the available treatment resources, the family should be able to make the painful decision concerning which course to follow. If any one of the following has a possibility of sufficing, it should be tried before commitment to a mental hospital; short-term treatment in a psychiatric unit of a general hospital, outpatient treatment in a mental health clinic, or a day care or night treatment center. There is increased awareness among mental health professionals that if possible, it is better to treat a person in his community on an outpatient basis.

Two guiding questions to ask in selecting treatment facilities are: (a) *Where will the person get intensive and appropriate treat-*

ment immediately? (b) *Which approach will tend to separate the person least from his geographical and familial setting and most briefly from his work?* Unless the state hospital treatment is obviously inadequate, families should be discouraged from acquiring a major debt to finance private hospitalization.

The most distressing situation for the family occurs when they must take responsibility for committing a relative involuntarily. "Commitment" is a legal procedure by which a court consigns a person to a mental hospital. His status becomes that of a child. He loses his adult rights to vote, marry, and enter into contracts. The hospital authorities, functioning as though they were his parents, grant him those liberties which they regard as constructive. He is restored to adult legal rights only when they release him, declaring that he is again competent to function as an adult. It is important for the family of a person who must be committed to recognize that mental illness has already deprived their loved one of the ability to make adult judgments. Commitment merely recognizes what has already happened and protects the person while he recovers adult competence through treatment.[4]

A minister should be familiar with commitment procedures in his state so that he can help interpret them to the family. The liberalization of some state laws permits increasing numbers of voluntary admissions to state hospitals. Application for such admissions may be by the person himself or by parents (or guardians), in the case of minors. If, after a psychiatric examination, the person is found to need hospitalization, he will be admitted. In most states he can leave at any time he chooses. In the case of involuntary commitments, in some states any adult relative or friend can file a request (with the court which handles such matters) that the allegedly mentally ill person be committed. The court appoints psychiatrists who examine the individual and report to the judge, who then makes the decision. If the individual wishes to contest the action, he can have a sanity hearing before a judge or jury, with his lawyer and with testimony from his own psychiatrist. After commit-

---

[4] A helpful discussion of the problems of hospitalizing a person with mental illness is found in *Counseling Your Friends* by Louis J. and Lucile Cantoni (New York: The William-Frederick Press, 1961), Chapter 7.

ment, in some states the person (or anyone on his behalf) may file a petition for his release, which initiates another court hearing.

If a person is violent and/or adamantly refuses to accept help, it may be necessary for the family to call the police who will transport him to a public psychiatric ward (in a county hospital) or to a mental hospital for observation. This is the least desirable method of getting the person to treatment, but it sometimes becomes necessary as a last resort. Unless there is no alternative, the clergyman should not be involved directly in involuntary commitment procedures since this tends to distort his future relationships with the sick person.

HELP DURING HOSPITALIZATION

The minister has important roles in helping both the hospitalized person and his family. With both, his ministry is primarily supportive and pastoral. Even though a mental hospital has an effective chaplaincy service the patient's minister should visit him as regularly as distance permits. This is assuming, of course, that such a call is desired by the person and there is no psychiatric reason why it would be disturbing. It is good procedure for the minister to phone the hospital in advance of a call to ascertain whether the medical staff feels that the person should have visitors at a certain stage in his recovery. Pastoral visits are usually encouraged by the medical staff. The minister is often allowed to visit during the first week or ten days within which visits by the family are not permitted in many mental hospitals.

An experienced mental hospital chaplain, Ernest E. Bruder, describes the importance of pastoral visits:

Much can be said about the deep psychological significance of a friendly visit from one's pastor. It can be one of the most constructive contributions to the patient's recovery. The very nature of the patient's illness has led him to believe himself to be ostracized. Thus, when a representative of the community calls—and that representative is a clergyman—it often encourages the patient to feel that he may not be as evil or wicked and hopeless as he felt himself to be. This is one of the most helpful contributions possible to the increase of the patient's self-esteem and as such—his ability to get well.[5]

[5] *The Church and Mental Health,* p. 189.

Chaplain Bruder recommends that calls be brief; that the patient not be argued with, admonished, or criticized; and that the minister avoid making any promises which cannot be met helpfully. Prayer and scriptures should be used only when they are welcome and when the pastor has some insight concerning what they mean to the patient. When used they should be brief, affirmative, and supportive in nature.

A talk with the patient's doctor, preferably before the first visit, can be helpful in ministering both to the patient and to his family. The minister's understanding of the nature and prognosis of the problem puts him in a stronger position to help guide the family and interpret the patient's behavior and the therapy to them. This can assist them in facing the realities of the situation while avoiding unnecessary anxieties.

In order to minister effectively to the family, the minister needs to strive for "heart-understanding" of their inner world. When the evidence becomes inescapable that a member of one's family is mentally ill, each family responds in its own unique way to this painful realization, depending on previous relationships within the family circle. Some families fragment while others unite under the crisis. Each individual responds with his own inner attitudes and feelings about mental illness. From his culture he has probably soaked up automatic responses of shame and stigma. Such feelings often are present even in persons with "enlightened" ideas about mental illness. People respond psychologically, not logically, to mental illness, particularly when it intrudes cruelly into their own family. Robert S. de Ropp's words, quoted at the beginning of this chapter, put the matter accurately and forcefully: "Madness severs the strongest bonds that hold human beings together . . . It is death without death's finality and without death's dignity."

The family's response is more than a reaction to the social stigma which still clings, leech-like, to mental illness. It is a response to the bizarre changes in the ill person himself which makes him a "stranger among his own people." It is a response to the disruption of essential family interaction, the disturbance of usual family patterns, the financial insecurity which arises from both the heavy costs of treatment and, in the case of the breadwinner, the loss of family income.

During the development of mental illness, family life may be a nightmarish chaos. The natural self-protective tendency of the family is to retreat from social contacts to escape the social stigma they fear. But drawing into a shell only compounds the sense of isolation and the spiraling fear and hostility within their closed windowless walls.

The pastor who has some understanding of the family's inner world can be of inestimable help to them. Just knowing that he understands, cares, and stands beside them in their darkness probably helps them more than anything he does. He can assist the family in avoiding the automatic response of hopelessness which the majority of us have when mental illness strikes. Such a response is no longer valid in the light of the dramatic progress that has been made during the last decade in treating mental illness (see Chap. 5). It is important to acquaint the family with the new hope and help that is available without reassuring them in ways that will leave them unprepared to handle the grim possibility that treatment of their loved one may not be effective.

There are other things a minister can do to help the family. He can help them ventilate and clarify their swirling chaotic feelings about what is happening. In many cases, these feelings have been accumulating during the long weeks, months, or even years of growing stress preceding hospitalization. Guilt, hostility, and fear usually form a vicious alliance in the deeper feelings of the family members. Mental illness has hit one whose life is merged with theirs at many points. Thus, the illness has struck a blow at a part of their own psychological fields. If they are particularly fortunate they will have access to a mental hospital which holds regular family orientation or, better, family counseling sessions. If not, their contacts with the hospital staff will probably be frustratingly brief and totally inadequate to give them the amount of help needed in handling their own crisis and in relating constructively with their patient. The sensitive clergyman's ministry of listening and interpretation can help fill this need.

As the minister functions in this way he may become gradually aware of the ways in which the problems of the ill person and those of the family intertwine. He should, of course, not suggest to the family that this is true. To do so would be to push a threatening truth on them at the very time they need most to deny it. Eventually, if they have the capacity to learn and grow from the experience, they will be able to examine and rectify their interaction with the ill person.

There is a variety of practical ways in which a minister and his key laymen can help the family. To illustrate, if it is the mother who is ill, someone can be found to care for the children while the father is at work or visiting the mother. If it is the father, guidance in finding financial help during the crisis is often needed. The congregation should be encouraged to rally around the family quietly, in order to help them resist the temptation to withdraw from the sustaining, perspective-giving relationships with the extended family (including the church), which they need desperately. Maintaining a web of meaningful relationships is crucially important to the family at this point.

A simple but effective way for a congregation to express its concern for a family reeling under a heavy blow is for a number of persons to take them gifts of food. Not only does this have practical value at a time when family members may not have the time or energy to fix meals but it also has a profound symbolic meaning on the level of feeding and nurturing. A casserole may have more meaning than a prayer under certain circumstances.

There are several books and pamphlets which are useful in ministering to the family of the mentally ill. The classic in the field is by Edith M. Stern, *Mental Illness: A Guide for the Family*.[6] It is a detailed manual which may help the family understand the various stages of hospitalization and posthospital care. *The Family and Mental Illness* by Samuel Southard [7] has a pastoral emphasis but lacks some of the detailed answers to the family's questions about hospitalization, which is the strength of the Stern book. A mental hospital chaplain and a psychiatrist collaborated in producing a valuable pamphlet, "Ministering to the Families of the Mentally Ill." [8] The

[6] (4th ed.: New York: Harper & Row, 1962).

[7] (Philadelphia: Westminster Press, 1957). This book contains an insightful description of the family crisis resulting from mental illness.

[8] By A. F. Ward and G. L. Jones. This pamphlet can be obtained from the National Association for Mental Health, 10 Columbus Circle, New York, New York.

Public Affairs pamphlet series includes "When Mental Illness Strikes Your Family" [9] which is helpful to the family in coping with this crisis.

THE PATIENT WHO DOES NOT RETURN

The most difficult adjustment a family can be required to make occurs when a mental patient does not respond to treatment and becomes chronically ill. To the family, the person is in a sense dead and yet he is not dead. The normal bereavement process—"grief work"—cannot proceed since the person is not gone and the grief wound is infected. Such a wound cannot heal. Even though pitifully crippled psychologically and unable to show his need, the patient continues to need attention from the family. Unfortunately, his negative responses may help alienate them. I recall one mental hospital in which some six hundred patients received not a single Christmas card. Many of these had been abandoned by their relatives.

Edith Stern's book contains a brief but helpful chapter on the chronic patient. She writes to the family:

No matter how remote you regard the possibility of recovery, never abandon a patient. . . . It is pitiful to see mental hospital inhabitants who have not had a caller for perhaps twenty years groom themselves and wait hopefully on visiting day. Often the fact that someone related by blood or marriage still cares is the only thing in life to which a patient clings—and this holds good even if he displays apparent indifference or antagonism to anyone and everyone. If the regular letter writer and visitor in your family dies, be sure that someone else takes over.[10]

This advice also applies to the ongoing ministry of pastoral care (by both laymen and clergymen). The chronically ill sheep are still members of the flock. Often, their need for shepherding is great. Fortunately, with newer methods of treatment (remotivation, for example), some persons who had been regarded as "hopeless" or "untreatable" for years are now responding.

A related problem is the pastoral care of the family in which there is a harmless, ambulatory psychotic who has been given all that psychiatry has to offer but has not been helped. A supportive ministry

[9] K. C. Doyle, Public Affairs pamphlet #172.
[10] *Mental Illness: A Guide for the Family*, p. 85.

to such a person and his family can be a godsend. Here, for instance, is the husband of a mildly and chronically paranoid woman. The help he receives from the worship services and an occasional talk with his minister is a major factor in helping him carry a staggering load.

It may help the families of persons with chronic mental illness to become involved in volunteer service in a community mental health project or a mental hospital. This can reduce the feelings of blind frustration and channel some of their blocked concern into socially constructive efforts.

WHEN THE PATIENT RETURNS FROM THE HOSPITAL

It is reliably estimated that readmission rates to mental hospitals could be reduced from almost thirty-five percent to around ten percent were adequate medical, social, and vocational aftercare facilities available. Unfortunately, few states provide more than minimal aftercare services to help patients bridge the yawning chasm between the moment of discharge and satisfying functioning in the community. The Joint Commission on Mental Health and Illness reported in 1961 that aftercare services were in a "primitive stage of development almost everywhere." [11] Halfway houses (where small groups of patients who are not ready to return to their homes live together and receive help in social rehabilitation), day hospitals, foster home services, rehabilitation centers, and ex-patient clubs are still in short supply in all parts of our country. Thousands of relapses could be prevented if there were an abundance of such facilities. This is one of the major mental health challenges of the 1960's.[12]

The acute shortage of community aftercare resources increases the responsibility of the local church in meeting this vital need. As shown by C. A. Chamber's research, churches can respond effectively to this need. A refreshing example of direct congregational action in providing aftercare facilities is Baker Street House in San Francisco. This is a halfway house sponsored by a Methodist church in that

[11] *Action for Mental Health,* p. xvii.

[12] For a graphic description of the problem of aftercare and examples of what is being done in scattered places, see "Mental Aftercare: Assignment for the Sixties" by Emma Harrison, Public Affairs Pamphlet #318. C. A. Chambers' dissertation "A Determination of the Extent to Which Certain Protestant Churches Can Meet the Needs of Former Mental Patients" (Temple University, 1960) describes the church's role.

area. It serves as a residence for young adults who have been released from mental hospitals and for those who are receiving treatment at outpatient psychiatric services. These persons live there with other young adults who have no major psychological problems. Residents participate in resident government, cook for themselves cooperatively, take part in both spontaneous and planned recreation and educational activities, and receive guidance they may desire in such matters as seeking employment and utilizing health and educational agencies in the community. Residents stay at least a month and no longer than 18 months. The setting is designed to serve as a springboard to more permanent living situations. The house is co-educational. House parents are responsible for program and administration. They fill the role which Erik Erikson calls the "adult guarantors." The sponsoring committee from the church takes responsibility for guiding the financial operation of the house. Committee members spend considerable time at the house interacting informally with the residents. The sponsoring committee and the houseparents receive regular training and counseling. (Twenty-three people from the church completed a sixteen-week training course in preparation for opening this facility.) The Glide Foundation launched the project and provides leadership-training. This halfway house provides a supportive interpersonal environment with a combination of peer group discipline and freedom. Here the recovering young adults may learn new social skills and test them out in actual relationships of the house. They can do reality-testing in an accepting group. This is a form of "social therapy" complementing the psychiatric treatment which is available in other facilities. Leaders of this project report that the church people involved have become excited with its obvious value. They believe that the churches can do a more effective job than any other agency in this area of great need and that such involvement can bring churches alive with a new sense of mission.

The minister can work with the family and with key laymen in his congregation to help prepare them to receive the discharged mental patient in a way that will contribute to his full recovery. Mental patients about to be discharged usually face the outside world with considerable anxiety about how their families, friends, and potential employers will react to them as "ex-mental patients." Families and friends are also anxious. How the ex-patient is received by the important people in his life (including, in many cases, his fellow church members) , and whether he is able to find a job are important factors in determining whether or not he suffers a relapse. Finding employment is often difficult because of prejudice against those who have had major psychiatric problems. In some cases a minister can help the mentally restored person by contacting potential employers in the congregation.

Edith Stern's *Mental Illness: A Guide for the Family* has an excellent chapter on what to do when the patient comes home. And Lauren H. Smith, former Chairman of the Council on Mental Health of the A.M.A. gives this list of "Do's and Don'ts" to help an ex-patient:

Do . . . Give support, encouragement, respect and affection . . . Expect in general the same kind of conduct you would from anyone else . . . Be optimistic about the ability to change . . . Recognize the right to disagree . . . Keep up prescribed medicine.

Don't . . . Be over solicitious or encourage dependency . . . Be demanding, disrespectful or rejecting . . . Threaten a return to the hospital . . . Agree with "extreme" talk or attitudes . . . Talk behind his back.[13]

There is almost always a period of readjustment to living outside the hospital and often the person has some residual symptoms. These take patience and understanding on the part of the family. Many families are "jumpy" with the ex-patient, fearing that every ripple of his emotional sea foretells a relapse. When they are beset by such worries, they should be encouraged to contact the psychiatrist who treated the person. The period of readjustment is especially difficult for many families because the mental illness is intimately related to family relationships. It behooves the minister to stay close to the families in his congregation who are in the throes of such an adjustment. The steadying influence of a concerned person from outside the family may be precisely what is needed.

The minister with training in counseling can perform a valuable service by being available to counsel with parishioners who are com-

[13] "When a Mental Patient Comes Home," *This Week* (January 6, 1963) .

pleting their recovery following discharge from a mental hospital. Before attempting anything beyond supportive counseling, it is wise to check with the psychiatrist, if possible. Ernest E. Bruder's volume, *Ministering to Deeply Troubled People* [14] should be regarded as prerequisite reading for counseling with the mentally ill. Bruder's depth understanding of the "wilderness of the lost" makes this book a moving experience. He points out that persons with mental illness can be our teachers if we dare get close to them. Any minister who is tempted to assume that counseling with persons who are in the process of recovering from mental illness should be entirely the province of the psychiatrist, will find himself confronted by this paragraph:

Mental illness . . . is involved with faith—faith in the Ultimate, faith in each other, faith in ourselves. Distortion and conflict in any one area affect all areas. Whether it is expressed in religious terms or not, the meaning of life, values, destiny—*ultimates*—are matters of faith and therefore are religious concerns. This is the area of the clergyman. Faith proceeds from trust and trust arises from the good relationships that we have with others.[15]

Anton Boisen's view that mental illness is often a religious crisis —a last-ditch effort of the psyche to find a new orientation of meaning—correlates with Bruder's view of mental illness.

Bruder recommends this approach to persons recovering from mental illness:

Fundamentally . . . the minister seeks to understand what the patient has experienced in his living which has made it necessary for him to become mentally ill. He does his best when he offers the patient the greatest gift he has—the gift of himself, rooted and grounded in the Being of God. His own friendly interest, his own reaching out with concern, his own desire to be helpful through a trained and understanding use of his unique religious resources—these are the things the patient needs. Being exposed to this attitude in the minister, the troubled person comes to feel encouraged to reach out of the loneliness of his isolation for the help which is available.[16]

[14] Ernest E. Bruder (Englewood Cliffs, N. J.: Prentice-Hall, 1963).
[15] *Ibid.*, p. 29.
[16] *Ibid.*, p. 70.

MINISTERING TO THE SUICIDAL PERSON

In the United States every sixty seconds, someone attempts to end his own life.[17] Some fifty times a day persons succeed in doing so. Suicide ranks ninth among the causes of death in our country. Each year some 18,000 persons destroy their lives. Probably five times this number attempt to do so. Reflecting on their experiences at the "Suicide Prevention Center" in Los Angeles, E. S. Schneidman and N. L. Farberow point out that all suicides, whether attempted or committed, "involves tremendous disruption of life, emotional turmoil, social discord." [18] Any minister who has dealt with the impact of suicide on a family can vouch for the accuracy of this statement.

Concerning the minister's role in preventing suicides, psychiatrist Herbert M. Hendin declares:

For some time now it has been evident that concerted effort and awareness on the part of those in close contact with the potential suicidal person could greatly reduce the number of actual suicides. Since members of the family are often too much involved themselves to see the oncoming development of suicide in one of their number, it is here that the minister may well save a life.[19]

How does one recognize a potential suicide? Suicides occur most often among the following: (a) *Those who threaten suicide.* The old belief that "those who talk about suicide don't commit suicide" is a deadly fallacy. Of every ten persons who kill themselves, eight have given definite warning of their intentions.[20] The only safe rule to follow is this—all suicidal threats must be taken seriously. Even the person who has no intention of killing himself, but who uses the threat to force others to take care of him, pay attention to him, or do what he demands, is emotionally disturbed and in serious need of psychiatric help. All suicide threats are serious, but they are especially dangerous if the person is an older male. Men kill themselves

[17] Karl Menninger in the Foreword to *Clues to Suicide* by E. S. Shneidman and N. L. Farberow (New York: McGraw-Hill Book Co., 1957).

[18] Norman L. Farberow and Edwin S. Schneidman (eds.), *The Cry for Help* (New York: McGraw-Hill Book Co., 1961), p. 4.

[19] "What the Pastor Ought to Know About Suicide," *Pastoral Psychology* (December, 1953), p. 41.

[20] "Some Facts About Suicide," Public Health Service Publication #852, 1961, p. 3.

twice as frequently as women, although women attempt suicide twice as often as men. In general suicide attempts are more apt to be successful among older persons. (b) *Persons who express feelings about their lives being empty, meaningless, worthless or "no longer needed" by anyone may be making suicide threats in disguise.* (c) *Any seriously depressed person, whatever the cause.* One or more of these signs may accompany psychological depression—feeling of a "heavy weight" on one's mind, loss of interest in normal activities, severe insomnia, undiminishing fatigue, feelings of "What's the use?", loss of appetites for food and sex, tension and agitation, social withdrawal, general motor retardation. (d) *Persons who have experienced major losses which deprive them of a dependency person or of a source of self-esteem such as a highly valued job.* (e) *Those with protracted illnesses.* Feelings of hopelessness and helplessness, particularly if the person is in intense pain, are danger signs. (f) *Persons who suddenly make plans for death* (making a will or getting their affairs in order). This is a warning sign if they are also generally unhappy or depressed. (g) *Those suffering from pathological grief reactions.* (h) *Those suffering from mental illness.* Suicides are frequent among schizophrenics, psychopathic personalities, alcoholics, and those with psychotic depressions. A suicide attempt may signal the onset of a psychotic episode.

If a minister knows or suspects that an individual is suicidal, he should inform the family or other responsible person and strongly recommend that psychiatric help be obtained at once. If no psychiatrist is available, any medical doctor will do. In an emergency, the person can be taken to a county hospital or the emergency service of any general hospital.

In talking with a person suspected or recognized as suicidal, the minister should encourage him to talk openly about it. This will tend to rob suicide of some of its distorted appeal to the person and give the minister an opportunity to help. The fear of suggesting suicide to a person who has no suicidal thoughts by raising the question, is largely unfounded. The minister should offer the person help and hope. If he does not respond to this offer, he has probably given up. If so, the minister should not let him out of his sight until some other responsible person has taken charge. If the person is intent on

257

killing himself, the minister (and others) should use whatever persuasion or coercion is necessary to block this. For example, if the suicidal person believes that he is doing what is best for his children, it should be pointed out forcefully that leaving them with the psychological burden of his suicide is the worst thing he could do for them. If a person is determined to destroy himself, and this feeling continues over a long period of time, it is often next to impossible to prevent his death. Hospitalization of such a person is essential. Fortunately, most suicidal persons have ambivalent feelings about dying and self-destructive impulses ordinarily diminish, given time. Sixty-five per cent of those who make one unsuccessful suicide attempt do not try suicide again. The majority of second attempts occur in the ninety days after the first. This is the most critical period.

The clergyman who has a community resource such as the Los Angeles Suicide Prevention Center [21] is very fortunate. The People's Church of Chicago sponsors a telephone answering service labeled simply "Emergency Call." The phone book carries this ad: "Emergency Call; Don't let worry end in tragedy. Call Longbeach 1-9595 day or night. A sympathetic minister will be happy to talk with you." When calls come from those in serious trouble, a minister in the caller's district is notified. If the case is urgent, the women who answer the phone try to hold the caller on the phone until a physician or the police can be alerted.[22]

ONE'S OWN ATTITUDE TOWARD THE SERIOUSLY DISTURBED

In the final analysis, one's own deep feelings about mental illness and suicide will determine one's effectiveness in this type of pastoral care. Because each of us is in our culture as a fish is in water, the stigma of mental illness is in our deeper feelings to some degree. If these feelings are strong, they will block our effectiveness in ministering to the mentally ill person and his family.

One of several values of clinical pastoral training in a mental hospital is that it provides an opportunity to work through feelings about oneself in relation to deeply disturbed persons. However it occurs a ministering person needs to achieve something of a fellow-

[21] For more information write Suicide Prevention Center, P. O. Box 31398, Los Angeles 31, California.

[22] V. A. Kraft, "Suicide Call," *Christian Advocate* (March 17, 1960), pp. 9-10.

feeling for the mentally ill person—to get beyond the labels he has been given and become aware of a suffering fellow human being. As psychiatrist Frieda Fromm-Reichmann once put it, "Unless one believes and feels that the most regressed catatonic, on the back ward of the mental hospital, is more alike than different from oneself, one will be of little help to the mentally ill person." [23]

There are a number of factors which converge to produce the attitudes of rejection which many ex-mental patients experience (See Chap. 5). These include the fear that the person's irrational side will break through again; fear of our own irrational impulses of which this illness reminds us; resentment of his irritating behavior; resentment of the threat to family pride which his former condition continues to pose; and the painful confrontation with the dark unknown in human life.[24]

In discussing the minister's work with the mentally ill, Ernest Bruder writes pointedly that "what a minister is in himself matters far more than what he does." He continues in this searching vein:

Only when he has dared to allow himself to experience something of the suffering and joys of his own living, when he has come to terms with his own experiences, is he in a position to appreciate similar feelings in others. . . . If the pastor has a keen awareness of what we have come to regard as *the interpersonal hurt* of his patient; knows the desperate and yet fatal need of the patient to evade further pain, no matter by what means, and often by striking out and hurting loved ones; feels something of the almost overwhelming and intolerable anxiety the patient experiences; is not too shaken by the terror evoked through what Kierkegaard expressed as "shut-up-ness unfreely revealed"; and can accept the consequent intense feelings of guilt and shame which isolate the patient from himself, from others and from God, then his ministry has within it the necessary element for a supportive and creative experience for the patient.[25]

A therapeutic attitude is essential for working redemptively with any troubled person—an alcoholic, a prisoner, a suicidal person, a mental patient, or the families of any of these. That the helping person possesses something of this attitude is vastly more important

---

[23] Lecturer at the William A. White Institute of Psychiatry, 1948.
[24] I am indebted to Camilla M. Anderson for pointing me to the two final factors.
[25] *Ministering to Deeply Troubled People*, p. 70.

than the particular counseling techniques he uses in such a relationship. The late Otis Rice who did some of the pioneering work in pastoral counseling with alcoholics once commented that to help an alcoholic, one must love him, and this isn't easy, since a drinking alcoholic can be very unlovable. One thing that had helped him, Rice reported, was "to remember that God loves the alcoholic, that he also loves Otis Rice, and then to remember how much God has to put up with in loving Otis Rice." [26]

A retired minister, Harold W. Ruopp of Minneapolis, while reflecting on his life, provided a striking illustration of what I mean by a therapeutic attitude. In retrospect, he identified three stages in his ministry. In the first stage, he tried to stand outside the life process as a spectator rather than a participant. He used an analogy to describe this stage—that of sitting on a riverbank preaching "helpful" sermons to the swimmers struggling in the current. In the second stage of his ministry a few years later he became a kind of lifeguard—a great helper "humbly proud" of his role, from time to time jumping into the river to put his arm around someone going down for the third time. As soon as he got him steadied to swim again, he would return to his place on the bank to wait for the next person who needed saving.

The third stage of his ministry came, he recalls, because of circumstances beyond his control in his own life. From then on, he was in the river all the time! Instead of always trying to hold someone else up, he glady permitted another person to hold him up. Instead of being the savior, he realized that he too needed saving. Again and again, he found that the humblest person had his arm around him, even as he tried to support that person. He concludes: "In the admission of great weakness, I found great strength. In the willingness to be helped, I became a better helper." [27]

This is the therapeutic attitude! A minister or layman who has it will be of genuine help to individuals and families who are "going through deep waters."

[26] Talk before the New York Academy of Medicine, 1952.
[27] The original form of this illustration appeared in Harold W. Ruopp's recently published book of sermons, *One Life Isn't Enough* (St. Paul, Minn.: Macalester Park Publishing Co., 1965), in the section "Postscript."

CHAPTER 12

Minister and Laymen Work Together for Mental Health

*The whole creation is on tiptoe to see the wonderful
sight of the sons of God coming into their own
—Rom. 8:19. (Phillips)
Is there no universal pastorhood to go along with
the universal priesthood of Protestantism?* [1]—*Seward
Hiltner*

A CREATIVE PARTNERSHIP

The key to the release of a church's mental health potentialities is
the development of a creative partnership between the minister and
a core-group of laymen who have caught a vision of these potentialities. Only thus can the healing-growth approach enter dynamically
into the life stream of a local segment of the Body of Christ.

Laymen outnumber clergymen approximately three hundred to
one. Obviously, any program must involve laymen as full partners
if it is to have more than superficial effects on a church and its community. One of the reasons why churches have not stimulated the
growth of their members more is the passive, follow-the-leader posture
of many lay persons and the one-man-show self-image of many ministers. This situation retards the spiritual maturing of everyone involved. Furthermore, it is profoundly unbiblical.

A deep-level cure for the "spectator-itis" of laymen and the one-
man-show orientation of ministers seems to be emerging in the "lay
renaissance"—a contemporary movement of profound significance

---

[1] *Preface to Pastoral Theology* (Nashville: Abingdon Press, 1958), p. 37.

for the mental health mission of our churches. This grassroots movement is growing spontaneously, on many fronts, with the rediscovery of the New Testament truth that *every Christian has a ministry simply because he is a Christian*. The New Testament Greek word "laos," from which "layman" and "laity" are derived, refers to all Christians! The "ministry of reconciliation" was given to the whole church (II Cor. 5:18), not to a set-apart, professional ministry. All are a vital part of the healing community. The layman is no second-class Christian. He is a minister in the life stream of his community and world. No Christian can really delegate his personal ministry to another. Every Christian is a shepherd (pastor) to others. The clergyman is simply a shepherd of shepherds, all under the great Shepherd. The clergyman is set apart by the church to provide leadership in the ministering community which is the church. His set-apartness is a matter of function, not a difference of spiritual responsibility. The clergyman's central job is to train his people for their ministry to the world. He is a teacher of teachers, a counselor of counselors, a pastor of pastors.[2] He is a "playing coach" on the team which is the church.[3] In the words of the author of Ephesians, the minister's primary job is "to equip God's people for work in his service" (Eph. 4:11-12, NEB).

During World War II the persecuted Christians threw a ringing challenge at comfortable, culture-adapted Christianity when they declared: "The first duty of the church is to *be* the church." It is my conviction that a local church works best for mental health when it is true to its mission as a church, not when it attempts to become a mental health agency. Its rich contribution to mental health is the result of the overflowing vitality of its spiritual and interpersonal life as a person-centered, God-oriented organism. The distinctive source of a church's vitality is the growing awareness among its members that they can become (in New Testament terms) the people of God (a community bound together by a glad commitment to the kingdom which is both among us and yet to be fully actualized), the fellowship of the Holy Spirit (a ministering family in which the life-renewing Spirit of God can be experienced), and the

---

[2] This conception was set forth in *The Purpose of the Church and Its Ministry*.

[3] This phrase is from Samuel Shoemaker's book, *Beginning Your Ministry* (New York: Harper & Row, 1963).

Body of Christ (his instrument for serving human need in all areas of life).[4]

When this New Testament picture of the church is taken seriously by Christians, salutary things begin to happen. Individuals and groups come alive. A new kind of minister-layman relationship emerges as the sense of mutual ministry grows. Laymen become "salty Christians" [5]—determined to be the "salt of the earth" by exerting a redemptive influence in their labor unions, corporations, clubs, or schools. Thus, the renewal of the church is coming with the pouring of its healing life into the world's wounds through the everyday ministry of dedicated laymen. This is the context within which a church's greatest contribution to mental health is made. Growing laymen, experiencing the empowering love of God, often see a dedication to mental health as a vital way of implementing their personal ministries of reconciliation.

THE MINISTER'S ROLES IN MENTAL HEALTH

As the respected leader of a church, the minister sets the tone of its program and its interpersonal climate. He does this by the kind of person he is, the quality of his relationships, the sort of people he attracts to the church, the motivational influence of his leadership, and his own passion for making that church a need-satisfying fellowship with a dynamic concern for helping lift the load of humanity. In order to be fully effective a church's mental health thrust requires the minister's enthusiasm. He is the key man in inspiring and training laymen for this ministry.

A revealing study of a cross-section of the Protestant ministry by sociologist Samuel W. Blizzard distinguished six practitioner roles in which parish ministers engage: *preacher, teacher, priest, organizer, administrator, pastor.*[6] I would add a seventh—*prophet.* As we have seen in the preceding chapters, each of these roles is a door opening into a whole realm of mental health opportunities.

Here is a summary of the major ways in which a minister can contribute to the mental health of his congregation and community:

[4] For a discussion of the New Testament conception of the church, see Grimes, *The Church Redemptive,* pp. 21-68.

[5] Hans-Ruedi Weber, *Salty Christians* (New York: Seabury Press, 1963), p. 33.

[6] These roles are discussed in S. W. Blizzard "The Minister's Dilemma," *The Christian Century* (April 25, 1956).

1. *Inform and motivate his congregation, with regard to both mental illness and positive mental health.* Many who hear him in his preaching and teaching roles are in attitude-molding positions as parents, teachers, and community leaders. Psychologist Gordon W. Allport writes:

Insofar as the clergy is better able to deal with issues of basic belief, values, and orientation toward life, he has an inescapable role to play in the conservation and advancement of mental health. . . . He can make psychological science his ally, and share with its practitioners the solution of a problem of joint concern.[7]

2. *Select and train a small group to become mental health leaders and infiltrators within the church and community.* If a number of dedicated laymen are exposed to the mental health needs of a community, particularly if these needs are personalized by visits to mental health facilities, some will respond with an Isaiah-like, "Here I am. Send me." An ad in the *London Times* read: "Brilliant speaker wants first-class cause." In every church there are members with unused talents who can be challenged by the freshness and obvious value of a church's mental health emphasis. A person serving on a committee charged with guiding a pastoral counseling service knows that his self-investment is paying significant dividends.

3. *Initiate action.* After the educational groundwork has been laid and a nucleus group trained, the minister is ready to work with that group in deciding on the most urgent unmet mental health need. After planning strategy, the group can move into action. The nature and goals of this mental health action should be determined by the unmet needs of a local situation. Organizationally the minister may prefer to work through an existing committee on social problems or create a new mental health task force responsible for this one area.

4. *Present the Christian message in a growth-stimulating way.* As a congregation's best trained interpreter of the message, the minister has a responsibility to test and retest his presentation of that message against criteria of healing and growth (see Chap. 2).

5. *Encourage the development of a growth-oriented program of Christian education by personally helping to motivate and train*

[7] *The Individual and His Religion,* p. 85.

healthy persons as teachers. From a mental health standpoint being a teacher of teachers is one of the minister's most important roles (see Chap. 6).

6. *Guide the development of a variety of creative groups including a network of small, family-modeled nurture groups.* The minister's personal involvement in leadership training activities may be his outstanding contribution in this area (see Chap. 7).

7. *Support persons in crisis and counsel with the disturbed.* The minister has both a preventive and a therapeutic opportunity in this area of service (see Chaps. 10 and 11). The "Mental Health Counselors" (called for in the Joint Commission's Report), a group between the psychiatrist and the "care-taking" professions, already exists to the extent that clergymen are effective counselors.

8. *Help to instill "unconditional positive regard" for persons into all the administrative procedures of the church, so that the total organism of the church can become an instrument for mental health.*

9. *Function as a community mental health leavener.* Because of the status which his position gives him in the community, a minister can have great influence in sparking mental health action by arousing a lethargic citizenry to their mental health responsibilities. Collectively, the country's 364,475 ministers represent a major community mental health resource (outnumbering psychiatrists thirty-three to one).[8] Unlike psychiatrists, clergymen are present and influential in almost every community. A professor of psychiatry accented the role of clergymen when he stated: "We recognize the minister as one of the first lines of defense in the mental hygiene movement.[9]

THE IMPORTANCE OF THE MINISTER'S MENTAL HEALTH

John Wesley once wrote: "You have need to be all alive yourselves, if you would impart life to others."[10] The minister's (or layman's) fundamental instrument of health or harm is interpersonal relationships. The quality of these determines his long-range influence on

[8] In 1960 there were approximately 11,000 psychiatrists.

[9] D. M. Kelley, Bowman Gray School of Medicine, quoted in "The Role of Religion in the Psychoses," by Wayne Oates, *Pastoral Psychology* (May, 1950), p. 36.

[10] From a letter to Zachariah Yewdall dated December 3, 1780, in *The Letters of John Wesley* Vol. 7 (London: The Epworth Press, 1931), p. 40. Of course it is not possible to be "all alive," if this means being perfectly mentally healthy. Nevertheless, Wesley's basic idea is valid and important.

people and this quality is determined by the degree of his own mental health. As Wayne Oates puts the matter: "Religion may either facilitate mental health or breed and maintain mental pathology, depending upon the mental health and methodology of the representatives of religion." [11]

A minister who suffered severe emotional deprivation in his childhood relationships, and whose self-esteem is therefore damaged, will subtly manipulate his flock in ways that will cause them to feed his exorbitant need for approval and love. If this need to manipulate is severe, he will become what Flanders Dunbar calls a "pathogenic agent." He will relate in ways that intensify guilt, dependence, and fear, blocking growth forces and infantilizing those around him. (An extreme example of this is the right-wing radio "prophet" whose paranoid message attracts a huge crowd of frightened, angry people. Such a person is a spawner of sickness who encourages hate and delusion in the name of religion.)

On the other hand, the relatively healthy minister naturally relates in ways that stimulate mutual trust and personal growth. As an accepting, loving person, he will automatically strengthen the mental health of those about him. To the degree that he really cares about people for their own sakes, he will be a source of health and growth. He will enter into honest (and sometimes painful) encounters with his people rather than stay in the detached safety of professionalism. Ross Snyder has said, "No person has earned the right to be pastor of a church or teacher of a class until he has risked himself with his people." [12]

The vast majority of ministers are reasonably mature, healthy persons. There are, however, certain mental health hazards in the ministry against which every minister needs to develop strategies of defense. One hazard is the contemporary *professional identity diffusion* of the ministry. Kaleidoscopic social changes have blurred the clearly focused pre-World War I sense of "who" and "why" the clergyman is in his community.

A part of some ministers' quiet sense of futility stems from the fact that the search for a new, relevant ministerial identity is far from

[11] "The Role of Religion in the Psychoses," p. 35.
[12] From "A Church as a Learning Community," a paper presented to the United Church Assembly (January 29, 1962), p. 6.

266

complete. It is helpful to be aware that at least some of one's inner uncertainties are symptomatic of broad historical uncertainties. The present situation makes it very important for the minister to find a sturdy sense of personal identity so that he will not need to lean so heavily on his professional identity.

Another ministerial health hazard consists of the variety of threats to his sense of self-worth. In our culture, where status and financial compensation are closely linked, ministers who are underpaid often suffer from gradual attrition of their self-esteem. However strong one's dedication to his calling, it is hard to escape the feeling that society puts a low value tag on one's services. A National Council of Churches study revealed that two thirds of our ministers are in substantial debt and that three fourths of these are not able to reduce their debt loads.[13] Since 1939, ministers' salaries have risen 105 percent as contrasted with 149 percent rise in the cost of living. 67 percent of ministers face serious problems in providing college educations for their children.[14]

Ministerial discounts, clergy fares on public conveyances, exemption from military service, and so forth, confront the clergyman with other mental health hazards. The first two of these are backdoor forms of remuneration which are distasteful to many self-respecting clergymen. Any form of special treatment by society exposes one to the trap of believing that one really is a special kind of human being. Such arrogance interferes with one's ability to establish authentic relationships.

Chronic loneliness poses another serious mental health hazard for ministers and their wives. Although he is surrounded by people, a minister may be hungry for relationships in which he can function as a peer rather than a professional leader. Some men find satisfying peer relationships with other professional people in the community. Others find renewal in a continuing small group experience with fellow ministers. One such group on the west coast hired a clinically trained chaplain to serve as therapist. Through honest sharing they were able to resolve some of their conflicting feelings about the

[13] W. A. Pleuthner, "Let's Pay Our Ministers a Living Wage," *This Week* (February 2, 1959).

[14] From a study by the Ministers' Life and Casualty Union.

ministry. Another group of ministers and their wives meet regularly with a well-trained clinical psychologist in a personal growth group.

Other mental health hazards faced by the minister and his family are the factors which make parsonage family life difficult. Since the minister's family is uprooted frequently, it is doubly important that family relationships be strong, supportive, and satisfying. Unfortunately, ministers sometimes sacrifice their families to the demands of their churches. The minister's wife faces more frustrations and fewer gratifications than her husband. It is essential for her mental health and his that they take a regular day off each week. Parsonage families who regularly set aside a block of time for shared activities are on the right track. A survey of ministers' wives showed that less than half of the churches encouraged their minister to take a regular day off.[15] One minister asked his officials to fill out questionnaires indicating how much time they felt he should spend each week on each area of his work. He found that to meet their desires would require an eighty-two hour work week.[16] In order to protect himself and his family from unwarranted demands, the minister has to master the fine art of saying "no."

The constant pressure to set a good example is another mental health hazard faced by ministers and their wives. Because they must please so many people and live an exemplary life they often feel that they must always hold themselves rigidly in line. Psychiatrist Harry Stack Sullivan once remarked, in his own inimitable way, that swallowing too much anger will ruin one's belly. As repressed ministers demonstrate, it will also deaden one's spontaneity and hamper one's relations with people. If a minister is to stay psychologically alive, he must find constructive ways of channeling his human feelings and drives. An understanding wife and a sharing group in which he can let down his hair are helpful. He also needs the "courage of his own imperfections" so that he can free himself from the need to please those who make unfair demands for neurotic reasons.

Closely related is the hazard of feeling that one must repress honest doubts. Some of the most tortured ministers I have met are

[15] J. G. Keohler, "The Minister as a Family Man," in *The Minister's Own Mental Health*, pp. 159-66.

[16] See the Reverend Wesley Shrader, "Why Ministers Are Breaking Down," *Life* (August 20, 1956), p. 95.

those from conservative churches who felt forced by the threat of job loss to mouth doctrines in which they no longer believed. Whatever one's doubts, the price of ignoring them is a reduction in the vitality of one's faith. Talking them over candidly with a trusted person outside one's church is one constructive way of handling doubts.

Another hazard faced by ministers and their wives is the tendency to restrict personal satisfactions and recreation. Any profession which demands as much giving as the ministry, requires time for taking-in activities—hobbies, reading, attending concerts, loafing, and non-church centered social relations. The ministry requires disciplined study and hard work, but creativity in these can be maintained only by alternating with periods for recharging the batteries. Samuel Johnson once remarked, "Sir, the life of a parson, of a conscientious clergyman, is not easy. I have always considered a clergyman as the father of a larger family than he is able to maintain." [17] The drain of having a considerable number of disturbed, dependent people constantly drawing on his emotional resources makes it imperative that a minister have replenishing experiences. One who brags (or complains) that he hasn't taken a day off in the last month is asking for serious trouble, as well as displaying his indispensability complex.

Hierarchical systems of church government pose mental health hazards for ministers who have not resolved their authority problems. Some comply with authority in ways that make them feel emotionally castrated; others defy authority in rebellious, self-hurting ways. Even if a minister's feelings toward authority are relatively mature, he may have problems in coping with whatever elements of the "stained glass jungle" are present in the ecclesiastical power structure of his denomination. Many men who resent hierarchical systems continue in them because they cannot relinquish the dependence and security they offer. Clergymen in denominations in which the ultimate authority is vested in the local congregation suffer from the insecurity of being vulnerable to the whims of power groups within their churches.

The most dangerous hazard to a minister's health is spiritual emptiness, the loss of a powerful sense of being the glad captive

---

[17] Quoted by C. W. Gilkey, "A Well-Proved Ministry," *Pastoral Psychology* (February, 1957) , pp. 9-10.

of one's mission in life. Young ministers sometimes leave seminary with heads full of facts about religion, but their hearts are strangely cool because they have not found a growing faith into which their knowledge can be integrated. Unless a maturing faith is found, the person either leaves the ministry or by middle age is like a salesman going through the motions of peddling a product in which he does not believe. The only way of avoiding this hazard is for a minister to work continually on his intellectual, emotional, and spiritual growth.

Fortunately, the vast majority of ministers and their wives overcome these hazards and live remarkably productive lives. Offsetting the frustrations are a host of deep satisfactions which rise from an effective ministry. These include the respect in which they are held in the community, the genuine appreciation they receive for work well done, the privilege of being invited to be with persons in their brightest and darkest hours, the satisfaction of communicating ideas that are important, the security of being surrounded by people who have affection for them, and the deep sense of well-being that comes from self-investment in significant work which helps lighten the load of humanity and makes for a better world.

PREPARATION FOR A PERSON-CENTERED MINISTRY

To some extent, the maximum release of a church's mental health potentialities depends on the caliber and character of its minister's training. Optimal training for a person-centered ministry includes three things: (a) *Experiences which lead to the understanding of one's religious heritage (through the study of Bible, theology, and church history) , of contemporary revelation regarding man (through the study of developmental psychology, anthropology, group dynamics, education, abnormal psychology, and so forth), and to the ability to meaningfully correlate these two bodies of truth.* (b) *A period of clinical pastoral training,* and (c) , *opportunities to discover and resolve one's inner problems (through individual or group psychotherapy) , and to develop a tough, growing faith.*

Seminary education is essentially conservative and therefore changes slowly. In spite of this, the basically interpersonal nature of the ministry is receiving some consideration (though not enough) in the rethinking of theological education which is occurring in many places. The Niebuhr-Williams-Gustafson report on theological education, states:

When one considers the revitalization of much in the theological curriculum today through new emphases in psychology and pastoral counseling, it must be concluded that a significant new turn in the education of the ministry has been taken. Powerful new resources are available throughout the curriculum because of work in this field. It is of first importance, therefore, that the field of pastoral care be accepted as the responsibility of the entire school and not be isolated as a subordinate department concerned with practical skills alone.[18]

To send a minister forth from seminary without his having confronted himself and human need at a deep level is to graduate him without the very insights which can allow him to make his message relevant to live human beings. Realizing this, some seminaries are using small, modified-therapy groups in which students experience self-encounter and gain awareness of their relationships. Several seminaries are requiring every student to have one quarter of clinical training—an experience of working for three months in a mental hospital, correctional institution, or general hospital under a carefully trained chaplain supervisor.[19] If all seminaries would do this, the mental health impact of the churches could be doubled in one generation.

Clinical pastoral training is, without a doubt, the most efficient way of vitalizing one's ministry to persons. Carl W. Christensen, instructor in neurology and psychiatry at Northwestern University Medical School, declares:

It should be as routine for a minister to have clinical training as for a physician to have an internship. Such training confronts the student with himself and his needs, and with others and their needs. It helps crystallize and make classroom work meaningful, it illustrates and illuminates the dynamics of person-to-person relationships. . . . If to this is added what contact with mental illness teaches about personal bias and prejudice, unrecognized illusion, ready answers, and pseudo-faith, the

[18] H. Richard Niebuhr, *et al, The Advancement of Theological Education* (New York: Harper & Brothers, 1957), p. 128.

[19] The two national, nondenominational clinical training groups are The Council for Clinical Training, Inc. (475 Riverside Drive, New York, New York) and The Institute of Pastoral Care (P. O. Box 57, Worcester 1, Massachusetts).

experience prepares the student for life. He has the courage to ask the right questions of religion, and the faith to search for the pertinent answers.[20]

Anyone who works as closely and constantly with people, as an effective minister must, benefits tremendously from the increased openness to himself and others which usually results from having psychotherapy. A west-coast minister gives this testimony concerning his personal analysis:

The parish minister has limitless opportunities to communicate with others from the center of his own life. It is assumed, often over-optimistically, that his life has a center and that he has not only found his way to it, but that he has found it to be reasonably acceptable. I would say that the most significant aspect of an Educative Analysis for the parish minister is that it helps him to accept the center of life and to speak from it. . . . It makes him more aware of himself as a person and more aware of others as persons. It gives him a deeper understanding of the forms and institutions of religion and helps him use those forms and institutions with more reliance on his feelings. . . . It helps him to shape them to ends of self-expression and self-realization.[21]

One of the major values of a period under a skilled therapist is that it gives one a delicious experience of grace—the unearned acceptance which is the heart of any genuinely therapeutic relationship. This experience can bring to life for the minister the central truth of the Christian faith. Unless it has come to life for him he cannot communicate it to others. It is true that any profound human experience confronts a person with himself and that any profound relationship brings grace to life. Unfortunately, profound experiences and relationships are rare in our society and most of us work overtime to avoid them. Clinical training and psychotherapy are two experiences in which self-confrontation and depth relationships are hard to avoid. In speaking of clinical training for theological students, Reuel Howe says: "They will be plunged deeply into life, many of them for the first time, and come up gasping and dripping,

---

[20] "The Minister's Own Mental Health," *The Christian Advocate* (March 31, 1960), pp. 7-8.
[21] H. B. Scholefield, "The Significance of an Educative Analysis for the Parish Ministry," *The Minister's Own Mental Health*, pp. 328-29.

ready to learn about life." [22] Both clinical training and psychotherapy are excellent means of enhancing the capacity to relate authentically and in depth.

Here are some of the ways a parish clergyman can sharpen his interpersonal skills:

1. *Clinical training.* If a minister has an enlightened congregation who will grant him a three-months "sabbatical" for a post-B.D. quarter of full-time clinical training, he will find this to be one of the great learning experiences of his life. Since it will add a depth dimension to his ministry, it is to the congregation's advantage that he have this experience. If full-time clinical training is impossible, a minister should enroll in a one- or two-days-per-week program in a nearby hospital. Several accredited chaplain supervisors have developed such programs for parish ministers, with valuable results.

2. *Supervision of one's counseling.* Clergymen in various parts of the country are discovering that one of the most rewarding forms of training is available at their doorstep. Individually, or in small groups, they simply make arrangements with a clinically trained person—psychiatrist, social worker, chaplain, psychologist, pastoral counseling specialist—to provide weekly or bi-monthly supervision of their counseling. Most mental health professionals are glad to participate, since it provides them with a stimulating opportunity to teach. Ideally, such supervision should extend over at least two years. The financial costs are modest, particularly if done in a group. Most ministers who have had supervision regard it as one of the most useful experiences in their entire educational careers.

3. *Personal psychotherapy.* If a minister is aware of creativity-depleting inner conflicts or is dissatisfied with his degree of effectiveness in relationships, he should not hesitate to enter individual or group psychotherapy. (It is crucial, of course, that the therapist be highly competent.) Though expensive, therapy will be among the best investments he has ever made, paying dividends in professional creativity and in both personal and marital happiness.

4. *An academic "retread" through seminary extension courses or graduate programs in pastoral care and counseling.* Sound degree

[22] *The Church and Mental Health,* p. 243.

programs include supervision and clinical experience. Disciplined reading in the mushrooming pastoral care literature and in the major journals, *Pastoral Psychology* and the *Journal of Pastoral Care,* is essential to continuing growth in one's interpersonal ministry. Exciting things are happening in this area, with which the pastor should keep abreast.

THE LAYMAN'S MENTAL HEALTH MINISTRY

As indicated earlier, the layman who is awakened to his opportunities plays a vital role in strengthening the mental health impact of his church. At many points, he has opportunities which the clergyman does not possess. Here are some facets of a layman's mental health ministry:

1. *He can help select an emotionally mature minister and then back him in a person-centered ministry.* The choice of an emotionally healthy minister is the essential factor in developing a church's mental health potentialities. An alert layman should utilize his influence in helping to select a man who gives evidence of a high degree of personal maturity and of the ability to be a "playing coach." The committee which interviews candidates should be composed of the most perceptive laymen in a church, including, if available, persons trained in interpersonal sensitivities. Such a committee should apply a typical criteria in considering a candidate: Does he care about people for their own sakes? Does he relate openly and honestly? Is he fully aware that he is a human being? What is the quality of his relationships with his wife and children? Would I like to be on a team of which he is coach? Is the gospel really good news to him personally? How sturdy is his self-esteem?

A layman should work to make sure that the salary which is offered is adequate to attract a minister with solid self-esteem and to prevent economic insecurity from hampering his effectiveness once he is hired. This is the only course consistent with the church's enlightened self-interest, not to mention Christian charity. A minister who is underpaid, who sees his family go without needed dental work, who cannot afford the books and recreation he must have to stay on his toes is crippled in his most basic function—establishing creative relationships.

A layman should encourage his minister's desire to take additional

274

clinical and academic training in pastoral counseling. (Seventy percent of ministers in one survey expressed a need for such training.) Like his counterpart in medicine, a growing minister needs regular post-graduate educational experiences to broaden his horizons and keep him up to date in his field. I shall always be grateful to the lay leaders of a Long Island church who made it possible for me, as their pastor, to have a quarter of clinical training ten years after completing seminary. Those years in the ministry had made me acutely aware of my inadequacies in meeting many pastoral care problems. This sense of need helped make that clinical training an invaluable experience.

Mental health concerns should motivate a layman to encourage his minister to do those things which are consistent with his mental health—a regular "preacher's sabbath" away from the telephone, at least a month's vacation for recharging his emotional and intellectual batteries, sufficient money and freedom to enjoy the legitimate recreational resources of the area, and enough privacy to protect the minister and his family from excessive living-in-a-goldfish-bowl pressure. I am not suggesting that a minister should be coddled. No self-respecting minister either wants or needs this. But all of us are sensitive to the expectations and approval of others. Healthy laymen can counterbalance the pressure of neurotic laymen who tend to heighten the mental health hazards of the ministry.

A layman should back the minister's efforts to increase the proportion of his time spent in person-centered activities. Providing adequate secretarial and janitorial staff is the place to start. Some churches have the best educated (though not the highest paid) mimeograph operators in town. A minister who spends his time in such ways is wasting both his training and his potential contributions to mental health.

2. *A layman should inform himself in the area of mental health and then let his pastor know that he stands ready to work alongside him in developing the church's mental health strategy.* If a clergyman knows that there are even one or two key laymen upon whose informed interest and leadership he can count, he is more likely to give immediate priority to a mental health emphasis or project.

3. *A layman should develop his own particular ministry to per-*

sons. Seward Hiltner's challenging question concerning a "universal pastorhood" in Protestantism must be answered affirmatively if a church's help- and health-giving potentialities are to be released. Early in this country's history, in Methodist class meetings the responsibility for pastoral care was with laymen.[23] A fellowship like A.A. is a refreshing example of the ability of nonprofessional persons to be of highly significant help to each other. Every local church has a largely untapped artesian well of latent helping resources in its laymen. If this stream is to be released, each concerned layman must discover his unique ministry of pastoral care.

Supporting fellow members and neighbors who are going through crisis experiences is the foremost pastoral care opportunity of laymen. An excellent means of increasing the effectiveness of key laymen in this work is for the minister quietly to establish a *pastoral care team.* Such a team consists of a carefully selected and trained group of laymen including a stable A.A. member and an Al-Anon member, a lawyer, a physician, and other intelligent, warmhearted persons with a dedication to following the Great Physician. The members of the team are on call to serve when the need arises at the discretion of the pastor. The team meets regularly for continuing training in the art of pastoral care.

How the members of the pastoral care team function depends on their training and their natural skills. Their help ordinarily consists mainly of supportive relationships and practical assistance such as finding employment for ex-prisoners and recovered mental patients. (Incidentally, studies have shown that the most important factor in the permanence of a patient's recovery from psychosis is having a job and doing well at it.[24]) Human need is everywhere! An alert pastoral care team working with a sensitive pastor will find no shortage of opportunities to serve.

The danger that well-meaning, but untrained persons will do harm while attempting to help is minimized by careful selection of team members, emphasis in their training on the limitations of their helping roles, and direct supervision by the pastor or some person from the mental health professions designated by him. There exists a broad group of troubled persons whose difficulties in living do

[23] *The Churches and Mental Health,* p. 57.
[24] *Mental Health Education: A Critique,* p. 39.

not require the services of a highly-trained professional person and yet who need more help than is available from random conversations with relatives and friends. The sick, the burdened, the handicapped, the bereaved, and the aged are among those to whom average team members can minister effectively. Several members of most pastoral care teams will have special helping competence by virtue of their professional training. Churchmen from one of the mental health professions should certainly be given an opportunity to serve on the team. The pastoral care team is a practical way of implementing the pastorhood of laymen concept.

A striking example of the effectiveness of lay shepherding is the work of the Committee on Institutions of the Louisville Council of Churches. Over twenty years ago, this group of laymen decided to take literally Christ's words, "I was sick and you visited me . . . in prison and you came to me" (Matt. 25:36). Over two hundred laymen have been involved in this project. Clergymen serve only as advisors. Thirteen groups of laymen provide a volunteer ministry in the police court, the jail, the reformatory, the general hospital, the tuberculosis sanatorium, the mental hospital, the juvenile court, and the children's homes. These dedicated laymen have helped countless sick and troubled persons. Their influence in the institutions has tended to upgrade the general treatment programs. Church women organized a committee to serve in the institutions for women. A volunteer presented a layette to a young, unwed mother in prison. The girl wept for the first time in years when she realized that someone cared about her.[25]

Another illustration of the effectiveness of lay pastoring is the sponsorship, over the past decade, of homeless alcoholics and ex-prisoners by a dozen or so Church of the Brethren congregations. In much the same manner that many churches have sponsored refugees from Iron Curtain countries, these "refugees" from behind another kind of curtain are provided with housing, helped to find employment, and, most important, made to feel accepted by the church fellowship. These experiences are reported to have had a profound educational effect on the congregations, in addition to helping some of society's rejects.

[25] George Stoll, *Laymen at Work* (Nashville: Abingdon Press, 1956).

Creative altruism is contagious. This is part of the answer to the question, "What can one person do?" A thirteen-year-old-son of a U. S. Army sergeant stationed in Italy read about Albert Schweitzer's hospital and decided to give a bottle of aspirin. An Italian radio station picked up the story. Not long after this, the boy was flown to Schweitzer's hospital with four and one-half tons of medical supplies worth $400,000 in planes provided by the Italian and French governments. His good-heartedness had started a chain-reaction of goodwill, causing many others to contribute.[26]

4. *A layman can implement his mental health ministry by accepting leadership in community mental health projects.* A churchman who served as chairman of a volunteer task force which completed a two-year survey of mental health needs and resources in Los Angeles County put his faith to work in a broadly influential manner. As a respected leader in industry, his name helped to protect the mental health program from serious damage at the hands of the reactionary forces of the area who were attacking it. The survey helped to motivate and guide an extensive program of strengthening the mental health resources of the county.

The "Friendly Visitors" program of Pasadena, California is an inspiring antidote to the common tendency to leave the responsibility for mental health mainly in the hands of professionals. Several years ago a grandmotherly appearing woman named Mara Moser began to wonder what was happening to the families of persons who are imprisoned. She discovered that society rejects or ignores them in most cases. Confused and embittered, the wife often retreats into her dingy house with blinds drawn. Economic pressures on the family are extreme. Frequently, the children fail in school and turn to delinquency.

Instead of stopping with an indignant question such as, "Why doesn't someone do something to help these victims of society's neglect?", Mara Moser decided to become that "someone" by doing whatever she could. At first the court authorities were suspicious of her motives and would not give her the names and addresses she needed. That her only motive was the honest desire to help apparently was hard for them to believe. Undaunted, she searched the

[26] *The Christian Century* (July 29, 1959), p. 870.

daily newspapers for the information. She persuaded the council of churches to give her efforts moral support. Eventually the council sponsored her work enthusiastically and gave her modest financial support.

Her approach was simple and direct—a visit to each family opened by the words, "I'm from the Friendly Visitors. I would like to talk with you." Often the frightened wives would peer suspiciously through barely opened doors before admitting her. Her lay ministry is mainly one of listening, support, and guidance. After a while, she started a weekly group where lonely wives could gather for fellowship and for learning some of the homemaking and personal grooming skills which many lack. This group experience helps to strengthen their shattered self-confidence. The fact that the group meets in the parish hall of a church is de-emphasized initially, since many of the women would not come to a church. To them, churches represent not the reconciling love of God but the society which has stood in judgment on them.

A number of volunteers from the churches have joined in the program. The court authorities, having seen the positive results of her work, now gladly give Mrs. Moser access to the names she needs. A plan for providing volunteer tutors for children from disturbed homes who are potential school dropouts has been implemented by the Friendly Visitor workers. What can one person, over sixty, with limited financial resources, no car, and the resistance of the authorities do? Mara Moser is the answer.

THE TIME IS NOW

At the beginning of this book I stated that the time is ripe for the churches to make a major breakthrough in the area of mental health. In the intervening chapters I have described how the contributions of a church to mental health can be multiplied in its various areas of work. Let me now reemphasize the strategic nature of our present situation.

For many years, the mental health movement limped along. Then came the end of World War II. The remarkable new vitality that has developed since then is apparent in the churches and in society at large. A ferment of interest in mental health matters is evident on every hand. Major advances in the treatment of the mentally ill are occurring. New, realistic hope is dawning on the horizon of this age-old problem. This moving tide of interest makes the timing right for a major advance in the churches' mental health ministries. Mental health is "an idea whose time has come."

Two factors facilitate the positive response of churches to this challenge. One is the existence of a substantial and growing group of ministers who are well trained in the field of pastoral care and counseling. Over 10,000 ministers now in churches and church-related institutions have had at least one quarter of full-time clinical training. The emergence of pastoral counseling as a specialty within the ministry and the development of new programs for advanced training in pastoral counseling both contribute to the rapid augmentation of the manpower pool of ministers who can provide competent leadership to the churches in their mental health programs. The other factor is the existence of a growing body of laymen who are knowledgeable and concerned about mental health. When these two groups come together, things begin to happen for mental health!

Over a century ago Thoreau sounded this note from a hut beside Walden Pond: "Man's capacities have never been measured; nor are we to judge of what he can do by any precedents, so little has been tried." [27] This is still true, both of men and of their churches. In the past, most churches have been like slumbering giants in the area of mental health. If fully awakened, they could release new forces of healing and wholeness in the stream of our world that could turn the tide for millions of persons toward that fullness of life which is mental health.

Think of the potential mental health influence of the 246,600 clergymen serving churches in our country.[28] As seminary and in-service training in personality development and counseling improves, clergymen will become increasingly significant contributors to mental health. Imagine the creative influences which can be released as more and more of the 319,240 churches and temples in our country become centers of healing, cells of sanity, helping to

[27] *Walden* (New York: The New American Library, 1942), p. 11.
[28] Benson Y. Landis (ed.), *Yearbook of Churches* (1964 ed.; New York: National Council of Churches, 1964), p. 258.

prevent mental and spiritual illnesses. The total job of fostering positive mental health obviously is too big to be done by any one group, including the churches. Every person and organization of goodwill has a role. The message of this book is that the role of the churches is much larger and more challenging than many of us had even dared to dream. If the churches, with their vast human resources of over 120 million persons, catch a vision of their potential strength in this area, they can become wellsprings of wholeness and health. What a magnificent opportunity!

Dorothea Lynde Dix[29] was probably the most remarkable woman our country has produced. A frail New England schoolteacher (retired early for health reasons) she seemed to be an unlikely candidate for the crusading role she was to fill. Yet singlehandedly she started a revolution of hope in the treatment of the mentally ill.

The day that changed her life was a cold Sunday in March, 1841, on which she taught a Sunday school class at the House of Correction in East Cambridge, Mass. There she was horrified by the sight of four insane persons chained like animals in dark, filthy, unheated cells. She returned to her home among Boston's bluebloods, too shocked to sleep, but with a fierce determination to pour whatever strength she had into a fight to correct this evil. Her struggle to achieve humane treatment for the mentally ill never faltered during the forty years which followed that momentous day in 1841.

First she collected facts, learning that treating the insane as dangerous animals was regarded by most people as perfectly appropriate, since they were considered depraved. Attendants at the jails and almshouses often charged visitors from 10 to 25 cents for visits to the "crazy house." For the entertainment of the visitors the insane were goaded to rage by being prodded with sticks. This is the way the mentally ill were treated in the United States of America, little more than a century ago!

Miss Dix proceeded to focus public attention on the situation in East Cambridge. Public officials condemned her conduct as "unwomanly," but after a vigorous battle, a stove and sanitary facilities were installed. For two years, she quietly collected a shocking dossier

[29] For a full account of the life of this amazing woman see Stewart Holbrook, *Lost Men of American History* (New York: The Macmillan Company, 1946).

of evidence concerning conditions in the rest of her state. Then she wrote a remarkable document, "Memorial to the Commonwealth of Massachusetts." In direct prose, she named places and described victims—a woman at Newton chained to the wall of a toilet, a youth at Groton with six feet of heavy steel chain connecting his neck to the wall. The gentlemen of the legislature, to whom she directed the report squirmed as she cited case after case of persons chained naked and beaten into obedience with rods. With dispatch, they set aside rooms for two hundred mentally ill patients at Worcester Hospital.

After collecting data in Rhode Island, she wrote an article for the Providence *Journal,* describing in vivid detail the treatment of one Abraham Simmons whom she had found chained in a seven by seven cell in Little Compton, with no window and no heat. The keeper admitted that his cell was double-walled so that he would not be disturbed by Simmons' piercing screams. She concluded her article by commenting that she supposed the citizens of Rhode Island considered themselves Christians, but she doubted if they could pray to the God of Abraham Simmons, imprisoned in his filthy, freezing cell. Overnight Simmons became a nationally known martyr. The state's legislators speedily provided better treatment for the mentally ill.

Eventually Miss Dix moved her fight to every state east of the Rocky Mountains and then to Canada. In three years, she traveled over ten thousand miles by stage, horseback, steamboats, and primitive trains, visiting over eight hundred jails, almshouses, and houses of refuge. Her courage was endless. Repeatedly she walked alone into filthy dungeons where alleged maniacs were chained; in New Jersey, after being warned that a certain man was extremely dangerous, she walked directly into his cell gently calling him by name. After staring in disbelief for a moment, the man broke down and cried. In two months he was recovered enough to work around the institution.

Everywhere she went, mental hospitals resulted from her work. She refused to have any hospitals named after her and shunned all personal publicity. She continued her fight until death stopped her at eighty. Dorothea Lynde Dix was a nonprofessional in the mental health field, and yet the impact of her remarkable life on the treatment of the mentally ill was stronger than that of any other person in our history. The fact that the task she so nobly began is still unfinished in the second half of the twentieth century should be a challenge to the conscience of every person of goodwill in our land.

To seize their present opportunities in mental health, our churches need laymen and ministers with something of the vision and courage of a Dorothea Lynde Dix. With such leaders, our churches increasingly will achieve that spirit of Christian community through which new streams of mental health will flow into our troubled world.

READING BY CHAPTERS

Chapter 1: The Mental Health Mission of the Local Church

Clebsch, W. A. and Jaekle, C. R. *Pastoral Care in Historical Perspective*. Englewood Cliffs, N. J.: Prentice-Hall, 1964.

Gurin, Gerald, *et al. Americans View Their Mental Health*. New York: Basic Books, Inc., 1960.

Jahoda, Marie. *Current Concepts of Positive Mental Health*. New York: Basic Books, Inc., 1958.

Maves, Paul B. (ed.) *The Church and Mental Health*. New York: Charles Scribner's Sons, 1953.

McCann, Richard V. *The Churches and Mental Health*. New York: Basic Books, Inc., 1962.

Chapter 2: The Christian Message and Mental Health

Allport, Gordon W. *The Individual and His Religion*. New York: The Macmillan Company, 1950.

Fromm, Erich. *Psychoanalysis and Religion*. New Haven: Yale University Press, 1950.

Loomis, Earl A. *The Self in Pilgrimage*. New York: Harper & Row, 1960.

Oates, Wayne E. *Religious Factors in Mental Illness*. New York: Association Press, 1955.

Roberts, David E. *Psychotherapy and a Christian View of Man.* New York: Charles Scribner's Sons, 1950.

Wise, Carroll A. *Religion in Illness and Health.* New York: Harper and Brothers, 1942.

Chapter 3: The Worship Service and Mental Health

Baker, Oren H. "Pastoral Psychology and Worship," *Pastoral Psychology,* March, 1960.

Carrington, W. L. *Psychology, Religion and Human Need.* Des Moines, Iowa: Meredith Press, 1957, Chap. 5.

Grimes, Howard, *The Church Redemptive.* Nashville: Abingdon Press, 1958.

Howe, Reuel L. *Man's Need and God's Action.* New York: Seabury Press, 1953.

Chapter 4: Preaching and Mental Health

Bartlett, Gene. *The Audacity of Preaching.* New York: Harper & Row, 1962.

Jackson, Edgar N. *A Psychology for Preaching.* Des Moines, Iowa: Meredith Press, 1961.

————. *How to Preach to People's Needs.* Nashville: Abingdon Press, 1956.

Kemp, Charles F. *Life-Situation Preaching.* St. Louis: Bethany Press, 1956.

————. *Pastoral Preaching.* St. Louis: Bethany Press, 1963.

Chapter 5: The Prophetic Ministry and Mental Health

Allport, Gordon W. *The Nature of Prejudice.* Boston: Beacon Press, 1954.

Fromm, Erich. *The Sane Society.* New York: Holt, Rinehart & Winston, 1955.

Joint Commission on Mental Illness and Health. *Action for Mental Health, A Program for Meeting the National Emergency.* New York: Basic Books, Inc., 1961.

Chapter 6: The Church School's Contribution to Mental Health

Allinsmith, Wesley, and Goethals, George. *The Role of Schools in Mental Health.* New York: Basic Books, Inc., 1962.

Cantor, Nathaniel. *Dynamics of Learning.* 3rd ed. Buffalo, N. Y.: Henry Stewart, 1956.

————. *The Teaching-Learning Process.* New York: The Dryden Press, 1953.

Kemp, Charles F. *The Church: The Gifted and the Retarded Child.* St. Louis: Bethany Press, 1958.

Manual of Procedures, Topics, and Materials for Discussions in Mental Health. New York: National Academy of Religion and Mental Health, 1956.

Ribble, Margaretha A. *The Rights of Infants.* New York: Columbia University Press, 1943.

————. *The Personality of the Young Child.* New York: Columbia University Press, 1955.

Ridenour, Nina. *The Children We Teach.* New York: Mental Health Materials Center, Inc., 1956.

Sherrill, Lewis J. *The Gift of Power.* New York: The Macmillan Company, 1955.

————. *The Struggle of the Soul.* New York: The Macmillan Company, 1951.

Chapter 7: Mental Health and the Group Life of a Church

Casteel, John L., ed. *Spiritual Renewal Through Personal Groups.* New York: Association Press, 1957.

Douglass, Paul F. *The Group Workshop Way in the Church.* New York: Association Press, 1956.

Knowles, Joseph W. *Group Counseling.* Englewood Cliffs, N. J.: Prentice-Hall, 1964.

Leslie, Robert C. "Small Groups in the Church." *Pastoral Psychology* (June, 1964).

Raines, Robert A. *New Life in the Church.* New York: Harper & Row, 1961.

Chapter 8: Creative Church Administration and Mental Health

Ashbrook, James B. "Creative Church Administration." *Pastoral Psychology* (October, 1957), p. 11.

Grimes, Howard. *The Church Redemptive.* Nashville: Abingdon Press, 1958. Chaps. X, XI.

Trecker, Harleigh B. *New Understandings of Administration.* New York: Association Press, 1961.

Chapter 9: Fostering Mental Health by Strengthening Family Life

Ackerman, Nathan W. *The Psychodynamics of Family Life.* New York: Basic Books, Inc., 1958.

Baruch, Dorothy W. *How to Live With Your Teen-ager.* New York: McGraw-Hill Book Company, 1953.

————. *New Ways in Discipline.* New York: McGraw-Hill Book Company, 1949.

————. *New Ways in Sex Education.* New York: McGraw-Hill Book Company, 1959.

Baruch, Dorothy W., and Miller, Hyman. *Sex in Marriage, New Understandings.* New York: Harper & Row, 1962.

Erikson, Erik H. *Identity and the Life Cycle.* New York: International Universities Press, 1959.

Fairchild, Roy W., and Wynn, John C. *Families in the Church.* New York: Association Press, 1961.

Howe, Reuel L. *The Creative Years.* New York: The Seabury Press, 1958.

Chapter 10: Pastoral Counseling and Mental Health

Alcoholics Anonymous. A. A. Publishing Co., 1955.

Brister, C. W. *Pastoral Care in the Church.* New York: Harper & Row, 1964.

Clinebell, Howard J., Jr. "Ego Psychology and Pastoral Counseling." *Pastoral Psychology* (February, 1963).

————, "Counseling with The Family of The Alcoholic," *Pastoral Psychology* (April, 1962).

————. "Philosophical-Religious Factors in the Etiology and Treatment of Alcoholism." *Quarterly Journal of Studies on Alcohol* (September, 1963).

————. *Understanding and Counseling the Alcoholic.* Nashville: Abingdon Press, 1956.

Hiltner, Seward. *Pastoral Counseling.* Nashville: Abingdon Press, 1952.

Hiltner, Seward, and Colston, Lowell G. *The Context of Pastoral Counseling.* Nashville: Abingdon Press, 1961.

Ikin, Alice G. *New Concepts of Healing.* New York: Association Press, 1956.

Irion, Paul E. *The Funeral and the Mourners.* Nashville: Abingdon Press, 1954.

Jackson, Edgar N. *Understanding Grief.* Nashville: Abingdon Press, 1957.

Johnson, Paul E. *Psychology of Pastoral Care.* Nashville: Abingdon Press, 1953.

Oates, Wayne E. *Protestant Pastoral Counseling.* Philadelphia: The Westminster Press, 1962.

Rogers, Carl R. *On Becoming a Person*. Boston: Houghton Mifflin Company, 1961.

Stewart, Charles W. *The Minister as Marriage Counselor*. Nashville: Abingdon Press, 1961.

Wise, Carroll A. *Pastoral Counseling: Its Theory and Practice*. New York: Harper & Row, 1951.

Chapter 11: Helping the Mentally Ill and Their Families

Bruder, Ernest E. *Ministering to Deeply Troubled People*. Englewood Cliffs, N.J.: Prentice-Hall, 1963.

Farberow, Norman L., and Schneidman, Edwin S., eds. *The Cry for Help*. New York: McGraw-Hill Book Company, 1961.

Southard, Samuel. *The Family and Mental Illness*. Philadelphia: Westminster Press, 1957.

Stern, Edith. *Mental Illness: A Guide for the Family*. 4th ed., New York: Harper & Row, 1962.

Chapter 12: Minister and Laymen Work Together for Mental Health

Grimes, Howard. *The Rebirth of the Laity*. Nashville: Abingdon Press, 1962.

Hofmann, Hans, ed. *Making the Ministry Relevant*. New York: Charles Scribner's Sons, 1960.

————. *The Ministry and Mental Health*. New York: Association Press, 1960.

Oates, Wayne E., ed. *The Minister's Own Mental Health*. Manhasset, N.Y.: Channel Press, 1961.

For further guidance on how a church can become an effective participant in the preventive and therapeutic aspects of the community mental health movement, the reader is directed to *Community Mental Health: The Role of Church and Temple*, Howard J. Clinebell, Jr., Editor (Nashville: Abingdon Press, 1970).

SOME NATIONAL MENTAL HEALTH ORGANIZATIONS, PUBLICATIONS, AND RESOURCES

Academy of Religion & Mental Health
16 E. 34th Street, N.Y., N.Y. 10016

Al-Anon Family Group Headquarters, Inc.
125 E. 23rd Street, N.Y., N.Y. 10010

Am. Assn. of Marriage Counselors
27 Woodcliff Drive
Madison, N.J.

Am. Assn. of Pastoral Counselors
201 East 19th St., N. Y., N.Y. 10003

Am. Group Psychotherapy Assn.
1790 Broadway, N.Y., N.Y. 10019

Am. Psychiatric Assn.
1700 Eighteenth St., N.W.
Washington, D.C. 20009

Am. Psychological Assn.
17 & Rhode Island Ave., N.W.
Washington, D.C. 20036

Children's Bureau
U.S. Dept. of Health, Ed. & Welfare
Washington 25, D.C.

Child Study Assn. of Am.
9 E. 89th St., N.Y., N.Y., 10028

Council for Clinical Training
475 Riverside Dr., N.Y., N.Y. 10027

Family Service Assn. of Am.
44 E. 23rd St., N.Y., N.Y. 10010

Institute of Pastoral Care
P.O. Box 57
Worcester, Mass.

Institute of the Crippled & Disabled
400 1st Ave., N.Y., N.Y. 10010

Journal of Pastoral Care
61 Lexington Ave.
Cambridge, Mass. 02138

Journal of Religion & Health
Academy of Religion & Mental Health
16 E. 34th St., N.Y., N.Y. 10016

Mental Health Film Board
164 E. 38th St., N.Y., N.Y. 10016

Mental Health Materials Center
1790 Broadway, N.Y., N.Y. 10019

National Assn. for Mental Health, Inc.
10 Columbus Circle, N.Y., N.Y. 10019

National Assn. for Retarded Children
386 Park Ave., S., N.Y., N.Y. 10016

National Assn. of Social Workers
2 Park Ave., N.Y., N.Y. 10016

National Council on Alcoholism
2 East 103rd St., N.Y., N.Y. 10029

National Council of Churches
Dept. of Family Life
475 Riverside Dr., N.Y., N.Y. 10027

National Council of Churches
Dept. of Pastoral Services
475 Riverside Dr., N.Y., N.Y. 10027

National Council on Family Relations
1219 University Ave., S.E.
Minneapolis, Minn.

National Institute of Mental Health
Bethesda 14, Maryland

The Pastoral Counselor
3 West 29th St.
New York, N.Y. 10001

Pastoral Psychology
400 Community Drive
Manhasset, N.Y. 11030

Public Affairs Pamphlets
381 Park Ave. S., N.Y., N.Y. 10016

U.S. Printing Office
Washington 25, D.C.

World Health Organization
Palais des Nations, Geneva

INDEX

47946